THE **BIG** BOOK OF
BARBECUING
& GRILLING

HILAIRE WALDEN

THE **BIG** BOOK OF BARBECUING & GRILLING

365

HEALTHY AND DELICIOUS RECIPES

DUNCAN BAIRD PUBLISHERS

LONDON

THE BIG BOOK OF BARBECUING AND GRILLING

Hilaire Walden

First published in the United Kingdom and Ireland
in 2006 by Duncan Baird Publishers Ltd
Sixth Floor
Castle House
75–76 Wells Street
London W1T 3QH

Conceived, created and designed by Duncan Baird Publishers Ltd

Managing Editor: Grace Cheetham
Editor: Gillian Haslam
Managing Designer: Manisha Patel
Photographic Art Direction: Sailesh Patel
Studio and Locational Photography: William Lingwood
Photography Assistant: Monica Larsen
Stylists: Tessa Evelegh and Helen Trent (props), Sunil Vijayakar and Joss Herd (home economists)

Library of Congress Cataloging-in-Publication Data is available

Distributed in the United States by Publishers Group West

ISBN-10: 1-84483-260-0
ISBN-13: 9-781844-832606

10 9 8 7 6 5 4 3 2 1

Typeset in Monitor
Colour reproduction by Scanhouse, Malaysia
Printed in China by Imago

CONTENTS

INTRODUCTION

The first sign of hot weather makes everyone long to cook outdoors over a fire. There is no need, though, to restrict grilling to the summertime. You can take advantage of sunny, still days at other times of year, and the 365 recipes in this book will provide you with such a selection to try that you'll want to cook outdoors as much as possible.

The various types of grills have improved in both quality and range, and there is now a wider choice of fuels. There are also many accessories that make grilling easier and extend the types of dishes that can be cooked—for example, hinged baskets to hold hamburgers and fish steaks, mesh sheets that prevent small pieces of food from falling onto the fire, and motorized rotisserie spits.

A big factor in grilling's popularity is that it is not a precise way of cooking. The choice of ingredients in a recipe, and their proportions, can be changed to suit your taste, budget, or what is available. The same applies to flavorings such as herbs and spices. Grilling is also a relaxed way of cooking— timings can vary according to many factors and you can cook at your own pace. As it is important to always ensure that meat and poultry are adequately cooked, the optimum internal temperatures are given on pages 14–15.

As with most things in life, grilling food just the way you like it is easy when you know how. For example, simply adjusting the height of the grill rack and/or moving the food to the side can slow or speed up the cooking. There are many more useful tips like this for troublefree, successful grilling on pages 12–13.

In the following chapters, you will find recipes to suit every occasion, taste, and diet. There are simple dishes, such as Steak with Roasted Garlic and Mushrooms, innovative dishes, such as Monkfish, Fennel, and Lemon Brochettes, and dishes inspired by cuisines around the world, such as Moroccan Chicken with Tabouleh. Children are sure to love Bacon-Wrapped Sausages, and vegetarians will find plenty of ideas to satisfy them, including Falafel Burgers with Yogurt and Mint Relish. If you want to make a special meal on the grill, you'll find recipes using ingredients such as scallops, tiger shrimp, lobster, and guinea fowl. And to finish, there are heavenly grilled desserts, including Chocolate Brioche Sandwiches.

HOW TO COOK ON A GRILL

There are two main methods used in grilling; direct heat and indirect heat. With direct heat the food is placed directly above an intense heat source and is usually turned during grilling so that it cooks evenly. This method is suitable for small items that take less than 25 minutes to cook, such as steaks, burgers, chops, and vegetables. For indirect-heat grilling, the charcoal fire or other heat source is on the opposite side, or on either side, of the food, or the heat is turned down, and the grill is usually closed, so that cooking is by reflected heat. This method is suitable for large pieces of meat or poultry that require long cooking.

GRILLING HEAT WITH CHARCOAL

Cooking can be done over a high, medium, or low heat, depending on the type of food.

• The charcoal fire is described as high when the flames have died down to glowing red coals covered with a fine layer of white ash. You should be able to hold your hand 6 inches above the fire for 2 seconds. High heat is used for cooking thin pieces of food, such as fish fillets.

• When the coals are covered by a thicker layer of white ash, the fire has reached the medium heat used for most cooking. You should be able to hold your hand over it for 4–5 seconds.

• If you can hold your hand over the fire for longer than 5 seconds, it is too cool for cooking, but can be used for keeping cooked food warm.

TYPES OF GRILLS

There is such a wide range of types and styles of grills available that it is worth spending time identifying your requirements: how often you will use the grill; where you will be siting it; the number of people you are likely to cook for most often; how sophisticated you want the equipment to be; and how much money you want to spend.

When it comes to choosing the grill, the main points to consider are the sturdiness of the construction, not only of the main part of the grill, but also any shelves, etc.; the spacing of the bars on the grid; whether the grid has a nonstick coating; the position of any air vents; ease of carrying, if it is portable; and, if not kept permanently outdoors, how easy it will be to store.

HIBACHI: these cast-iron, troughlike grills are heavy but portable. They have short legs and can be used on the ground or on a heat-resistant surface at a comfortable working height. The distance of the cooking rack from the fire is adjustable.

DISPOSABLE FOIL GRILLS: easy to use and cheap, these grills consist of a heavy-duty aluminum foil tray filled with charcoal briquettes and a firelighter, covered with a grid. Their limitations are their size, the fact that you cannot adjust the height of the grid or move the food to a cooler part for slightly slower cooking, and a burning time of only about 1 hour.

PEDESTAL GRILLS: these may be fueled by charcoal or gas, and occasionally by electricity. The firebox with its grid sits on a pedestal. These grills may be simple constructions, such as those commonly seen in parks and other recreational areas, or very sophisticated—and expensive—models.

BARREL GRILLS: made from cast-iron, these resemble pot-bellied stoves. They are very stable and are used at table height. They have adjustable grill racks and often a stand for a spit, are easy to light (with newspaper or kindling), and can be ready for cooking in just 10–15 minutes.

KETTLE GRILLS: these reliable grills come in a range of sizes, from table-top models to free-standing versions; most use charcoal, but there are also some powered by gas. They have a domed metal lid that reflects the heat onto the food, thus cooking it quickly and evenly and enabling large pieces of meat or whole chickens to be grilled by indirect heat. The cover excludes air, thus reducing flareups. With the cover in place, smoke is contained within, which heightens the flavoring of the food. The cover can be left off for conventional grilling by direct heat.

GRILL CARTS: these are sophisticated, usually large, rectangular grills set on a moveable cart, and with a hinged lid. They come with a temperature gauge, dampers to regulate the airflow, and moveable grates and cooking grids. Spits for rotisserie cooking, warming racks, and side shelves are also available. They work in much the same way as a kettle grill.

BUILT-IN GRILLS: choose a sheltered site with easy access to the kitchen, but not too near the house. Ordinary house-bricks can be used in the construction, but it is a good idea to line them with firebricks, as these withstand the heat better. You will also need a metal container to hold the fire, and a grill or grid, preferably with pegs, nails, or bricks projecting from the walls for adjusting its height. Or, simply buy a pack containing everything you need from a hardware store.

INDOOR GRILLS: some ranges have a grill section, while others come with a grate accessory that can be fixed in place of the range's burners. With a range-top grill you can grill food indoors, although you need a very efficient exhaust fan to remove smoke from the kitchen. Another option is to use a Tuscan grill—a metal frame with an adjustable grill rack—in a fireplace.

FUELS

CHARCOAL: there are two main types for grilling:

Natural hardwood charcoal: this is hard wood—hickory, mesquite, oak—that has been fired in a kiln without igniting the wood but driving out all the by-products, resulting in a very light, black, combustible form of carbon. Good-quality hardwood charcoal normally comes in larger pieces than charcoal briquettes; it also lights more easily, burns cleaner and slower, and produces a higher heat than briquettes, or than gas grills. Once it is alight, more fuel can be added to the grill if and when necessary to give a bigger, hotter fire.

Charcoal briquettes: cheaper than natural hardwood charcoal, these uniformly shaped lumps of fuel are made from particles of waste charcoal combined with sawdust. Some charcoal briquettes are impregnated with a starter for instant lighting and others contain bits of wood to provide a hardwood flavor. There are also other, cheaper briquettes made from alternative sources of fuel, with products such as sand and clay as fillers and bound with a petroleum-based substance. Needless to say, they do not burn as well or for as long as charcoal briquettes.

GAS: gas grills, fueled by liquid propane, are easy to use and heat up very quickly. The heat can be regulated, giving good control of the cooking, and they do not produce ash. However, they don't burn at as high a temperature as charcoal and do not generally give the food the same "grilled" taste, although wood chips, and modifications such as "flavorizer" bars, can create the authentic aroma and taste. Portable gas grills are also available, but the height of the grill rack may be static.

AROMATIC ADDITIVES: you can add excellent flavor to grilled foods by burning aromatics in the fire. Note, though, that the food needs to be on the grill long enough for the fragrant smoke to have time to penetrate.

Wood chips and chunks: small pieces of wood can be burned on charcoal fires to give off a pleasant aroma and to flavor the food being grilled. Hardwoods such as oak, hickory, mesquite, almond, apple, cherry, and olive, burn more slowly than softwoods such as redwood and pine, which can also produce sparks. For a strong smoky flavor, use the wood chips or chunks dry; soak them first for a more subtle flavor. The wood chips can be added directly to the hot coals, or they can be put in a drip pan or wrapped in heavy-duty foil. You can also add wood chips to a gas grill—put them in the smoker box.

Herbs and spices: Woody herbs, such as rosemary, thyme, sage, fennel, and bay, grapevine cuttings, and large whole spices, such as cinnamon sticks and star anise, produce a deliciously fragrant smoke. Soak the herbs sprigs or spices in water for at least 15 minutes, then drain and throw them onto the hot coals.

GRILLING EQUIPMENT

Accessories can be divided into those few essentials that you will need to get you started, and extra items you can buy as the grilling bug takes hold.

ESSENTIAL

Long-handled tongs, large spatulas, and long-pronged fork: use the fork only toward the end of cooking to test if the food is done. If the food is pierced while it is cooking, it will let juices escape and the food will become dry.

Long-handled basting brush: choose one with natural bristles.

Skewers: choose long, flat metal skewers for meat, poultry, and firm-textured fish brochettes, and for keeping butterflied birds and roasts flat during cooking. Metal skewers should be oiled before use, to prevent food from sticking to them. Long and short bamboo and wooden skewers are best for quicker-cooking, smaller, and more delicate items; they should be soaked in water for 30 minutes before use to prevent them from burning. Wooden toothpicks will secure stuffed foods and hold rolled items in place; toothpicks should also be soaked before use.

Oven mitts: choose mitts with extra long cuffs.

USEFUL BUT NOT ESSENTIAL

Hinged baskets: these are useful for cooking a whole large fish or several small fish, or foods such as hamburgers and corn on the cob. They facilitate the turning of foods and help prevent large or more delicate items from breaking up. Look for hinged baskets that are adjustable, with nonstick bars and long handles.

Fine, wire-mesh racks: these rest on the grill rack, and are ideal for cooking smaller items that might otherwise break up or fall through the grid.

Grill-cleaning brush: choose a model that is also fitted with a scraper.

Digital thermometer: this instantly checks the internal temperature of meat and poultry.

Heavy-duty foil drip tray: when grilling by indirect heat, place under the food to catch any drips and thus prevent flareups.

Kabob rack

SITING AND LIGHTING THE GRILL

Here are a few essential guidelines to help you get the best from your grill.

- Always read the manufacturer's directions for the grill and the fuel.
- In the backyard, choose a place away from overhanging trees or bushes; set up free-standing models where they won't wobble; and place portable grills on the ground or a heatproof surface.
- Do not light an open fire in high winds.
- Start building a charcoal fire 45–60 minutes before you want to start cooking (30–35 minutes for instant-lighting briquettes). Open all the air vents or dampers. Arrange a heap of smaller pieces of fuel in the bottom of the fire basket. Make a well in the center and put in a solid cube of paraffin lighter. Light the cube with a taper or long match and, using larger pieces of fuel, build an igloo-shaped dome on top, enclosing the fire but leaving an airspace. Leave the fire undisturbed for 30–40 minutes. Once the flames have subsided and the coals are covered with fine white ash, rake them evenly over the bottom of the grill. The fire is now ready for cooking.
- Chimney or flue starters, which resemble a large coffee can with a handle, will hasten the initial heating of charcoal. The bottom section is filled with crumpled newspaper, charcoal is packed inside the top, and the chimney is set in the center of the grill. The newspaper is set alight and the flames heat the charcoal. Once the charcoal is ready, it is poured out into the grill.
- To replenish a charcoal fire, place extra fuel on top of the burning coals and wait for the fresh coals to burn down a bit before resuming cooking.

FOOD SAFETY

Here are a few rules to which you should always adhere:

- Don't leave raw or precooked food out in the sun.
- Keep cooked food well away from raw food, and use separate equipment for preparing and handling each type.
- Always let frozen food thaw completely before cooking.
- Keep food cool before cooking; make use of coolers.
- Meat is a poor conductor of heat, so thick pieces will take a surprisingly long time to cook. Always check internal temperature with a digital thermometer to be sure it is cooked through. Do this with poultry too, both large pieces and whole birds.

COOKING SAFETY

To ensure your grilling is safe and fun, follow these guidelines:

• Never spray liquid starter such as lighter fluid on an already lit charcoal fire. When it ignites, the fire can run back to the can and cause an explosion.

• Check the hose and regulator on a gas grill.

• Keep matches away from a lit fire.

• Have a spray bottle of water handy to douse flareups.

• If there are more serious flames, smother them with a fireproof lid or other cover.

• Lift a grill cover away from you, to avoid being burned by the steam and blinded by the smoke.

• Do not wear flowing or very loose clothes (be especially careful with sleeves).

• Wear long, flame-retardant mitts and use long-handled tools, such as tongs, spatulas, and basting brushes (use separate tools for moving coals).

• Never leave the grill unattended, and keep children and pets away from the fire.

• When the cooking is completed, spread out the coals to speed the cooling (or cover the grill). Charcoal takes a long time to go out; embers that look gray may still be hot.

• Do not move or pack up a charcoal grill until the fire is out and the coals are cold.

• Clean the grill rack thoroughly with a stiff wire brush and scraper before putting it away.

• Never use a charcoal grill indoors or anywhere there is not adequate ventilation.

HINTS AND TIPS

Before starting to cook, always:

• Make sure you have enough fuel for the amount of food you want to cook.

• Have everything you will need.

• Heat the fire in plenty of time, according to the fuel being used.

• Position the grill rack about 2 inches above the heat.

• Brush the grill rack or basket with oil and put it over the fire to heat for a few minutes.

• Soak wooden skewers in water for 20–30 minutes (use them for foods that need shorter cooking times). Oil metal skewers (long, flat ones are best for meat, fish, and poultry and brochettes that require longer cooking).

• When making kabobs and brochettes, use foods that take the same amount of time to cook and cut them to the same size so they will cook evenly. Do not pack meat and poultry too tightly onto skewers, otherwise they will not cook through properly.

• If food has been left to marinate in the refrigerator, move it to room temperature 30–45 minutes before cooking.

• Brush surplus marinade from foods before cooking them (to keep food moist, brush with leftover marinade during grilling).

During cooking:

• Don't put too much food on the grill rack at one time, because the food will steam and have a soft surface rather than a crisp, caramelized, tasty one.

• Let the food cook for at least 1 minute after you place it on the grill. Don't try to turn or move it until it can be moved easily.

- Place longer-cooking food on the grill rack first, then add quicker-cooking items.
- Sear meat, poultry, and thicker pieces of fish over the hottest part of the fire, then move them to a cooler part, or raise the grill rack, to finish cooking.
- The heat from the fire crisps the surface of the food quickly, but the food itself cooks more slowly and steadily. Meat, poultry, and fish in particular will cook better on a relatively cool fire that is glowing gently, usually referred to as medium-hot.
- If fat, oil, or marinade drips onto the hot fire and flareups occur, remove the food, then either sprinkle the flames with water or wait until they die down before continuing the cooking.
- Cook thicker pieces of food toward the edge of the fire, because this allows plenty of time for the heat to penetrate to the center before the outside becomes tough.
- If food seems to be cooking too quickly, raise the rack, or move the food to the edge of the grill rack. If cooking too slowly, lower the grill rack, or move the food over the center of the fire.
- To cool a fire that's too hot, push the hot coals apart. Conversely, to increase the heat, heap the coals together.
- Keep an eye on the cooking and check frequently for doneness. Start checking before the food is due to be ready, because once it has become dry and tough it's beyond repair.
- Metal skewers will retain heat for quite a while after being removed from the grill rack, so be sure to warn diners about this.
- Be careful about brushing nearly cooked food with marinade containing raw juices, especially a marinade that has been used for chicken or pork.

COOKING TIMES

These cooking times and those given in the recipes are only a guide: the time depends on the thickness of the food; the temperature of the food and the surroundings; the type of grill used; the choice of fuel; the intensity of the heat; the height of the grill rack from the heat source; and whether there are any drafts.

Roasts and whole birds can be tested to see if they are done to your satisfaction by inserting a digital instant-read thermometer into the thickest part. Meat and poultry to be sliced for serving should be removed from the grill rack to a ridged meat platter or a board, covered with foil, and left to rest for 5–10 minutes before being carved or cut up.

These timings and those given in the recipes are for foods that are at room temperature before being cooked, then grilled over medium-hot coals using the direct-heat method (see page 8), unless otherwise stated.

POULTRY

Cook skin-on chicken and duck breasts on the skin side first until it is crisp, then turn them over to complete the cooking. To check if chicken is cooked through, pierce the thickest part, next to the bone if appropriate, with a skewer or the point of a sharp knife. If the juices run out clear, the chicken is ready. If the juices are at all pink, it needs more cooking. For dark thigh and leg meat, the internal temperature should be 170°F; for breast meat, the temperature should be 160°F.

Breast and leg quarters, bone in: 10–11 oz: 25 minutes, turning regularly

Boneless breast halves, skin on: 7 minutes skin-side down, then 5 minutes on the other side

Drumsticks/thighs, bone in: 8 oz: 15–20 minutes, turning regularly

Boneless thighs: 6 oz: 4–5 minutes on each side

Large wings: 15–20 minutes, turning regularly

Brochettes and kabobs: 5 minutes on each side

Squab chickens, butterflied: 25 minutes

Whole chicken: cook over indirect heat for 15 minutes per pound plus an extra 15 minutes, to the required internal temperature (check with a digital thermometer)

Duck breasts, skin on: 5 minutes skin-side down, then 8–10 minutes on the other side

PORK

These timings produce pork that is well done but still juicy. The internal temperature should be 170°F. If you prefer pork slightly rosy, grill until the internal temperature is 160°F.

Boneless steaks: 1 inch thick: 7–8 minutes on each side

Sirloin or loin chops: 1 inch thick: 8–10 minutes on each side

Brochettes and kabobs: 12–15 minutes, turning once

Tenderloin: 1 lb: 25 minutes, turning once

Larger roasts: cook over indirect heat for 25–30 minutes per pound plus an extra 25 minutes, or to the desired degree of doneness (check internal temperature)

BEEF

For rare beef, the internal temperature should be 130°F, for medium-rare 135°F, for medium 150°F, for medium-well 165°F, and for well done 185°F.

Boneless sirloin steaks: 1½ inches thick: rare: 3–4 minutes on each side; medium-rare: 4–5 minutes on each side; medium: 5–6 minutes on each side

Filet mignons: 2 inches thick: rare: 6 minutes on each side; medium-rare: 8 minutes on each side; medium: 10 minutes on each side

Brochettes and kabobs: 8–10 minutes, turning regularly

Roasts: cook over indirect heat for 20 minutes per pound plus an extra 20 minutes for rare, 25 minutes per pound plus an extra 25 minutes for medium, and 30 minutes per pound plus an extra 30 minutes for well done (check doneness with a digital thermometer).

Hamburgers: 1 inch thick: rare: 3 minutes on each side; medium: 4 minutes on each side; well done: 5 minutes on each side

LAMB

These timings are for medium-rare lamb (internal temperature of 130°–135°F). Decrease the timings slightly for rare meat and increase slightly for medium (140°–150°F).

Loin chops, bone in: 1 inch thick: 6–7 minutes on each side

Boneless loin chops: 3 minutes on each side

Leg steaks or shoulder chops: 1½ inches thick: 5–7 minutes on each side

Brochettes and kabobs: 8–10 minutes, turning regularly

Leg of lamb, butterflied: 12–15 minutes on each side

Roasts: cook over indirect heat for 20 minutes per pound (check for desired doneness with a digital thermometer)

FISH AND SEAFOOD

As a general rule, allow 8–10 minutes for each 1 inch of thickness (half that time for ½-inch-thick fillets). Fish is generally considered to be cooked when the flesh in the center is just changing from translucent to opaque, although there are some exceptions: salmon is often served less well done, and tuna may be preferred fairly rare.

Steaks: 7–8 oz, 1 inch thick: 4–5 minutes on each side

Fillets: 3–4 minutes on each side, depending on thickness

Brochettes and kabobs: 3–4 minutes on each side

Whole fish: 10–12 oz: 6–7 minutes on each side; 3 lb: 12–15 minutes on each side

Raw large shrimp and tiger shrimp: 2–3 minutes on each side

Sea scallops, shucked: 2–3 minutes on each side

APPETIZERS AND SNACKS

In this chapter you will find a huge range of enticing snacks and mouthwatering appetizers to keep both cooks and guests happy while you are pouring the drinks and waiting for the main course dishes to be cooked.

If you prefer not to eat a heavy meal, though, there is a wonderful choice of recipes here for lighter snacks. Dip into Chicken, Papaya, and Rice Noodle Salad, for example, or Scallops with Thai Dipping Sauce. You might even like to make a meal out of a selection chosen from this chapter. Combine Red Pepper, Feta, and Olive Wraps with Chicken Bruschettas with Prosciutto and Figs, and Butterflied Shrimp with Italian Dip. There are also tempting dishes for children, such as Skewered Potato Chip Scrolls and Sausage and Cheese Grills.

The recipes are all very quick and simple to cook and many can even be prepared in advance, leaving you to enjoy a lazy afternoon in the sunshine.

001 BUTTERFLIED SHRIMP WITH ITALIAN DIP

PREPARATION TIME *10 minutes, plus 30-60 minutes marinating* **COOKING TIME** *4-6 minutes* **SERVES 3-4**

1 lb raw tiger shrimp or large shrimp in shell	5 tbsp extra-virgin olive oil	1 tbsp chopped fresh basil
½ garlic clove, finely chopped	2 tbsp sun-dried tomato paste	salt and freshly ground black pepper
juice of 1 lemon	pinch of paprika	basil sprigs for garnish

1 Remove the heads and fine legs from the shrimp. Using sharp scissors, cut the shrimp lengthwise almost in half, leaving the tail end intact. Lay them in a shallow dish, sprinkle the garlic over, and pour on half the lemon juice and 2 tablespoons of the oil. Stir to ensure the shrimp are evenly coated. Cover and let marinate in a cool place for 30-60 minutes.

2 Meanwhile, to make the dip, stir together the remaining lemon juice and oil with the tomato paste, paprika, and chopped basil in a small bowl. Add a little seasoning.

3 Lift the shrimp from the dish. Thread onto skewers for easier turning, if desired. Grill on an oiled rack until the shrimp turn pink, 2-3 minutes on each side .

4 Remove the shrimp from the grill and sprinkle with salt and black pepper. Either pour the dip over or serve it separately. Garnish the shrimp with the basil sprigs.

002 POTATO SKINS WITH CHIVE DIP

PREPARATION TIME *10 minutes* **COOKING TIME** *1½ hours* **SERVES 2-4**

2 large baking potatoes, scrubbed and dried	CHIVE DIP	1½ tbsp snipped fresh chives
olive oil for brushing	2 tbsp thick, plain yogurt	salt and freshly ground black pepper
coarse sea or kosher salt	½ cup cottage cheese, pressed through a sieve	

1 Preheat the oven to 400ºF. Pass a metal skewer through each potato, then bake until the potatoes are tender but the skins are still soft, about 1¼ hours.

2 Meanwhile, make the dip by stirring the yogurt into the cottage cheese. Add the chives and seasoning to taste. Cover and chill until required.

3 Remove the potatoes from the oven and leave until cool enough to handle, then cut each one into quarters lengthwise. Using a teaspoon, scoop out most of the flesh, leaving a thin layer next to the skin. (Use the removed flesh in another recipe.)

4 Brush the potatoes with olive oil and sprinkle the skins with coarse salt. Grill on an oiled rack until golden, 4-6 minutes on each side . Season with black pepper and serve with the dip.

003 CROQUE M'SIEUR

PREPARATION TIME *10 minutes* **COOKING TIME** *4-6 minutes* **MAKES** *6 sandwiches*

12 slices firm bread	wholegrain mustard for spreading	1 cup grated Gruyère cheese
unsalted butter, softened, for spreading	6 thin slices good-quality ham	

1 Spread one side of half of the slices of bread with butter, then with mustard. Top with a slice of ham, then some cheese. Cover with the remaining bread and press together.

2 Grill on an oiled rack until the bread is browned and the cheese is melting, 2-3 minutes on each side. Press down on the sandwiches with a metal spatula during cooking.

3 Remove the crusts and cut the sandwiches in half. Serve warm.

004 SPINACH-FILLED TOMATOES WITH ROQUEFORT TOPPING

PREPARATION TIME *10 minutes* **COOKING TIME** *15 minutes* **SERVES 4**

4 large roma tomatoes, halved lengthwise	1 garlic clove, finely chopped	salt and freshly ground black pepper
2 tsp olive oil	6 oz frozen chopped spinach, thawed and squeezed dry	2–3 oz Roquefort cheese, sliced
1 shallot, finely chopped		

1 Carefully scoop the pulp from the tomatoes. Sprinkle the inside of the shells with salt, then turn them upside down and let drain. Chop the tomato flesh.
2 Heat the oil in a small frying pan, add the shallot and garlic, and fry until softened, stirring occasionally. Add the chopped tomato flesh and heat, stirring, until the moisture has evaporated. Stir in the spinach, season, and heat through.
3 Stand the tomatoes on a plate, cut-side up. Pack the spinach mixture into the tomato cups and top each with a slice of cheese. Season with black pepper.
4 Transfer the tomatoes to an oiled grill rack and grill until they are lightly charred and slightly softened, 4–6 minutes. Do not let them become too soft, or they will be difficult to transfer to serving plates.

005 ZUCCHINI TUBES WITH RICOTTA AND SUN-DRIED TOMATOES

PREPARATION TIME *10 minutes* **COOKING TIME** *15 minutes* **SERVES 2–4**

3 large zucchini, about 6 oz each, ends trimmed	½ cup ricotta cheese	2 sun-dried tomatoes in oil, drained and chopped
1 tbsp peanut oil, plus extra for brushing	3 tbsp freshly grated Parmesan cheese	salt and freshly ground black pepper
1 plump garlic clove, finely chopped	2 tbsp fresh white bread crumbs	
2 shallots, finely chopped	½ tbsp snipped fresh chives	
	½ tbsp chopped fresh basil	

1 Cut each zucchini across in half. Using an apple corer, carefully remove the center from each zucchini piece, but keep the zucchini intact. Chop the removed flesh.
2 Heat the oil in a frying pan and add the zucchini flesh, garlic, and shallots. Cook gently until the shallots are tender, stirring occasionally. Remove the pan from the heat and stir in the cheeses, bread crumbs, herbs, sun-dried tomatoes, and seasoning.
3 Stand the zucchini tubes on end and pack in the cheese filling. Brush the outsides of the tubes with oil. Grill at the side of an oiled rack until softened and lightly charred, 6–8 minutes, turning frequently. Do not let them become too soft.

006 GRILLED PIZZA WITH RED PEPPERS, EGGPLANT, AND CHORIZO

PREPARATION TIME *20 minutes, plus rising time* **COOKING TIME** *20–30 minutes* **SERVES 4**

about 3 cups white bread flour
2 tsp rapid-rise active dry yeast
1 tsp salt
freshly ground black pepper
scant 1 cup warm water
2 tbsp olive oil, plus extra for brushing

TOMATO SAUCE
2 tbsp olive oil

1 small onion, finely chopped
2 garlic cloves, finely chopped
1 tsp dried oregano
28-oz can crushed tomatoes
about 2 tsp sun-dried tomato paste, or to taste
1½–2 tbsp chopped fresh herbs, such as parsley, thyme, oregano, tarragon, rosemary

TOPPING
2 large, red bell peppers, halved lengthwise
1 eggplant, sliced across into rounds
olive oil for brushing
6-oz piece smoked Spanish chorizo, chopped
3 oz feta cheese, crumbled
3 oz mozzarella cheese, grated
small handful of fresh basil leaves, torn

1   Stir the flour, yeast, salt, and some pepper together in a bowl. Make a well in the center and pour in the water and oil. Bring the flour mixture into the liquids to make a soft dough. Knead on a floured surface until firm and elastic, 10–12 minutes.
2   Turn the dough over in an oiled bowl, cover, and let rise until doubled in volume.
3   Meanwhile, make the sauce: Heat the oil, add the onion and garlic, and fry until softened and translucent. Add the dried oregano. Stir in the tomatoes and simmer until thickened. Add the sun-dried tomato paste, fresh herbs, and seasoning to taste. Let cool.
4   Grill the red peppers on an oiled rack, or under a preheated broiler, until charred and blistered. Leave until cool enough to handle, then remove the skins. Slice the peppers.
5   Brush the eggplant slices with oil, then grill or broil until tender and lightly charred on both sides.
6   Punch down the dough and divide it in half. Roll out each piece to an even 10-inch circle. Brush each circle with olive oil, then transfer, oil-side down, to two flat baking sheets.
7   Carefully slide the pizzas, oil-side down, onto the oiled grill rack. Grill until the underside of each base is marked with charred lines, 2–3 minutes. Transfer the pizza bases, grilled-side up, back to the baking sheets. Brush with oil and spread on the tomato sauce, leaving a ½-inch border. Arrange the red pepper and eggplant slices evenly over the top, then scatter on the chorizo and feta and mozzarella cheeses. Season with plenty of black pepper and sprinkle with the basil. Drizzle some more oil over the top.
8   Slide the pizzas back onto the oiled grill rack and grill until the bases are browned underneath and cooked through and the cheeses have melted, 3–4 minutes longer.

007 CHEESE AND CHIVE BAGUETTES

PREPARATION TIME *10 minutes* **COOKING TIME** *8 minutes* **SERVES 4**

6 tbsp unsalted butter, softened
2 plump garlic cloves, crushed

2 cups grated aged Cheddar cheese
2½ tbsp snipped fresh chives

freshly ground black pepper
4 baguette rolls (half baguettes)

1   Beat the butter until smooth, then mix in the garlic, cheese, chives, and some black pepper.
2   Cut the rolls in half lengthwise and spread the cut sides with the flavored butter.
3   Wrap each roll in heavy-duty foil, twisting the edges together tightly. Place on the grill rack and cook until the butter has melted and the bread is warm, about 8 minutes. Serve at once.

008 SHRIMP PINWHEELS

PREPARATION TIME *10 minutes, plus 2 hours marinating* **COOKING TIME** *5–6 minutes* **SERVES 6**

24 raw tiger shrimp	1 tbsp fenugreek seeds	⅛ tsp ground turmeric
2 tsp cumin seeds	3 tbsp peanut oil	salt and freshly ground
1 tbsp crushed dried chiles	4 shallots, chopped	black pepper
1 star anise	4 garlic cloves, chopped	lemon wedges for serving

1 Remove the heads from the shrimp and peel them, leaving the last tail section in place. Put them in a shallow, nonreactive dish.

2 Toast the cumin seeds, chiles, and star anise in a frying pan for 1 minute, stirring. Grind finely in a spice grinder, or crush using the end of a rolling pin in a small bowl. Set aside.

3 Fry the fenugreek seeds in 1 tablespoon of the oil until they start to crackle. Add to the spices.

4 Put the shallots, garlic, turmeric, and remaining oil into a blender and add the spice mixture, some salt, and plenty of black pepper. Mix to a coarse paste. Spread evenly over the shrimp. Cover and let marinate in a cool place for 2 hours.

5 Curl each shrimp into a tight spiral, then thread onto an oiled skewer, inserting it at the base of the tail end. Grill the shrimp on an oiled rack until pink, 3–4 minutes, turning once. Squeeze the lemon wedges over the shrimp and serve. (If desired, the lemon wedges can be lightly charred on the grill alongside the shrimp.)

009 HONEY AND HOISIN SPARERIBS

PREPARATION TIME *5 minutes, plus 2 hours marinating* **COOKING TIME** *50–55 minutes* **SERVES 6**

3½–4½ lb pork spareribs, cut into individual ribs
2 tbsp mild honey
⅔ cup apple cider or apple juice

⅔ cup hoisin sauce
¼ cup cider vinegar
3 tbsp ketchup *(see page 184)*

1 tsp prepared English mustard

1   Line a roasting pan with heavy-duty foil. Put the ribs in the pan.
2   Combine the remaining ingredients and spoon evenly over the ribs; don't worry if there seems to be inadequate liquid, as the ribs will yield fat during cooking. Cover the pan with plastic wrap and let marinate in a cool place for 2 hours, if possible.
3   Preheat the oven to 400°F. Uncover the pan and cook the ribs in the oven for 30–35 minutes, turning them over occasionally.
4   Remove from the oven, brush the ribs with the cooking juices, and transfer to an oiled grill rack. Grill until cooked through and dark golden brown, 20–25 minutes, turning and brushing occasionally with the cooking juices.

010 SKEWERED POTATO CHIP SCROLLS

PREPARATION TIME *10 minutes* **COOKING TIME** *10–15 minutes* **SERVES 4–6**

2 baking potatoes, about 8 oz each, peeled

olive oil for brushing
freshly ground black pepper

coarse sea or kosher salt and paprika for sprinkling

1   Using a mandoline or fine slicing blade in a food processor, cut the potatoes into wafer-thin slices lengthwise. Put immediately into a bowl of salted hot water. Stir to separate the slices, then leave until pliable, 3–4 minutes .
2   Drain and dry the slices thoroughly, then carefully roll up each slice, from the narrowest end. Thread onto oiled long skewers, leaving at least ½ inch between each scroll.
3   Brush the scrolls with oil and sprinkle with black pepper. Grill on an oiled rack until crisp, 10–15 minutes, turning occasionally.
4   Remove from the grill rack and sprinkle with salt and paprika.

011 ITALIAN BLT

PREPARATION TIME *5 minutes* **COOKING TIME** *8 minutes* **SERVES 4**

1 plump garlic clove, halved lengthwise
1 large focaccia loaf, split in half horizontally

virgin olive oil for brushing
8 slices of pancetta, or very thinly sliced bacon
4 tomatoes, halved lengthwise

¾ cup ricotta cheese
fresh basil leaves for garnish

1   Rub the cut surface of the garlic over the cut surfaces of the focaccia, then brush lightly with olive oil. Lightly toast the focaccia on both sides on an oiled grill rack.
2   At the same time, grill the pancetta on the rack until crisp; cook the tomatoes near the side of the grill rack until lightly charred and beginning to soften, about 4 minutes on each side. Remove with a metal spatula.
3   Transfer the focaccia base to a platter. Top with the pancetta and spread on the ricotta, then add the tomatoes. Scatter the basil over. Put on the top of the focaccia and press lightly together.

012 TANDOORI SHRIMP ROLLS

PREPARATION TIME *10 minutes, plus 30–60 minutes marinating* **COOKING TIME** *4–5 minutes* **SERVES 4**

8 oz shelled raw tiger
   shrimp or large shrimp
4 French or sourdough
   bread rolls or
   burger buns
butter for spreading
crisp lettuce leaves
¼ red onion, rinsed and
   thinly sliced

lemon wedges and fresh
   cilantro for serving

MARINADE
1 tbsp lemon juice
1 tbsp thick, plain yogurt
1 small garlic clove, finely
   chopped

½ tsp grated fresh
   gingerroot
large pinch of paprika
pinch of ground cumin
pinch of garam masala
½ tbsp peanut oil

1 Make the marinade by mixing all the ingredients together in a nonreactive bowl. Stir in the shrimp, ensuring they are evenly coated. Cover and leave in a cool place for 30–60 minutes.
2 Lift the shrimp from the marinade and spread out on an oiled grill rack. Grill until they have turned pink, 2–2½ minutes on each side.
3 Meanwhile, split the rolls open and warm them on the side of the grill rack.
4 Remove the shrimp from the grill. Squeeze some lemon juice over them.
5 Butter the warm rolls liberally. Fill with lettuce leaves, red onion slices, shrimp, and cilantro leaves. Squeeze the halves of the rolls together and serve.

013 GRILLED CHEESE, HERB, AND TOMATO SANDWICHES

PREPARATION TIME *5 minutes* **COOKING TIME** *4–6 minutes* **MAKES** *4 sandwiches*

8 slices bread
4 slices Fontina, Taleggio,
   Gruyère or aged
   Cheddar cheese, or
   use them grated
3–4 tomatoes, sliced
olive oil or melted unsalted
   butter for brushing

HERB SPREAD
½ cup wild arugula
⅓ cup fresh flat-leaf
   parsley leaves
⅓ cup fresh basil leaves
½ tsp capers
½ tsp wholegrain mustard
½ tbsp olive oil

salt and freshly ground
   black pepper

1 First make the herb spread: Put the arugula, parsley, and basil in a food processor or blender and pulse six or seven times until coarsely chopped, then add the remaining ingredients and mix for about 30 seconds to make a coarse paste.
2 Spread one side of each slice of bread with a little of the herb spread. Lay four slices on the work surface and divide the cheese among them. Top with the tomato slices, then press the other bread slices on top. Brush the outer surfaces of the bread with oil or melted butter.
3 Grill on an oiled rack until browned and the cheese is melting, 2–3 minutes on each side. Press down on the sandwiches with a metal spatula during cooking to help them stick together. Remove the crusts and cut the sandwiches in half. Serve warm.

014 EGGPLANT AND MOZZARELLA ROLLS

PREPARATION TIME *15 minutes, plus 30–60 minutes draining* **COOKING TIME** *6–8 minutes* **SERVES 4-6**

2 eggplants
salt and freshly ground
  black pepper
1 tbsp extra virgin olive oil,
  plus extra for brushing
6 tbsp Pesto *(see page 172)*

12 oil-cured black olives,
  pitted and cut into
  slivers
6 sun-dried tomatoes in oil,
  drained and sliced
3 tbsp finely shredded
  fresh basil

5 oz buffalo mozzarella
  cheese (mozzarella di
  bufala), diced
3 tbsp freshly grated
  Parmesan cheese

1. Cut each eggplant lengthwise into six ¼-inch-thick slices. Sprinkle salt over the slices and let drain for 30–60 minutes. Rinse off the salt and dry the slices thoroughly.
2. Brush the slices with extra virgin olive oil and grill on an oiled rack until lightly charred and softened, 2–3 minutes on each side, turning once. Remove from the grill.
3. Using half of the pesto sauce, spread a little over each eggplant slice. Scatter the olives, sun-dried tomatoes, basil, and mozzarella on top. Sprinkle with black pepper.
4. Roll up the eggplant slices, starting at a short end. Secure with soaked wooden toothpicks (see page 10). Sprinkle with the Parmesan and return to the oiled grill rack. Grill until warmed through and lightly golden, about 2 minutes on each side.
5. Meanwhile, mix the tablespoon of extra virgin olive oil with the remaining pesto sauce. Transfer the eggplant rolls to plates, drizzle the pesto dressing over them, and serve immediately.

015 MIXED SATAY

PREPARATION TIME *15 minutes, plus 1–8 hours marinating* **COOKING TIME** *17–23 minutes* **SERVES 4**

1½ lb mixed boneless meats and skinless, boneless chicken, cut into 1-inch-wide strips	2 tsp ground coriander	SATAY SAUCE
	2 tsp ground cumin	½ cup shelled unsalted peanuts
	1 tsp turmeric	1 garlic clove, chopped
	1 tbsp dark brown sugar	2 tbsp red Thai curry paste
12 raw medium shrimp, shelled but with the last tail section left on	¼ cup canned coconut milk	1¾ cups canned coconut milk
squeeze of lemon juice	lemon or lime wedges for serving	2 tbsp dark brown sugar
1 garlic clove, crushed and chopped		squeeze of lemon juice
		dash of hot pepper sauce

1   Put the meat, chicken, and shrimp into a shallow, nonreactive dish. Sprinkle with lemon juice.
2   Combine the garlic, spices, sugar, and coconut milk to make a fairly stiff paste. Rub evenly into the meat mixture. Cover and let marinate in a cool place for at least 1 hour, preferably 8 hours.
3   Meanwhile, make the sauce: Toast the peanuts under a preheated broiler, stirring frequently to ensure they brown evenly. Transfer to a blender or food processor. Add the garlic, curry paste, and a little of the coconut milk. Blend until smooth, then add the remaining ingredients and blend well. Pour into a saucepan. Bring to a boil and boil for 2 minutes, then lower the heat and simmer for 10 minutes, stirring occasionally. If the sauce thickens too much, add a little water.
4   Thread the meat, chicken, and shrimp onto separate skewers. Grill on an oiled rack for 5–10 minutes; beef and lamb will still be slightly pink inside, but pork and chicken should be cooked through. Grill shrimp until they just turn pink, 3 minutes on each side.
5   Warm the sauce on the side of the grill rack, thinning if necessary with a little more water, then pour into a warm serving bowl.
6   Serve the skewers with lemon or lime wedges and the satay sauce.

016 CHICKEN YAKITORI

PREPARATION TIME *10 minutes* **COOKING TIME** *13–15 minutes* **SERVES 6**

6 boneless chicken thighs, cut into 1-inch pieces	YAKITORI SAUCE	1½ tbsp sugar
	¾ cup dark soy sauce	freshly ground black pepper
12 baby leeks, outer leaves removed, then cut into 1-inch lengths, or 12 fat scallions, green parts trimmed	⅓ cup sake	
	⅓ cup chicken stock	
	¼ cup mirin	
	1 small garlic clove, finely chopped	

1   Make the sauce by heating the ingredients in a saucepan, stirring until the sugar has dissolved. Bring to a boil, then simmer for 1 minute. Remove from the heat and let cool, then strain.
2   Thread the chicken, skin-side out, and the leeks or scallions alternately onto skewers.
3   Pour about one-quarter of the sauce into a small bowl to serve as a dipping sauce.
4   Grill the skewers on an oiled rack for 2 minutes. Brush with the remaining sauce and grill for 6–8 minutes longer, basting with the sauce frequently and turning once.
5   Serve the skewers with the dipping sauce.

017 CHICKEN, PAPAYA, AND RICE NOODLE SALAD

PREPARATION TIME *15 minutes, plus 1 hour marinating* **COOKING TIME** *4–5 minutes* **SERVES 4**

8 oz skinless, boneless chicken breast halves, cut into strips

4 oz thin rice noodles

1 small zucchini, cut into thin strips

2 heaped tbsp fresh cilantro leaves, coarsely torn

1 small papaya, peeled, seeded, and cut into wedges

MARINADE

1 garlic clove, crushed

1 tbsp Thai fish sauce

1 tsp Thai red curry paste

1 tsp toasted sesame oil

1 tsp clear honey

DRESSING

3 tbsp peanut oil

3 tbsp lime juice

1½ tbsp Thai fish sauce

few drops of hot pepper sauce

2–3 tsp sugar

1 Put the chicken strips in a nonreactive bowl. Make the marinade by combining the ingredients. Stir into the chicken, cover, and let marinate in a cool place for 1 hour, stirring occasionally.

2 Meanwhile, pour boiling water over the noodles and let soak for 4–5 minutes, or according to package directions. Drain well and tip into a large bowl. Add the zucchini and cilantro.

3 Make the dressing by combining the ingredients. Pour half over the noodles and toss, then chill.

4 Lift the chicken from the marinade and grill (in an oiled fine wire mesh, if possible) on the rack for about 2 minutes on each side.

5 Grill the papaya wedges at the side of the rack for 5 minutes. Remove from the rack and cut into bite-sized pieces.

6 Divide the noodles among four bowls. Mix the chicken and papaya together, pile on top of the noodles, and trickle the remaining dressing over.

018 LIME AND HONEY-GLAZED CHICKEN WINGS

PREPARATION TIME *5 minutes, plus 4–8 hours marinating* **COOKING TIME** *20–25 minutes* **SERVES 4**

12 large chicken wings

lime wedges for serving

MARINADE

2 tbsp olive oil

3 tbsp honey

6 tbsp lime juice

2 tbsp dry white wine

2 tsp chopped fresh marjoram

1 tsp fresh thyme leaves

freshly ground black pepper

1 Place the chicken wings in a shallow, nonreactive dish.

2 Make the marinade by mixing all the ingredients together. Pour evenly over the wings and turn them over to ensure they are evenly coated, then cover and let marinate in a cool place for 4–8 hours, turning occasionally.

3 To make it easier to turn the chicken wings on the grill rack, cut off the tips of the wings, then thread the wings onto parallel skewers, three wings to each pair of skewers.

4 Transfer the wings to an oiled grill rack (reserve the marinade) and grill for 20–25 minutes, turning and brushing with the reserved marinade. Serve the wings with lime wedges.

019 VEGETABLE AND PROSCIUTTO BRUSCHETTAS

PREPARATION TIME *15 minutes* **COOKING TIME** *10–15 minutes* **SERVES 6**

2 heads Belgian endive, quartered	6 baby leeks	BASTING SAUCE
1 red bell pepper, cut into 6 pieces	3 plump garlic cloves, halved lengthwise	3 tbsp virgin olive oil
6 bottled or canned artichoke hearts, halved lengthwise	6 slices sourdough bread	1 plump garlic clove, crushed
	6 slices prosciutto*	1 tbsp soy sauce
	chopped fresh cilantro for garnish	½ tbsp harissa sauce
		½ tbsp dried marjoram

1 Put all the vegetables, except the garlic, in a large dish.
2 Make the basting sauce by combining the ingredients. Stir into the vegetables. Lift the vegetables from the sauce (reserve the sauce), thread alternately onto oiled skewers and grill on an oiled rack until flecked with brown and tender, 10–15 minutes, turning and brushing with the reserved sauce occasionally. When they are cooked, transfer them to a bowl and keep warm.
3 Meanwhile, spear the garlic halves onto soaked wooden toothpicks (see page 10) and grill until tender.
4 Toast the bread on the side of the grill rack. Squash a garlic half over each slice of toast. Lay the prosciutto on top and spoon on a mixture of vegetables, sliding them off the skewers. Sprinkle with the chopped cilantro.
* If preferred, instead of, or as well as, the prosciutto, the bruschetta slices can be spread with soft goat cheese or ricotta cheese.

020 SHRIMP WITH LEMON GRASS AND PAPAYA SALSA

PREPARATION TIME *15 minutes, plus 1 hour marinating* **COOKING TIME** *4–6 minutes* **SERVES 4–6**

4 lemon grass stems, peeled and finely chopped	1 fresh, hot red chile, seeded and chopped	4 scallions, chopped
1 plump garlic clove, chopped	28 raw tiger shrimp or large shrimp, shelled but last tail section left on	handful of fresh cilantro leaves, finely chopped
5 tbsp virgin olive oil	1 papaya, peeled and halved	salt and freshly ground black pepper
1½ limes		lime wedges for serving

1 Combine the lemon grass, garlic, 2 tablespoons of the oil, the juice of 1 lime, and two-thirds of the chile in a bowl. Stir in the shrimp, cover, and let marinate in a cool place for 1 hour.
2 Meanwhile, scoop the seeds from the papaya and dice the flesh. Mix with the juice of the remaining half lime, the remaining chile, the scallions, cilantro, and seasoning.
3 Lift the shrimp from the marinade and spread them on an oiled grill rack. Grill until they turn pink, 2–3 minutes on each side. Serve with the salsa and lime wedges.

021 VEGETABLE WRAPS

PREPARATION TIME *10 minutes* **COOKING TIME** *12–16 minutes* **MAKES 4**

4 slim asparagus spears	1 small eggplant, cut	2 tbsp chopped fresh
8 cremini mushrooms	lengthwise into	herbs, such as flat-leaf
2 zucchini, cut on the	½-inch slices	parsley, cilantro, basil
diagonal into	8 scallions	¼ cup Rouille *(see page 183)*
½-inch slices	olive oil for brushing	salt and freshly ground
3 heads baby bok choy	4 pita breads	black pepper

1   Trim the asparagus spears, then blanch in boiling water for 2 minutes. Rinse under running cold water, drain, and dry well.
2   Brush the vegetables with oil and grill on an oiled rack: Grill the mushrooms for 6–10 minutes (depending on their size), the zucchini for 6–8 minutes on each side, the bok choy for 4 minutes on each side, the eggplant for 5 minutes, and the scallions for 3 minutes.
3   Meanwhile, split the pita breads open and separate the two halves.
4   Combine all the vegetables with the herbs and rouille, and season. Divide among the pita breads, leaving about a 1-inch border all around. Fold over ½ inch on opposite sides, then roll up tightly, starting at one of the unfolded sides, and serve.

022 RED PEPPER, FETA, AND OLIVE WRAPS

PREPARATION TIME *10 minutes* **COOKING TIME** *10 minutes* **SERVES 4**

6 red bell peppers	8 oz feta cheese,	2 tbsp balsamic vinegar
4 flour tortillas	crumbled	fresh basil leaves for
Basil and Broiled Tomato	12 oil-packed black	serving
Pesto *(see page 172)*	olives, pitted	

1   Grill the peppers on an oiled rack until the skin is charred and blistered, about 10 minutes. Leave until cool enough to handle, then remove the skins. Slice the flesh.
2   Meanwhile, warm the tortillas at the side of the grill rack for 30 seconds.
3   Spread the pesto sauce over the tortillas. Divide the peppers, cheese, and olives among the tortillas, sprinkle with the vinegar, and add a few fresh basil leaves. Roll up and serve.

023 NORTH AFRICAN LAMB BITES

PREPARATION TIME *10 minutes, plus 1 hour marinating* **COOKING TIME** *10–14 minutes* **SERVES 4**

2 tbsp caraway seeds	½ tbsp freshly ground	8 oz boneless leg of lamb,
1 tbsp cumin seeds	black pepper	cut into 16 cubes
½ tbsp coriander seeds	pinch of crushed dried	small pita breads and
salt	chiles	plain yogurt for serving

1   Toast the seeds in a small, heavy frying pan over medium heat until fragrant. Crush fairly finely, then mix with some salt, the black pepper, and chiles. Rub into the lamb. Cover and let marinate in a cool place for 1 hour.
2   Thread the lamb onto four skewers. Grill on an oiled rack until browned and cooked to the desired degree of doneness, 5–7 minutes on each side, turning occasionally.
3   Meanwhile, warm the pita breads on the side of the grill rack for 30 seconds on each side. Serve the bites with the pita breads and yogurt.

024 SCALLOPS WITH THAI DIPPING SAUCE

PREPARATION TIME *10 minutes* **COOKING TIME** *4–6 minutes* **SERVES 4**

20 sea scallops, shucked
toasted sesame oil
  for brushing
20 fresh cilantro leaves
20 thin slices of pickled
  ginger *(see page 167)*

THAI DIPPING SAUCE
2 tbsp Thai fish sauce
1 tbsp lime juice
1 tsp finely chopped garlic
1 tsp finely chopped fresh,
  hot red chile
1 scallion, thinly sliced

2 tsp finely chopped
  peanuts
2½ tsp chopped peeled
  English cucumber
1½ tbsp palm sugar or
  dark brown sugar

1 Make the dipping sauce by stirring the ingredients together until the sugar has dissolved, then
   pour into a small serving bowl.
2 Brush the scallops lightly with sesame oil. Lay them on the grill rack and grill until they just
   change color, 2–3 minutes on each side, turning once. Take care not to overcook.
3 Remove from the rack and pierce each scallop onto a toothpick, adding a cilantro leaf and a slice
   of pickled ginger. Serve with the dipping sauce.

025 CHICKEN BRUSCHETTAS WITH PROSCIUTTO AND FIGS

PREPARATION TIME *10 minutes* **COOKING TIME** *10 minutes* **SERVES 4**

2 large, boneless chicken
  breast halves
2 tbsp balsamic vinegar
1 tsp clear honey
2 tbsp extra virgin olive oil,
  plus extra for trickling

salt and freshly ground
  black pepper
4 large, ripe but firm figs,
  halved from top to
  bottom

1 garlic clove, halved
  lengthwise
4 large slices sourdough
  bread
4 slices prosciutto
handful of arugula leaves

1   Make four slashes on each side of each chicken breast.
2   Combine the balsamic vinegar with the honey, oil, and seasoning. Brush half of the mixture over
    the chicken and fig halves; reserve the remaining mixture.
3   Grill the chicken on an oiled rack until lightly charred and cooked through, about 4 minutes
    on each side. Add the figs to the grill when you turn the chicken over and cook until softened,
    1–2 minutes. Remove the chicken and figs from the grill and keep warm.
4   Rub the cut sides of the garlic over one side of each slice of bread, then cook on the oiled grill
    rack until toasted. At the same time, grill the prosciutto until crisp. Remove the bread from the
    grill and trickle some oil over. Keep the bread and prosciutto warm.
5   Slice the chicken and arrange on the toasted bread with the arugula, prosciutto, and figs. Trickle
    the remaining balsamic mixture over and serve.

026 GOAT CHEESE-FILLED GRAPE LEAVES

PREPARATION TIME *10 minutes* **COOKING TIME** *5 minutes* **SERVES 3-6**

6 large, fresh grape leaves*,
  or vacuum-packed grape
  leaves, very well rinsed

6 small goat cheeses,
  such as St. Marcellin
  crottins, or 3 milder,
  softer cheeses,
  4 oz each, halved
  horizontally

virgin olive oil for brushing
fresh thyme for sprinkling
freshly ground black
  pepper
crusty bread for serving

1   Dry the grape leaves well.
2   Lay each leaf flat on the work surface. Brush each goat cheese with virgin olive oil and place
    in the center of a leaf. Sprinkle lightly with thyme and with plenty of black pepper. Fold the
    leaf over to enclose the cheese completely and secure with a soaked wooden toothpick (see page
    10). Brush with more olive oil and sprinkle with black pepper.
3   Grill on an oiled rack until the cheese begins to melt, about 2½ minutes on each side. Lift from
    the grill with a metal spatula and eat with crusty bread.
*   Use fresh, tender grape leaves, if available. Blanch until they become supple, about 2 minutes,
    then drain and dry well.

027 CHEESE-FILLED RED PEPPERS

PREPARATION TIME *10 minutes* **COOKING TIME** *10 minutes* **SERVES 4**

½ cup chopped oil-cured
  black olives
2 heaped tbsp chopped
  fresh basil or flat-leaf
  parsley leaves
2 tbsp chopped capers

4 red bell peppers, halved
  lengthwise, deseeded
6 oz mixed Taleggio cheese
  and buffalo mozzarella
  (mozzarella di bufala),
  sliced

7 tbsp herb vinaigrette
freshly ground black
  pepper
4 slices ciabatta
virgin olive oil
arugula leaves for serving

1   Combine the olives, basil or parsley, and capers in a bowl.
2   Grill the pepper halves on an oiled rack until very lightly charred, about 6 minutes. Remove from
    the grill and divide the Taleggio and mozzarella cheeses among the pepper halves. Return to the
    grill and cook until the cheese has melted. Sprinkle with the olive mixture, trickle the vinaigrette
    over, and grind on some black pepper.
3   Meanwhile, toast the ciabatta slices on the grill rack. Remove from the grill and brush with olive
    oil. Serve the filled peppers with the ciabatta toasts and arugula leaves.

028 GRILLED TOMATO BRUSCHETTA

PREPARATION TIME *10 minutes* **COOKING TIME** *6 minutes* **SERVES 2-4**

4 sun-ripened tomatoes,
  halved
salt and freshly ground
  black pepper
olive oil for brushing

1 large ciabatta loaf,
  halved horizontally
¼ cup tapenade
1 tbsp extra virgin
  olive oil

1 peppadew (bottled
  mild pepper piquante),
  thinly sliced
small handful (about 10)
  fresh basil leaves

1   Brush the tomatoes with olive oil and season. Grill on a rack for 3 minutes on each side.
2   Meanwhile, cut each length of ciabatta across in half and toast on the grill rack. Remove from the
    grill and spread the cut sides with tapenade.
3   Squash the tomatoes onto the ciabatta. Trickle the extra virgin olive oil over and sprinkle with the
    peppadew and basil leaves.

029 SAUSAGE AND CHEESE GRILLS

PREPARATION TIME *15 minutes, plus 30 minutes chilling* **COOKING TIME** *10-15 minutes* **SERVES 4**

8 thin slices bread, crusts
  removed
Dijon mustard for
  spreading

8 oz good-quality pork
  sausage (or use the
  meat from sausages)
4 slices Gruyère cheese or
  aged Cheddar cheese

all-purpose flour
2 eggs, beaten
1 cup fresh white
  bread crumbs

1   Spread one side of each bread slice with mustard. Divide the sausage into eight portions and
    spread over the mustard. Keeping the sausage on the outside, sandwich pairs of bread slices
    together, inserting a cheese slice in the center.
2   Spread flour on one plate, put the egg on another plate, and spread the bread crumbs on a third.
    Dip the sandwiches lightly in the flour, then in the egg; allow the excess egg to drain off, then dip
    into the bread crumbs to coat evenly. Refrigerate for 30 minutes to firm up.
3   Grill on an oiled rack until the sausage is cooked and golden brown and the cheese has melted,
    5-8 minutes on each side .

030 MARINATED HALLOUMI SALAD

PREPARATION TIME *10 minutes, plus 1–4 hours marinating* **COOKING TIME** *2–3 minutes* **SERVES 4**

12 oz halloumi or
cut into ½-inch thick
slices
1 tbsp salted capers, well
rinsed and dried
12 mixed black and green
olives, pitted
fresh flat-leaf parsley

for garnish
lemon wedges for serving
sourdough bread or
crusty country bread
for serving

MARINADE
½ cup virgin olive oil

1 tsp Dijon mustard
2 tsp balsamic vinegar
1 tbsp fresh thyme
pinch of sugar
1 fresh, hot red chile,
seeded and finely
chopped

1 Lay the cheese slices in a shallow, nonreactive dish.
2 Combine the marinade ingredients and pour over the cheese. Turn the slices over, then cover and let marinate in a cool place for 1–4 hours, turning the slices occasionally.
3 Lift the cheese from the marinade and grill on an oiled rack until golden, 1–1½ minutes on each side, turning carefully.
4 Transfer to plates and scatter the capers and olives over. Garnish with the parsley and serve immediately, with lemon wedges and sourdough bread.

031 GLAMORGAN SAUSAGES

PREPARATION TIME *10 minutes, plus 1 hour chilling* **COOKING TIME** *10–15 minutes* **SERVES 4**

4 cups fresh white bread crumbs	3 scallions, finely chopped	about 2 tbsp milk
1 cup shredded cheese, such as Welsh Caerphilly, Emmental, aged Cheddar, or firm goat	1 tbsp minced fresh parsley	all-purpose flour for dusting
	½ tsp fresh thyme leaves	
	1 egg, beaten	
	salt and freshly ground black pepper	

1 Combine the bread crumbs, cheese, scallions, herbs, egg, and seasoning in a bowl, adding enough milk to bind the ingredients together. The mixture should be soft enough to gather into balls, but do not make it too soft.

2 Roll into eight sausage shapes. Roll the sausages in the flour to coat evenly, pressing the flour in lightly. Refrigerate for 1 hour.

3 Grill the sausages at the side of an oiled rack over medium-low heat until browned and cooked through, 10–15 minutes, turning frequently.

032 BREAD, BASIL, AND CHEESE KABOBS

PREPARATION TIME *10 minutes, plus 24 hours marinating* **COOKING TIME** *4–5 minutes* **SERVES 4**

8 oz halloumi cheese, cut into ½-inch slices	1 plump garlic clove, crushed and finely chopped	1 long French loaf, cut into ½-inch slices
¼ cup virgin olive oil		about 24 fresh basil leaves
2 tsp lemon juice	freshly ground black pepper	

1 Put the halloumi cheese in a shallow, nonreactive dish. Add the olive oil, lemon juice, garlic, and plenty of black pepper. Stir together, then cover and let marinate for 24 hours.

2 Drain off and reserve the marinade. Thread the pieces of cheese and bread alternately on skewers, interspersing them with basil leaves and packing them quite tightly.

3 Brush with the reserved marinade and grill on an oiled rack over medium-high heat for 4–5 minutes, turning and brushing occasionally with the reserved marinade.

033 SMOKY CHICKEN WINGS

PREPARATION TIME *5 minutes* **COOKING TIME** *20–25 minutes* **SERVES 4**

2 tbsp olive oil	2 tsp sweet chile sauce	fresh thyme leaves for sprinkling
1 tbsp sun-dried tomato paste	juice of ½ lemon	salt and freshly ground black pepper
1 garlic clove, finely crushed	1 tsp pimenton (smoked Spanish paprika)	
	12 large chicken wings	

1 Combine all the ingredients, except the chicken, thyme, and seasoning, to make a thick sauce.

2 To make it easier to turn the chicken wings on the grill, cut off the tips of the wings, then thread them onto parallel skewers, three wings to each pair of skewers.

3 Grill on an oiled rack for 10 minutes, turning twice. Brush liberally with the sauce and grill until cooked through and a rich golden brown, 10–15 minutes longer, turning and brushing with the sauce occasionally.

4 Remove from the grill, sprinkle with the thyme leaves and seasoning, and serve.

FISH AND SEAFOOD

Grilling over a high heat is ideal for fish, as the intense heat improves the flavor by charring the surface. The most suitable fish are firm species, such as cod, haddock, monkfish, and swordfish, and oily types like tuna, salmon, and sardines. Salmon is best served a little translucent, while tuna is best on the rare side, but if you prefer them cooked through, remove from the grill just before the inside is opaque—they will continue to cook off the heat.

Fish steaks should be at least 1 inch thick so that they will not cook too quickly. With the exception of oily fish, which should be cooked close to the fire until the skin is crisp, grill fish on a rack at the highest notch. Allow 8–10 minutes per 1 inch thickness of fish, but do watch carefully, as fish can quickly overcook. Delicate white fish, such as sole and flounder, and thin fillets are difficult to grill, because they disintegrate when you try to turn them over. Large fish are easier to handle if cooked in a double-sided hinged basket. They can also be wrapped in foil, although they will lose some of the characteristic grill flavor.

Shellfish are ideal for grilling—it is difficult to make a fire too hot for them, as by the time you char the exterior they are invariably done to perfection. They are best grilled with the shells on to retain their juices and keep them moist.

CHAPTER 2

034 SALMON BURGERS

PREPARATION TIME *15 minutes, plus 2–3 hours cooling and chilling* **COOKING TIME** *8 minutes* **SERVES 4**

1 lb skinless salmon fillet
salt and freshly ground
   black pepper
1½ cups mashed, freshly
   boiled potato
½ tbsp unsalted butter

1–2 tbsp chopped fresh
   dill*, to taste
grated zest and juice
   of ½ large lemon
all-purpose flour for
   coating

2 eggs, beaten
6–8 tbsp cornmeal or
   fine dry bread crumbs
Tomato Tartar Sauce *(see
   page 179)* **for serving**

1 Put the salmon in a pan with barely enough water to cover. Season and bring to a boil. Remove the pan from the heat, cover, and let the salmon cool in the liquid. Drain off the liquid. Skin the salmon and flake the flesh into a bowl.

2 Mash the warm potato with the butter, then combine with the salmon, dill, lemon zest and juice, and seasoning. With well-floured hands, form the mixture into four patties.

3 Tip the beaten eggs onto one plate and the cornmeal or bread crumbs onto another. Coat the patties in the egg; allow the surplus egg to drain off, then coat in the cornmeal or bread crumbs, patting them firmly in place. Cover and refrigerate for 1–2 hours.

4 Place the burgers in an oiled hinged basket and grill until golden and crisp, 4 minutes on each side. Alternatively, grill the burgers directly on the oiled rack, turning them carefully with a metal spatula.

* Dill's strength of flavor can vary quite considerably, especially in winter.

035 SEA BASS WITH SAUCE VIERGE

PREPARATION TIME *10 minutes, plus 20 minutes marinating* **COOKING TIME** *25 minutes* **SERVES 4**

4 sea bass fillets, skin on,
   about 6 oz each
olive oil for brushing
salt and freshly ground
   black pepper

SAUCE VIERGE
6 vine-ripened roma
   tomatoes, finely diced
2 garlic cloves, finely
   chopped
3 small shallots, finely
   chopped

⅔ cup virgin olive oil
1 tsp lemon juice
3 tbsp shredded fresh
   basil leaves

1 First make the sauce: Put the tomatoes, garlic, and shallots in a bowl, sprinkle with a little salt, and leave until the juices run, about 20 minutes. Add the virgin olive oil, lemon juice, basil, and black pepper to taste.

2 Brush the sea bass fillets with olive oil and sprinkle with seasoning. Grill the fish in an oiled hinged basket, or on an oiled grill rack, skin side down first, for 3 minutes, then turn over and grill the other side until the fish is cooked through.

3 Remove the fish to plates and spoon the sauce over.

036 TERIYAKI TUNA

PREPARATION TIME *5 minutes, plus 1–2 hours marinating* **COOKING TIME** *4 minutes* **SERVES 4**

	MARINADE	1 garlic clove, crushed
4 tuna steaks, about 6 oz each	2 tbsp mirin	through a garlic press
lightly toasted sesame seeds, lightly crushed, for serving	2 tbsp soy sauce	½–¾ tsp Sichuan peppercorns, ground
	2 tbsp sake	
	2 tsp grated fresh gingerroot	

1 Lay the tuna steaks in a nonreactive dish.
2 Make the marinade by mixing all the ingredients together. Pour it over the tuna and turn the steaks over to make sure they are evenly coated, then cover and let marinate in a cool place for 1–2 hours, turning occasionally.
3 Lift the steaks from the marinade. Reserve the marinade.
4 Grill the tuna on an oiled rack for about 2 minutes. Brush with the reserved marinade, turn the steaks over, and brush again with the marinade. Grill for 2 minutes longer, or until done to your taste. Sprinkle with the sesame seeds and serve.

037 ROSEMARY-SKEWERED MONKFISH WITH GARLIC AND LEMON BASTE

PREPARATION TIME *5 minutes* **COOKING TIME** *35-40 minutes* **SERVES 6**

1½ lb monkfish fillet, cut
   into chunks
freshly ground black
   pepper
1 tsp pimenton (smoked
   paprika)

12 strong, fresh rosemary
   stems without leaves
coarse sea salt
6 slices firm white bread,
   cut on the diagonal
lemon wedges for serving

GARLIC AND LEMON BASTE
1 cup olive oil
2 large garlic bulbs, divided
   into cloves, unpeeled
1 lemon, halved and cut
   into chunks
3 fresh rosemary sprigs

1 To make the baste, cook the ingredients together very gently in a saucepan for 30 minutes; do
   not let the oil become too hot, or the garlic will fry. Strain the oil; return the garlic cloves to the
   oil and reserve.
2 Carefully pierce a hole through each chunk of fish. Sprinkle the fish with black pepper and
   pimenton, then brush with garlic-flavored oil. Thread the fish chunks onto the rosemary stems.
3 Grill on the rack until the fish is browned at the edges, 6–8 minutes, turning occasionally and
   brushing with garlic oil. Remove from the grill rack and sprinkle with coarse sea salt.
4 While the fish is grilling, toast the bread at the side of the grill rack. Using a slotted spoon, lift the
   garlic from the oil and either squash the garlic flesh from the skins onto the toasts, or remove
   the skins and eat the cloves with the fish. Serve the lemon wedges alongside.

038 SEA BREAM WITH FIVE-SPICE POWDER, LIME, AND GINGER

PREPARATION TIME *10 minutes, plus 1 hour marinating* **COOKING TIME** *20-25 minutes* **SERVES 4**

2 shallots, chopped
1-inch piece fresh
   gingerroot, peeled
   and chopped
1 tbsp Chinese five-spice
   powder

1 tbsp soy sauce
grated zest and juice
   of 2 limes
coarse sea salt

2 sea bream or porgy,
   about 1½ lb each,
   cleaned

1 Put the shallots and ginger into a blender and mix to a paste. Add the five spice-powder, soy
   sauce, and lime zest and juice, and mix briefly.
2 With a sharp knife, cut two slashes in both sides of each fish, going right through to the bone.
3 Brush the five-spice paste over the fish, making sure it goes into the slashes. Cover and let
   marinate in a cool place for 1 hour.
4 Grill the fish in an oiled hinged basket, or directly on an oiled grill rack, for 20–25 minutes,
   turning halfway through the cooking time.

039 SEAFOOD BROCHETTES WITH DILL

PREPARATION TIME *10 minutes, plus 1 hour marinating* **COOKING TIME** *6–8 minutes* **SERVES 4**

1 lb skinned cod fillet, cut
    into 1-inch cubes
16 raw large shrimp,
    shelled but last tail
    section left on
1½ limes, sliced
2 small zucchini, sliced
    on a diagonal
16 large cherry tomatoes

MARINADE
¼ cup virgin olive oil
1 tbsp white wine vinegar
    juice of ½ lime
2 garlic cloves, crushed
2 tbsp chopped fresh dill
salt and freshly ground
    black pepper

DILL TARTAR DIP
⅔ cup sour cream
2 tbsp tartar sauce
2 tbsp mayonnaise *(see
    page 179)*
1 tsp chopped fresh dill

1   Make the marinade by combining all the ingredients.
2   Thread the cod, shrimp, lime slices, zucchini, and cherry tomatoes alternately onto eight skewers. Lay them in a shallow, nonreactive dish and pour the marinade over. Turn the brochettes to coat them, then cover and let marinate in a cool place for 1 hour, turning occasionally.
3   Meanwhile, make the dip by mixing all the ingredients together. Season to taste. Cover and chill.
4   Lift the brochettes from the marinade (reserve any remaining marinade) and grill on an oiled rack until the shrimp have turned pink and the cod is cooked, 6–8 minutes, turning occasionally and brushing with the marinade. Serve with the dip.

040 RED MULLET WITH FENNEL AND LEMON

PREPARATION TIME *15 minutes* **COOKING TIME** *8–10 minutes* **SERVES 4**

1 fennel bulb	3 garlic cloves, thinly sliced	1 tsp fennel seeds
4 red mullet or other firm fish fillets, about 6 oz each	2 tbsp chopped fresh flat-leaf parsley	salt and freshly ground black pepper
	1 lemon, halved and sliced	1 tbsp olive oil

1 Trim the stems from the fennel bulb, saving the feathery green fronds. Discard the core. Halve and thinly slice the fennel bulb. Blanch in boiling salted water for 2 minutes. Drain very well.
2 Using a sharp knife, cut several slashes in the skin side of each fish.
3 Cut four double-thickness sheets of heavy-duty foil, each large enough to enclose a fillet. Put one-quarter of the garlic, sliced fennel, and parsley on each sheet of foil, spreading in an even layer. Lay a fillet on top, skin-side up. Insert a lemon slice in each slash and put the rest on top. Sprinkle with the fennel seeds, reserved feathery fronds, and seasoning, and trickle the oil over. Fold the foil loosely over the fish and twist the edges together firmly to seal.
4 Cook on an oiled grill rack for 8–10 minutes, turning the packages over halfway through the cooking time.

041 MONKFISH, FENNEL, AND LEMON BROCHETTES

PREPARATION TIME *10 minutes, plus 30–60 minutes marinating* **COOKING TIME** *6–8 minutes* **SERVES 4**

1¼ lb monkfish fillet, cut into 1-inch cubes	2 tsp finely grated lemon zest	salt and freshly ground black pepper
2 tsp fennel seeds, crushed	2 tbsp lemon juice	1 lemon, thinly sliced
2 tbsp chopped fresh fennel herb	3 tbsp olive oil	

1 Put the monkfish into a nonreactive bowl.
2 Combine the fennel seeds, chopped fennel, lemon zest, lemon juice, oil, and seasoning. Stir into the fish, cover, and let marinate in a cool place for 30–60 minutes.
3 Lift the fish from the marinade (reserve any remaining marinade) and thread onto skewers, alternating with folded lemon slices.
4 Grill on an oiled rack until evenly browned, 6–8 minutes, turning once and basting with any remaining marinade.

042 SHRIMP WITH SPANISH TOMATO SAUCE

PREPARATION TIME *10 minutes* **COOKING TIME** *40 minutes* **SERVES 4**

24 raw tiger shrimp or large
   shrimp in shell
olive oil for brushing

SPANISH TOMATO SAUCE
4 tbsp olive oil
1 onion, chopped

4 garlic cloves, chopped
2 ripe roma tomatoes,
   chopped
1 red bell pepper, chopped
dash of hot pepper sauce
2 tbsp dry sherry
¼ cup fish stock

10 blanched almonds,
   toasted
lemon juice, to taste
sea salt and freshly ground
   black pepper

1   First make the sauce: Heat half the olive oil, add the onion and three-quarters of the garlic, and fry until softened, stirring frequently. Add the tomatoes, red pepper, pepper sauce, sherry, and fish stock. Bring to a boil, then cover and simmer for 30 minutes, stirring occasionally.

2   Put the almonds into a blender or food processor and grind coarsely. Add the remaining olive oil and garlic, and blend until evenly combined. Add the sauce and blend until smooth. Add lemon juice and seasoning to taste. Set aside until required.

3   Brush the shrimp with oil. Thread onto pairs of parallel skewers and grill on an oiled rack until the shells turn pink, 3 minutes on each side.

4   Meanwhile, heat the sauce at the side of the grill rack. Remove the shrimp from the skewers and serve with the sauce.

043 CRAB BURGERS

PREPARATION *10 minutes, plus 1–2 hours chilling* **COOKING TIME** *6–8 minutes* **SERVES 4**

1 potato, about 8 oz, baked
   in its skin
½ tbsp unsalted butter
8 oz freshly cooked flaked
   crab meat

1 small, fresh, hot red chile,
   seeded and minced
8 plump scallions, finely
   chopped
1 tsp harissa sauce

2 tsp Thai fish sauce
1 extra large egg white,
   lightly beaten
about 1 cup cornmeal
2 tsp sesame seeds

1   Scoop the flesh from the baked potato and mash it with the butter. Let cool, then mix with the crab meat, chile, scallions, harissa, fish sauce, and egg white. Divide the mixture into eight portions and form into patties.

2   Mix the cornmeal with the sesame seeds, then use to coat the patties. Chill for 1–2 hours.

3   Grill the burgers in an oiled hinged basket until they are golden and thoroughly hot, 3–4 minutes on each side. Alternatively, grill directly on an oiled rack, turning the burgers carefully with a metal spatula.

044 SEARED SQUID SALAD

PREPARATION TIME *15 minutes, plus 2–4 hours marinating* **COOKING TIME** *4 minutes* **SERVES 6**

2 lb small squid, cleaned

MARINADE
1 tbsp peanut oil
1 tsp toasted sesame oil
1 tbsp lemon juice
1 fresh, hot red chile,
    seeded and finely
    chopped

1 garlic clove, crushed
salt

FOR SERVING
handful of frisée
12 cherry tomatoes,
    quartered
1 bunch watercress,
    trimmed

½ English cucumber, peeled,
    halved, seeded, and cut
    into fine strips
peanut oil and lime juice
    for dressing
salt and freshly ground
    black pepper
2–3 tbsp fresh cilantro
    leaves

1   Cut the squid bodies lengthwise along one side to open them out flat. Using the point of
    a knife, score diagonal parallel lines on the squid bodies, but do not cut right through. Put into
    a nonreactive bowl. Leave the tentacles whole and add them to the bowl.
2   Make the marinade by combining all the ingredients. Pour this over the squid and stir everything
    together, then cover and let marinate in a cool place for 2–4 hours.
3   Lift the squid from the marinade and grill on an oiled rack until just opaque, about 2 minutes on
    each side, turning once.
4   Meanwhile, toss the frisée, tomatoes, watercress, and cucumber together. Trickle a little peanut
    oil and lime juice over, just to moisten. Season.
5   Slice the squid into rings and pile onto the salad. Garnish with fresh cilantro.

045 THAI FISH BURGERS

PREPARATION TIME *10 minutes, plus 1 hour chilling* **COOKING TIME** *8–10 minutes* **SERVES 4**

1 shallot, coarsely chopped	1 plump garlic clove,	pinch of sugar
½-inch piece fresh	coarsely chopped	2 scallions, coarsely
gingerroot, peeled and	2 Kaffir lime leaves, or 1 tsp	chopped
coarsely chopped	grated lime zest	2 tbsp chopped fresh
1 fresh, hot red chile,	2 tbsp Thai fish sauce	cilantro
seeded and coarsely	1 lb white fish fillets,	chopped fresh cilantro and
chopped	chopped	lime wedges for serving

1 Combine the shallot, ginger, chile, garlic, lime leaves, and fish sauce in a food processor. Add the fish and process until reduced to a paste.

2 Add the sugar, scallions, and cilantro. Pulse a few times until combined but not chopped further.

3 Knead the mixture with your hands until smooth, then form into 1-inch-thick patties. Refrigerate for at least 1 hour.

4 Grill the burgers in an oiled hinged basket until they are golden, 4–5 minutes on each side; they will be rare to medium in the center. Alternatively, grill directly on an oiled rack, turning the burgers carefully with a metal spatula. Serve with cilantro and lime wedges.

046 TIGER SHRIMP, BACON, AND AVOCADO KABOBS

PREPARATION TIME *10 minutes* **COOKING TIME** *6–8 minutes* **SERVES 4**

8 lean bacon slices	8 scallions, green parts	freshly ground black
2 large avocados, pitted,	only, chopped	pepper
peeled, and cubed	1 garlic clove, finely	chopped fresh cilantro
12 raw tiger shrimp, shelled	chopped	and lime wedges
but last tail section	2 tbsp olive oil	for serving
left on	1 tbsp soy sauce	

1 Stretch the bacon slices on a cutting board with the back of a knife, then cut each slice across into three pieces. Wrap each bacon piece around an avocado cube. Thread the cubes onto skewers, alternating with the shrimp.

2 Stir together the scallions, garlic, oil, soy sauce, and black pepper. Brush over the kabobs and grill on an oiled rack until the shrimp have turned pink and the bacon is cooked, 6–8 minutes, turning regularly and brushing with the oil mixture. Serve with chopped cilantro and lime wedges.

047 BACON-WRAPPED SCALLOPS

PREPARATION TIME *10 minutes* **COOKING TIME** *4–6 minutes* **SERVES 4**

12 sea scallops, shucked, with coral if possible	**6 bacon slices** **Worcestershire sauce**	**lemon wedges for serving**

1 Remove the corals from the scallops and set aside.
2 Stretch the bacon slices on a cutting board with the back of a knife, then cut across in half. Wrap a piece of bacon around each scallop. Thread three wrapped scallops lengthwise onto a soaked bamboo skewer (see page 10), putting a coral between each one. Repeat with the remaining scallops and corals.
3 Season the bacon with Worcestershire sauce and grill on an oiled rack until the bacon is crisp and the scallops just opaque, 2–3 minutes on each side. Take care not to overcook the scallops. Serve with lemon wedges.

048 COD WITH SPICED ORANGE MARINADE

PREPARATION TIME *10 minutes, plus 2–3 hours marinating* **COOKING TIME** *8–10 minutes* **SERVES 4**

4 cod steaks, 1 inch thick, about 6 oz each **chopped fresh fennel herb for garnish** **lime wedges for serving**	MARINADE **¼ cup orange juice** **¼ cup dry vermouth** **¼ cup hoisin sauce** **¼ cup soy sauce** **1 garlic clove, crushed**	**½ tsp ground cumin** **½ tsp Chinese five-spice powder** **freshly ground black pepper**

1 Lay the cod steaks in a shallow, nonreactive dish just large enough to hold them.
2 Make the marinade by mixing all the ingredients together. Pour this over the cod and turn the steaks to coat evenly, then cover the dish and let marinate in a cool place for 2–3 hours.
3 Lift the cod from the marinade (reserve the marinade) and grill on an oiled rack for 4–5 minutes on each side, brushing occasionally with the marinade. Serve garnished with chopped fennel and accompanied by lime wedges.

049 HERBED FISH BURGERS

PREPARATION TIME *15 minutes* **COOKING TIME** *8–10 minutes* **SERVES 4**

12 oz haddock fillet, skinned **1–2 tbsp lemon juice** **1 tbsp Worcestershire sauce** **1 tsp horseradish sauce**	**½ cup milk** **1 tbsp snipped fresh chives** **1 tbsp chopped fresh parsley**	**2 cups cooked potatoes, mashed with a little butter** **1 cup fresh white bread crumbs**

1 Put the fish, lemon juice, Worcestershire sauce, horseradish sauce, and milk in a food processor or blender and blend until smooth. Transfer to a bowl and mix in the herbs and mashed potatoes until evenly combined.
2 Shape into four patties. Coat evenly in the bread crumbs.
3 Grill the fish burgers in an oiled hinged basket until golden and crisp, 4–5 minutes on each side. Alternatively, grill the burgers directly on an oiled rack, turning carefully with a metal spatula.

050 TROUT WITH TARRAGON

PREPARATION TIME *10 minutes, plus 1–2 hours marinating* **COOKING TIME** *12 minutes* **SERVES 4**

4 trout, about 12 oz each, cleaned	2 small shallots, finely chopped	½ tbsp coarsely chopped fresh flat-leaf parsley
	1 garlic clove, finely chopped	1 tsp Dijon mustard
MARINADE		1 tsp Pernod or Ricard
6 tbsp virgin olive oil	½ tbsp coarsely chopped fresh tarragon leaves	1 tsp dark soy sauce
1½ tbsp lemon juice		

1 Using the point of a sharp knife, cut three slashes in both sides of each trout.
2 Make the marinade by combining all the ingredients. Brush liberally over the inside as well as the skin of the trout, going into the slashes. Cover and leave in a cool place for 1–2 hours.
3 Grill the trout in an oiled hinged basket, or directly on an oiled rack, for about 6 minutes. Turn the fish over, brush liberally with the marinade, and grill on the other side for about 6 minutes longer. Test for doneness by inserting the point of a sharp knife near the head; the flesh should flake easily. If necessary, move the fish to the side of the grill rack to ensure even cooking.
4 Transfer the trout to plates and pour any remaining marinade over.

051 SPICED SHRIMP WITH TOMATO AND CILANTRO SALSA

PREPARATION TIME *10 minutes, plus 30 minutes marinating* **COOKING TIME** *6 minutes* **SERVES 4**

1 tsp cayenne pepper	½ tsp onion powder	2 tbsp olive oil
1 tsp black pepper	1 tsp salt	Tomato and Cilantro
1 tsp white pepper	20 raw large shrimp in shell	Salsa *(see page 66)*
½ tsp garlic granules		for serving

1 Stir together the cayenne, black, and white peppers, garlic granules, onion powder, and salt.
2 Rub a little of this mixture over the shrimp (reserve the rest for another time or discard) and trickle the oil over. Let marinate in a cool place for 30 minutes.
3 Thread the shrimp onto pairs of parallel skewers and grill on an oiled rack until the shells have turned pink, about 3 minutes on each side.
4 Meanwhile, taste the salsa for seasoning. Serve the shrimp accompanied by the salsa.

052 TROUT WITH BLACK OLIVADE

PREPARATION TIME *10 minutes* **COOKING TIME** *12 minutes* **SERVES 4**

4 trout, about 12 oz each, cleaned	BLACK OLIVADE	**1 tbsp capers, preferably salt-packed, well rinsed**
olive oil for brushing	**1 cup pitted Kalamata olives**	**6 tbsp virgin olive oil**
coarse sea salt and freshly ground black pepper	**7 anchovy fillets, drained**	**about 3 tbsp chopped fresh basil**
lemon wedges for serving	**¼ cup sun-dried tomatoes in oil, drained**	

1 Make the olivade: Put the olives, anchovies, sun-dried tomatoes, and capers into a blender and pulse to chop coarsely. Add the oil and pulse again until just combined. Transfer to a bowl and stir in the basil. Season with black pepper. Set aside.

2 Using the point of a sharp knife, cut three slashes in both sides of each trout. Brush the fish with oil, going into the slashes. Season with black pepper.

3 Grill the trout in an oiled hinged basket, or directly on an oiled rack, for about 6 minutes. Turn the fish over and cook on the other side for about 6 minutes longer. Test for doneness by inserting the point of a sharp knife near the head; the flesh should flake easily. If necessary, move the fish to the side of the grill rack to ensure even cooking.

4 Transfer the trout to serving plates, sprinkle with a little sea salt, and serve with the olivade and lemon wedges.

053 SHRIMP SPIEDINI WITH GREMOLATA

PREPARATION TIME *10 minutes* **COOKING TIME** *3–4 minutes* **SERVES 4**

1 large lemon	**salt and freshly ground black pepper**	**20 raw large shrimp, shelled**
3 garlic cloves, minced	**chile powder (optional)**	**virgin olive oil for brushing**
¼ cup chopped fresh flat-leaf parsley		

1 To make the gremolata, pare the zest from the lemon with a sharp potato peeler. Stack the pieces, a few at a time, into a pile and cut across them to make short, fine strips. Combine with the garlic, parsley, and salt and black pepper to taste. Set the gremolata aside.

2 Slice along the underside of the shrimp from the thickest part toward the tail, but take care not to cut all the way through. Gently press the shrimp to flatten them (butterfly).

3 Brush the shrimp with virgin olive oil, then season with salt and either black pepper or chile powder. Thread lengthwise onto pairs of parallel skewers.

4 Grill the shrimp on an oiled rack until the flesh is opaque, 3–4 minutes, turning once.

5 Meanwhile, cut the lemon in half and squeeze the juice from one half. Remove the shrimp from the rack, trickle the lemon juice over them, and sprinkle with the gremolata.

054 MUSSELS EN PAPILLOTE WITH COCONUT, GINGER, LEMON, AND LIME

PREPARATION TIME *10 minutes* **COOKING TIME** *10 minutes* **SERVES 4**

¼ cup chopped fresh
   gingerroot
2 lemon grass stems,
   crushed and finely
   chopped
grated zest and juice of
   1 lemon

grated zest and juice of
   1 lime
4 garlic cloves, finely
   chopped
leaves from a small sprig
   of thyme

salt and freshly ground
   black pepper
2½ lb mussels, cleaned
1 cup canned coconut milk

1   In a large bowl, mix together the ginger, lemon grass, lemon and lime zest and juices, garlic,
    thyme, and seasoning. Add the mussels and stir thoroughly.
2   Cut four large pieces of heavy-duty foil and pile one-quarter of the mussel mixture onto each
    one. Trickle the coconut milk evenly over the mussels. Fold the edges of the foil loosely over the
    mussels and twist the edges firmly together to seal.
3   Cook on the grill rack until all the mussels have opened, about 10 minutes, turning the packages
    over a couple of times. Discard any mussels that remain stubbornly closed. Serve the mussels
    in their foil packages.

055 FISH SATAY

PREPARATION TIME *10 minutes, plus 1 hour marinating* **COOKING TIME** *12–15 minutes* **SERVES 4**

1-inch piece fresh
gingerroot, chopped
1 garlic clove
2 tsp light soy sauce
1 tbsp lime juice
1 fresh, hot red chile,
seeded and minced
salt and freshly ground
black pepper

1¼ lb mahi mahi, cut
into 1-inch cubes
½ papaya, cubed
fresh cilantro leaves,
shredded

SATAY SAUCE
3 tbsp coarsely chopped
peanuts

1 tbsp peanut oil
1 garlic clove, chopped
1 fresh, hot red chile,
seeded and chopped
1 shallot, chopped
½ cup canned coconut milk
grated zest and juice of
1 lime

1   Press the ginger in a garlic press to extract the juice into a bowl, then crush the garlic in the press, adding the extract to the bowl. Stir in the soy sauce, lime juice, chile, and seasoning. Add the fish and stir to ensure all the pieces are evenly coated. Cover and let marinate in a cool place for 1 hour, stirring several times.
2   Meanwhile, make the sauce: Fry the peanuts in the oil until lightly browned. Put the garlic, chile, and shallot in a small blender or food processor and blend until smooth. Add to the peanuts and fry for 5 minutes, stirring to prevent sticking. Stir in the coconut milk and lime zest and juice. Set aside.
3   Lift the fish from the marinade and thread onto skewers, adding a piece of papaya to the ends of each one. Grill on an oiled rack for 6–8 minutes, turning to brown evenly.
4   Meanwhile, heat the sauce at the side of the grill rack. Serve the fish sprinkled with cilantro and accompanied by the satay sauce.

056 MEXICAN FILLET BURGERS

PREPARATION TIME *10 minutes, plus 30 minutes marinating* **COOKING TIME** *6–8 minutes* **SERVES 6**

2 lb thick, firm white fish
fillets, such as haddock
or cod
1 bunch fresh cilantro,
coarsely chopped
1 garlic clove, chopped
1 fresh, hot red chile,
seeded and chopped

2 tsp paprika
1 tsp ground cumin
grated zest of 1 lime
5 tbsp olive oil
6 hamburger buns
baby spinach leaves and
red onion slices for
serving

LIME MAYO
½ cup mayonnaise *(see
page 179)*
2 tbsp lime juice
dash of hot pepper sauce
salt and freshly ground
black pepper

1   Cut the fish into six pieces that are slightly larger than the buns. Put into a nonreactive dish.
2   Mix the cilantro, garlic, chile, paprika, cumin, lime zest, and olive oil in a blender. Season to taste. Coat the fish evenly with the paste, then cover and let marinate in a cool place for 30 minutes.
3   Meanwhile, mix all the mayo ingredients together. Adjust the seasoning, if necessary.
4   Grill the fish on an oiled rack until opaque and just cooked through, 3–4 minutes on each side.
5   While the fish is cooking, toast the buns at the side of the grill rack. Spread some of the mayo on the cut sides of the buns, then put spinach leaves and red onion slices on the bases of the buns. Add a piece of fish to each and cover with the bun tops.

057 FISH WITH HERBS AND LEMON

PREPARATION TIME *10 minutes* **COOKING TIME** *6 minutes* **SERVES 4**

4 white fish fillets, such as monkfish, cod, or halibut, skin on and at least 1 inch thick, about 8 oz each	salt and freshly ground black pepper	lemon wedges for serving
1½ tbsp extra virgin oil, plus extra for rubbing	2 tbsp chopped mixed fresh herbs, such as parsley, basil, thyme, chervil, or fennel	
	1 tbsp lemon juice	

1   Rub the fish lightly with extra virgin olive oil and sprinkle with some seasoning. Mix the 1½ tablespoons of extra virgin olive oil with the herbs to make a paste.
2   Grill the fish, flesh side down, in an oiled hinged basket, or directly on an oiled grill rack, for about 3 minutes. Turn the fish over, spread with the herb paste, and grill until the flesh flakes easily when tested with the point of a sharp knife, about 3 minutes longer.
3   Remove from the heat and sprinkle with the lemon juice. Serve with extra lemon wedges.

058 OYSTERS WITH PROSCIUTTO AND RED PEPPER

PREPARATION TIME *10 minutes* **COOKING TIME** *3–5 minutes* **SERVES 2-3**

3 slices prosciutto	2 tsp hot pepper sauce	12 oysters, freshly shucked and on the half shell
½ red bell pepper, roasted until soft *(see page 20)*, then finely chopped*	1 tsp Worcestershire sauce	3-4 tbsp freshly grated Parmesan cheese
	salt and freshly ground black pepper	

1   Grill the prosciutto on the rack until frazzled. Chop finely and mix with the red pepper, pepper sauce, Worcestershire sauce, and salt and pepper, to taste.
2   Divide among the oysters and sprinkle with the Parmesan. Put at the side of the grill rack and grill until the oysters are just opaque, 3–5 minutes.
*   ½ bottled red bell pepper could be used instead.

059 SEARED TUNA

PREPARATION TIME *10 minutes, plus 30 minutes marinating* **COOKING TIME** *4 minutes* **SERVES 4**

4 tuna steaks, about 4 oz each	2 tbsp chopped fresh cilantro	¼ cup lime juice
½-inch piece fresh gingerroot, peeled and finely chopped	2 tbsp chopped fresh basil	1 tbsp toasted sesame oil
	1 fresh, hot red chile, finely chopped	1 tbsp Thai fish sauce
2 tbsp chopped fresh mint	1 garlic clove, crushed	salt and freshly ground black pepper
		lime wedges for serving

1   Lay the tuna steaks in a nonreactive dish.
2   Mix the ginger, herbs, chile, garlic, lime juice, sesame oil, fish sauce, and seasoning together. Pour onto the tuna, turn the steaks over, cover, and leave in a cool place for 30 minutes, turning once.
3   Lift the steaks from the marinade. Reserve the marinade.
4   Grill the tuna on an oiled rack for 2 minutes. Brush with the reserved marinade, turn over, and grill until done to your taste, about 2 minutes longer. Serve with lime wedges.

060 MOROCCAN SPICED HALIBUT

PREPARATION TIME *10 minutes, plus 30-60 minutes marinating (optional)* **COOKING TIME** *8-10 minutes*
SERVES 4

¼ cup olive oil
2 tbsp lemon juice
3 garlic cloves, crushed
2 tbsp chopped fresh
   cilantro
1 tbsp chopped fresh
   parsley

1 tbsp chopped fresh mint
1 tsp harissa sauce
1 tsp ground cumin
pinch of saffron threads,
   lightly toasted and
   pounded

4 halibut steaks, 1 inch
   thick, about 7 oz each
lime wedges for serving

1   Combine all the ingredients, except the fish and lime wedges, in a bowl.
2   Lay the fish steaks in a single layer in a nonreactive dish, pour the marinade over them, and
    turn to ensure they are evenly coated. If time permits, cover and let marinate in a cool place for
    30-60 minutes, turning occasionally.
3   Lift the fish from the marinade and grill in an oiled hinged basket, or directly on an oiled rack,
    until cooked through, 4-5 minutes on each side. Serve with lime wedges.

061 SHRIMP WITH ASIAN PESTO

PREPARATION TIME *10 minutes, plus 1 hour marinating* **COOKING TIME** *6 minutes* **SERVES 4-6**

1½ lb raw large shrimp
   in shell

ASIAN PESTO
1½-2 tbsp peanut oil

2 tbsp each finely chopped
   garlic, fresh gingerroot,
   and fresh basil
1½ tbsp finely chopped
   fresh, hot chile

2 tsp rice wine
1 tbsp toasted sesame oil
salt and freshly ground
   black pepper

1   Make the pesto by mixing the ingredients to a paste in a blender.
2   Remove the legs from the shrimp, keeping the shells intact. Using the point of a small, sharp
    knife, cut a few slits in the shells of the shrimp. Rub the pesto thoroughly over the shrimp, then
    let marinate in a cool place for 1 hour.
3   Grill the shrimp on an oiled rack until the shells turn pink, about 3 minutes on each side.

062 HADDOCK WITH BASIL OIL

PREPARATION TIME *5 minutes* **COOKING TIME:** *8-10 minutes* **SERVES 4**

4 haddock steaks, 1 inch
   thick, about 7 oz each
olive oil for brushing
Wilted Tomatoes *(see
   page 168)* and lemon
   wedges for serving

BASIL OIL
7 tbsp virgin olive oil
1 bunch of fresh basil
1 garlic clove, chopped
juice of ½ lemon
salt and freshly ground
   black pepper

1   Make the basil oil by puréeing all the ingredients in a small blender or food processor.
2   Brush the haddock with olive oil and sprinkle with seasoning. Grill, skin side down first, in an oiled
    hinged basket, or directly on an oiled rack, for 4-5 minutes on each side.
3   Remove the fish from the grill and serve with some of the basil oil poured over and the rest served
    separately, and accompanied by the wilted tomatoes and lemon wedges.

063 LOBSTER WITH ALMOND, CHEESE, AND HERB DRESSING

PREPARATION TIME *15 minutes, plus 20 minutes soaking* **COOKING TIME** *9 minutes* **SERVES 4**

2 raw lobsters,
1½–2¼ lb each
olive oil for brushing
lemon wedges for serving

DRESSING
3 tbsp blanched almonds
⅓ cup fresh flat-leaf
parsley leaves
½ cup mixed fresh herbs,
such as chervil, dill,
fennel, mint, and chives

1 garlic clove, chopped
1 cup mild olive oil
6 tbsp freshly grated
Parmesan cheese
about 1 tsp lemon juice
salt and freshly ground
black pepper

1 Make the dressing: Put the almonds into a blender or food processor, add all the herbs and garlic, and process until finely chopped. With the motor running, slowly pour in the oil in a thin, steady stream. Add the cheese and blend briefly, then season with lemon juice, salt, and pepper. Transfer to a bowl.

2 Put the lobsters on a heavy cutting board, stomach down. Using a large, sharp knife, slice them lengthwise in half, from head to tail. Discard the stomachs and intestines. Crack the claws with the back of the knife, or use a hammer.

3 Brush the lobster meat and shells with olive oil. Lay the lobsters, flesh side down, on the grill rack over a medium-hot fire and grill for 30 seconds. Turn them over and grill until the shells have turned bright red and the flesh has become white, about 8 minutes longer.

4 Add a little dressing to each lobster half and serve the rest separately with the lemon wedges.

064 SARDINES WITH ZUCCHINI, LEMON, AND DILL

PREPARATION TIME *15 minutes, plus 2 hours chilling* **COOKING TIME** *12–14 minutes* **SERVES 4**

8-12 sardines, depending on size, cleaned	virgin olive oil for brushing	DRESSING
coarse sea salt	salt and freshly ground black pepper	2 tbsp lemon juice
4 zucchini, sliced thinly lengthwise	lemon wedges for serving	2 tbsp extra virgin olive oil
		fine leaves from 3 fresh bushy dill sprigs

1 Bury the sardines in sea salt. Set aside in a cool place for 2 hours.
2 Lift the sardines from the salt and brush them clean.
3 Brush the zucchini slices with olive oil and grill on a rack until tender and nicely marked, about 3 minutes on each side. Remove to a serving dish.
4 Meanwhile, make the dressing by whisking together the lemon juice, oil, and seasoning. Add the dill. Trickle this over the zucchini slices and set aside while cooking the sardines.
5 Brush the sardines with olive oil and sprinkle with black pepper. Put into a hinged basket, or thread onto pairs of oiled parallel skewers, alternating the heads and tails, and place on an oiled grill rack. Grill on one side for 3–4 minutes, then turn them over and cook the other side until the skin is scorched and bubbling. Serve the sardines with the zucchini and lemon wedges.

065 CHINESE-STYLE SEA BASS

PREPARATION TIME *10 minutes, plus 2–3 hours marinating* **COOKING TIME** *30–35 minutes* **SERVES 6**

1 sea bass, weakfish, or red snapper, about 3 lb, cleaned	salt and freshly ground black pepper	6 scallions, finely chopped
3 tbsp grated fresh gingerroot	¼ cup rice wine vinegar	several sprigs of fresh cilantro
	3 tbsp toasted sesame oil	lime wedges for serving

1 Cut three or four slashes in both sides of the fish, going right down to the bone. Insert a small amount of the ginger in each slash. Season inside and out, then transfer the fish to a large sheet of heavy-duty foil and fold up the sides.
2 Pour the rice wine vinegar and sesame oil over the fish and sprinkle with the scallions. Lay some cilantro sprigs on top of and around the fish. Wrap the foil loosely around the fish and twist the edges together tightly to make a secure packet. Leave in a cool place for 2–3 hours.
3 Cook the packet on the grill rack for 15 minutes, then turn the packet over and cook until the flesh in the slashes is opaque, 15–20 minutes longer. Serve the fish with the cooking juices spooned over and accompanied by lime wedges.

066 SALMON WITH LIME, TOMATO, AND MUSTARD DRESSING

PREPARATION TIME *10 minutes* **COOKING TIME** *8 minutes* **SERVES 4**

4 thick salmon steaks, skin
   on, about 7 oz each
virgin olive oil for brushing
salt and freshly ground
   black pepper

fresh flat-leaf parsley
   leaves for garnish

DRESSING
2 vine-ripened roma
   tomatoes, halved

juice of 2 limes
1 heaped tsp wholegrain
   mustard
¼ cup olive oil
2–3 tsp sugar

1 Make the dressing: Slice the tomatoes into thin strips. Shake the remaining ingredients with salt and pepper to taste in a lidded jar. Taste and add more sugar, if necessary. Add the tomato strips and set aside.
2 Brush the salmon with virgin olive oil and sprinkle with seasoning. Grill, flesh side down, for 4 minutes, then turn the steaks over and grill the other side until the skin is crisp and the flesh barely cooked.
3 Remove from the grill, garnish with the parsley, and serve with the dressing.

067 GRILLED COD WITH CHERMOULA

PREPARATION TIME *10 minutes, plus 1–2 hours marinating* **COOKING TIME** *6 minutes* **SERVES 4**

4 cod fillets, skin on, about
   6–7 oz each
pita breads for serving

CHERMOULA
1 fresh, hot red chile,
   seeded and chopped

2 garlic cloves, chopped
2 tbsp chopped fresh
   cilantro
1 tbsp chopped fresh
   flat-leaf parsley
1 tbsp chopped fresh mint
½ tbsp toasted cumin seeds

1 tsp saffron threads
1 tsp paprika
juice of 1 lemon
5 tbsp olive oil
salt

1 Lay the fish in a shallow, nonreactive dish.
2 Make the chermoula by blending all the ingredients in a small blender or food processor until smooth. Spoon the chermoula over the cod fillets and turn to coat them. Cover and let marinate in a cool place for 1–2 hours, turning occasionally.
3 Lift the fish from the dish and grill in an oiled hinged basket, or directly on an oiled grill rack, until lightly browned and cooked through, about 3 minutes on each side.
4 Meanwhile, warm the pita breads at the side of the grill rack for about 30 seconds on each side. Serve the cod with the pita bread.

SPICED SARDINES WITH ORANGE
AND OLIVE SALAD

PREPARATION TIME *15 minutes, plus 2–3 hours marinating* **COOKING TIME** *6–8 minutes* **SERVES 4**

4 garlic cloves, crushed
1 tbsp olive oil
1 tbsp lemon juice
1 tsp ground Sichuan
 peppercorns
½ tsp hot paprika
salt and freshly ground
 black pepper

12–16 sardines, depending
 on size, cleaned

ORANGE AND OLIVE SALAD
5 oranges
1 small red onion, very
 thinly sliced

16 large salt-packed black
 olives, pitted
½ cup coarsely chopped
 fresh flat-leaf parsley
 leaves
extra virgin olive oil for
 trickling

1   Mix together the garlic, olive oil, lemon juice, peppercorns, paprika, and seasoning. Rub
    thoroughly over the sardines, then cover and let marinate in a cool place for 2–3 hours.
2   Make the salad: Peel and section the oranges, removing all the pith and membranes. Put the
    sections in a bowl with the red onion, olives, and parsley. Season and trickle some oil over.
3   Grill the sardines in an oiled hinged basket, or thread them onto pairs of oiled parallel skewers,
    alternating the heads and tails, and grill on an oiled rack. Cooking time is 3–4 minutes on each
    side. Serve with the orange and olive salad.

069 GRILLED SPICED SALMON

PREPARATION TIME *10 minutes, plus 2 hours marinating* **COOKING TIME** *8-9 minutes* **SERVES 4**

2 lb salmon fillet, skin on	seeds from 6 cardamom pods	peanut oil for brushing lime wedges for serving
1 tsp cumin seeds	½ tsp black peppercorns	
1 tsp coriander seeds	coarse sea salt	

1 Using a sharp knife, cut a diamond pattern in the salmon skin.
2 Grind the seeds, peppercorns, and salt, or pulverize in a bowl using the end of a rolling pin.
3 Brush the salmon with the oil and press the spice mixture into the skin. Cover and let marinate in a cool place for 2 hours.
4 Place the salmon fillet in an oiled hinged basket and grill for 4-5 minutes on each side. Serve with lime wedges.

070 TROUT WITH PANCETTA

PREPARATION TIME *10 minutes* **COOKING TIME** *12-14 minutes* **SERVES 4**

4 trout, about 1 lb each, cleaned	salt and freshly ground black pepper	6-8 slices pancetta Herb Sauce *(see page 67)*

1 Sprinkle the trout inside and out with a little salt and plenty of black pepper.
2 Stretch the pancetta with the back of a knife, then use to wrap each fish. Secure the loose ends with wooden toothpicks that have been soaked in water for 20 minutes.
3 Cook in an oiled hinged basket, or directly on an oiled grill rack, for 6-7 minutes, then turn the fish over (take care if not using a hinged basket) and grill on the other side until the pancetta is crisp and the fish cooked through, 6-7 minutes longer. If necessary, move the fish to the side of the grill rack to ensure even cooking. Serve with the herb sauce.

071 SALMON WITH ANCHOVIES AND CAPERS

PREPARATION TIME *10 minutes, plus 2-3 hours marinating* **COOKING TIME** *7-8 minutes* **SERVES 4**

2 lb salmon fillet, skin on	2½ tbsp coarsely chopped fresh parsley	freshly ground black pepper
8 anchovy fillets	1 tsp grated lemon zest	virgin olive oil for brushing
1 tbsp salt-packed capers, rinsed	1½ tbsp lemon juice	lemon wedges and arugula salad for serving

1 Using the point of a sharp knife, cut several deep slashes through the skin side of the salmon.
2 Finely chop the anchovy fillets, capers, parsley, and lemon zest together. Mix with the lemon juice and black pepper. Press well into the slashes in the fish. Season the salmon with black pepper and brush with olive oil. Cover and let marinate in a cool place for 2-3 hours.
3 Place the fish in an oiled hinged basket and grill for 7-8 minutes, turning halfway through the cooking. Serve with lemon wedges and an arugula salad.

072 BLACKENED PASTRAMI-STYLE SALMON WITH GRILLED LEMONS

PREPARATION TIME *10 minutes, plus 24 hours marinating* **COOKING TIME** *8 minutes* **SERVES 8**

2 tbsp sugar
2 tbsp coarse sea salt
2 tbsp chopped fresh dill
1 tbsp paprika
1 tsp garlic granules
1 tsp onion salt

1 tsp ground allspice
1 tsp freshly ground black
   pepper
1 tsp English mustard
   powder

2 pieces salmon fillet, skin
   on, about 2 lb each
4 lemons, halved
olive oil for brushing
salad leaves dressed with
   olive oil for serving

1   Combine the sugar, salt, dill, paprika, garlic granules, onion salt, allspice, pepper, and mustard powder. Rub over both sides of the salmon fillets. Wrap in a large piece of plastic wrap and place in a long dish or tray. Put a heavy cutting board on top and leave in a cool place for 24 hours.

2   Unwrap the salmon, brush with olive oil, and place in an oiled hinged basket. Grill, skin-side down, near the coals for 5 minutes. Turn carefully and grill for 2½ minutes longer. If you prefer salmon well done, grill for another couple of minutes, but take care not to overcook, as it will become dry.

3   Meanwhile, brush the lemon halves with olive oil and grill at the side of the grill rack until they are flecked with brown.

4   Remove the salmon from the grill and cut into eight portions. Serve with the grilled lemons and dressed salad leaves.

073 FRAGRANT WHOLE SALMON

PREPARATION TIME *10 minutes, plus 8 hours marinating* **COOKING TIME** *15–20 minutes* **SERVES 8**

1 salmon, about 5½ lb,
   cleaned
lime wedges, cilantro
   leaves, and sliced
   scallions for garnish

MARINADE
¾ cup rice wine vinegar
¾ cup soy sauce
3 tbsp clear honey
1 fresh, hot red chile,
   seeded and finely
   chopped

5 garlic cloves, thinly sliced
   into slivers
4 whole star anise, lightly
   crushed
3-inch piece fresh
   gingerroot, peeled
   and grated

1   Make the marinade by putting all the ingredients into a blender and blending to mix.

2   Cut three or four diagonal slashes in both sides of the salmon, then lay the fish in a nonreactive dish. Pour some of the marinade over the fish, making sure that it goes into the slashes. Turn the fish over and pour on the remaining marinade, again making sure that it goes into the slashes. Cover and let marinate in a cool place for 8 hours, turning the fish occasionally.

3   Transfer the salmon to a large piece of heavy-duty foil. Fold the foil loosely over the fish and twist the edges together firmly to seal completely. Slash the foil at an angle once or twice down each side, but be careful not to cut right around.

4   Cook the fish on the grill rack for 15–20 minutes, turning halfway through, or for longer if the fire begins to cool down.

5   Serve the salmon garnished with the lime wedges, cilantro leaves, and sliced scallions.

074 RED SNAPPER WITH PIQUANT SAUCE

PREPARATION TIME *5 minutes* **COOKING TIME** *6 minutes* **SERVES 4**

4 red snapper fillets, skin on, about 6 oz each olive oil for brushing salt and freshly ground black pepper	PIQUANT SAUCE 1-2 garlic cloves, crushed leaves from a sprig of fresh mint, chopped 1 tbsp sun-dried tomato paste	1 tbsp white wine vinegar 1 tsp Dijon mustard pinch of sugar ⅔ cup olive oil

1 Make the sauce: Put the garlic, mint, tomato paste, vinegar, mustard, and sugar into a small blender or food processor. Blend together until smooth, then, with the motor running, slowly pour in the oil until completely amalgamated. Season to taste.

2 Brush the fish fillets with oil. Grill in an oiled hinged basket, or directly on an oiled grill rack, until the flesh is opaque, about 3 minutes on each side. Transfer to plates and serve with the sauce.

075 SWORDFISH WITH THYME AND ANISE

PREPARATION TIME *10 minutes, plus 1-2 hours marinating* **COOKING TIME** *6 minutes* **SERVES 4**

4 swordfish steaks, about 7 oz each	MARINADE 2 tsp fennel seeds 3 tbsp Pernod 2 tbsp olive oil 2 tsp fresh thyme leaves	1 tsp crushed dried chiles 4 sun-dried tomato halves in oil, drained and finely chopped salt

1 Lay the swordfish steaks in a shallow, nonreactive dish.

2 Make the marinade: Heat a small, heavy frying pan, add the fennel seeds, and toast until they begin to darken. Crush lightly, then mix with the remaining ingredients.

3 Pour the marinade over the fish steaks and turn to coat them evenly, then cover and let marinate in a cool place for 1-2 hours, turning once or twice.

4 Lift the fish from the marinade and grill on an oiled rack for 3 minutes or so on each side; they will still be slightly pink in the center.

076 SICILIAN RED MULLET

PREPARATION TIME *15 minutes* **COOKING TIME** *12-14 minutes* **SERVES 4**

4 red mullet or other small whole fish, about 12 oz each, cleaned olive oil for brushing	1 tsp fennel seeds ½ tsp cumin seeds 1 tsp dried oregano ½ tsp black peppercorns	1 lemon, quartered and thinly sliced 12 fresh bay leaves salt

1 Using a sharp knife, cut three deep slashes on each side of all the fish. Brush them with olive oil.

2 Using a mortar and pestle, crush together the fennel and cumin seeds, oregano, and black peppercorns.

3 Rub into the fish, making sure the mixture goes into the slashes. Push a lemon slice and bay leaf into each slash. Brush the fish again with oil and sprinkle with salt.

4 Grill the fish in an oiled hinged basket, or directly on an oiled grill rack, until cooked through, 6-7 minutes on each side, turning once.

077 BLACKENED SEA BASS

PREPARATION TIME *10 minutes* **COOKING TIME** *6 minutes* **SERVES 4**

4 sea bass fillets, skin on, about 6 oz each	SPICE RUB	FOR SERVING
	1½ tbsp paprika	Avocado, Tomato, and Red
4 tbsp unsalted butter, melted	2 tsp garlic granules	Pepper Salsa (see
	½ tsp dried oregano	page 174)
salt and freshly ground black pepper	½ tsp dried thyme	lime wedges
	½ tsp cayenne pepper	

1 Make the spice rub by mixing all the ingredients together, with some seasoning, and spread out on a plate.
2 Brush the fish with melted butter, then press both sides onto the spice rub, making sure it adheres.
3 Grill the fish, flesh side down first, in an oiled hinged basket, or directly on an oiled grill rack, for 3 minutes. Turn the fish over and cook until the skin is blistered and browned, about 3 minutes longer. Serve with the salsa and lime wedges.

078 TUNA WITH TOMATOES, MINT, AND BASIL

PREPARATION TIME *10 minutes* **COOKING TIME** *35 minutes* **SERVES 4**

2 very ripe beefsteak tomatoes	1 garlic clove, finely chopped	cracked black pepper
5 tbsp extra virgin olive oil	2 tsp finely chopped fresh mint	4 tuna fillets, about 7 oz each
2 tbsp soy sauce	½ cup fresh basil leaves, shredded	olive oil for brushing
2 tbsp lemon juice		salt and freshly ground black pepper

1 Cut the tomatoes into 2-inch cubes. Mix with the extra virgin olive oil, soy sauce, lemon juice, garlic, mint, basil, and black pepper in a small saucepan and warm gently for 30 minutes.
2 Brush the tuna with olive oil and sprinkle with seasoning. Grill, skin-side down, on an oiled rack for about 2 minutes, then turn over and grill until the flesh is rare, 2 minutes longer, or until done to your taste. Remove to plates.
3 Stir the sauce and spoon it over the tuna.

079 GREEK-STYLE SWORDFISH

PREPARATION TIME *5 minutes, plus 30 minutes marinating* **COOKING TIME** *6 minutes* **SERVES 4**

4 swordfish steaks, about 5 oz each	¼ cup Greek virgin olive oil	1 tsp dried oregano
	juice of ½ lemon	salt and freshly ground black pepper

1 Lay the fish steaks in a single layer in a nonreactive dish.
2 Combine the remaining ingredients. Pour over the fish steaks and turn them over to make sure they are evenly coated, then cover and let marinate in a cool place for 30 minutes.
3 Lift the steaks from the marinade. Reserve any remaining marinade.
4 Grill the swordfish in an oiled hinged basket, or directly on an oiled grill rack, for 3 minutes. Brush with the reserved marinade, turn the steaks over, and grill for 3 minutes longer.

080 RED SNAPPER WITH SESAME, GINGER, AND CILANTRO

PREPARATION TIME *10 minutes, plus 1–2 hours marinating* **COOKING TIME** *14 minutes* **SERVES 6**

½ cup peanut oil

1 tbsp toasted sesame oil

1 tbsp soy sauce

2 tbsp rice wine vinegar

½-inch piece fresh gingerroot, peeled and grated

leaves from a small bunch of fresh cilantro, chopped

juice of 1 lime

salt and cracked black pepper

6 red snapper or other small whole fish, about 1 lb each, cleaned

sesame seeds for serving

1 Combine the peanut and sesame oils with the soy sauce, vinegar, ginger, cilantro, lime juice, and salt and black pepper to taste.

2 Cut two diagonal slashes in each side of the fish and place in a nonreactive dish. Pour the cilantro mixture over the fish and turn them to coat them evenly, then cover and let marinate in a cool place for 1–2 hours, turning occasionally.

3 Grill the fish in an oiled hinged basket until the undersides are blistered and brown, about 7 minutes. Turn the fish over and grill until the flesh near the head flakes easily when tested with the point of a sharp knife, about 7 minutes longer. Remove the fish to plates, sprinkle with sesame seeds, and serve.

081 MAHI MAHI WITH CAPERS AND LEMON

PREPARATION TIME *10 minutes, plus 1 hour marinating* **COOKING TIME** *6–8 minutes* **SERVES 4**

4 mahi mahi steaks, or
  other firm fish steaks,
  about 7 oz each
1 tsp chopped fresh thyme
1 tsp chopped fresh
  tarragon

2 garlic cloves, finely
  chopped
salt and freshly ground
  black pepper
2 tbsp olive oil
1 cup dry white wine

SAUCE
2 tbsp capers in wine
  vinegar, drained
1 tsp grated lemon zest
juice of 2 small lemons
5 tbsp olive oil

1 Lay the fish steaks in a single layer in a nonreactive dish. Sprinkle the herbs, garlic, and some seasoning over the fish, then pour the oil and wine over. Cover and let marinate in a cool place for 1 hour, turning a couple of times.

2 Meanwhile, make the sauce: Briefly blend the capers with the lemon zest and juice in a small blender or food processor. With the motor running, slowly pour in the oil. Season to taste.

3 Lift the fish from the dish and grill, skin-side down first, in an oiled hinged basket, or directly on an oiled grill rack, until the flesh flakes easily when tested with the point of a sharp knife, 3–4 minutes on each side. Transfer the fish to plates and pour the sauce over.

082 PIZZA-STYLE FISH PACKETS

PREPARATION TIME *10 minutes* **COOKING TIME** *25 minutes* **SERVES 4**

1 cup canned crushed
  Italian tomatoes
1 garlic clove, finely
  chopped
pinch of crushed dried
  chiles
2 tbsp coarsely chopped
  fresh basil

4 firm, white fish fillets,
  such as cod or haddock,
  about 6 oz each
5 oz mozzarella cheese,
  coarsely grated
1 pepperoni sausage,
  thinly sliced
2 tbsp capers, drained

¼ cup freshly grated
  Parmesan cheese
freshly ground black
  pepper

1   Cook the tomatoes, garlic, and chile in a small saucepan over low heat until most of the liquid has evaporated and the tomatoes are pulpy, 10–12 minutes. Stir in the basil.
2   Cut four pieces of heavy-duty foil large enough to enclose a fish fillet. Place a fillet on each piece of foil and spread one-quarter of the tomato mixture over the fish. Top with the mozzarella, sausage, and capers. Sprinkle with the Parmesan and black pepper. Fold the foil loosely over the fish and twist the edges together firmly to seal them.
3   Cook on a grill rack for about 10 minutes, turning over halfway through. Just before the end of the cooking time, carefully open one packet to check if the fish is done: the flesh should flake easily when tested with the point of a knife.

083 BASS WRAPPED IN GRAPE LEAVES

PREPARATION TIME *10 minutes, plus 2 hours marinating* **COOKING TIME** *20 minutes* **SERVES 4**

1 sea bass, about 4½ lb,
  cleaned, with head and
  tail left on
salt and freshly ground
  black pepper
4 garlic cloves, sliced
  lengthwise

leaves from 1 large bunch
  of fresh herbs, such as
  chervil, fennel, dill,
  oregano, and rosemary
7 tbsp virgin olive oil
2 tbsp white wine vinegar

1 package grape leaves
  preserved in brine,
  drained and rinsed
lemon wedges for serving

1   Cut deep slashes in several places on both sides of the fish. Sprinkle seasoning deep into the slashes and insert the garlic slivers and herbs into the slashes. Put any remaining herbs in the fish cavity. Lay the fish in a nonreactive dish.
2   Whisk together the oil, vinegar, and seasoning. Pour this over the fish, cover, and let marinate in a cool place for 2 hours, turning a few times.
3   Meanwhile, pour boiling water over the grape leaves to cover and leave for 5 minutes, then drain.
4   Remove the fish from the dish and wrap in the grape leaves. Place in an oiled hinged basket. Grill until the flesh flakes easily when tested with the point of a knife, about 20 minutes, turning once. Adjust the height of the grill rack to ensure the fish cooks evenly. Serve with lemon wedges.

084 MONKFISH WITH INDIAN SPICES

PREPARATION TIME *10 minutes, plus 1 hour marinating* **COOKING TIME** *6–8 minutes* **SERVES 4**

2 monkfish fillets, about 12 oz each each	MARINADE	RAITA
salt and freshly ground black pepper	2 tsp garam masala	½ English cucumber, halved lengthwise and seeded
	1 tsp ground cumin	1 small garlic clove, finely chopped
	½ tsp chile powder	
	½ tsp turmeric	⅔ cup thick, plain yogurt
	3 tbsp chopped fresh cilantro	2 tbsp chopped fresh mint
	1–2 tbsp peanut oil	

1 Put the monkfish into a nonreactive dish.
2 Make the marinade by stirring all the ingredients together. Rub into the monkfish to coat evenly and thoroughly. Cover and let marinate in a cool place for 1 hour.
3 To make the raita, shred the cucumber on the coarse side of the grater. Drain on paper towels. Mix the cucumber with the garlic, yogurt, mint, and seasoning.
4 Grill the monkfish in an oiled hinged basket, or directly on an oiled grill rack, until cooked through, 6–8 minutes, turning once.
5 Remove from the grill, cut each fillet in half, and serve with the raita.

085 TUNA BURGERS

PREPARATION TIME *10 minutes, plus 1 hour chilling* **COOKING TIME** *4 minutes* **SERVES 4–6**

1½ lb tuna steaks or fillets, skinned	1 tbsp soy sauce	dash of hot pepper sauce
	5 scallions, minced	salt
1 tsp grated fresh gingerroot	1 tbsp chopped fresh cilantro	
1 garlic clove, finely chopped	1 tbsp chopped fresh flat-leaf parsley	

1 Chop the tuna evenly by hand until it has the texture of coarsely ground meat. Put into a bowl.
2 Combine the remaining ingredients with 1–1½ tablespoons of cold water, then stir carefully into the tuna until just evenly mixed. Divide into four or six equal portions. With wet hands, form into patties about 1 inch thick. Cover and refrigerate for at least 1 hour to firm up, or longer to let the flavors develop fully.
3 Grill the burgers in an oiled hinged basket until they are golden, about 2 minutes on each side; they will be rare to medium in the center. Alternatively, grill the burgers directly on an oiled rack, turning them carefully with a metal spatula.

086 MACKEREL WITH SWEET CHILE AND MINT

PREPARATION TIME *10 minutes, plus 2 hours chilling* **COOKING TIME** *10 minutes* **SERVES 4**

4 mackerel, about 11 oz each, cleaned	2 tbsp sugar	1½ tbsp chopped fresh mint
coarse sea salt	1 large, fresh, mild red chile, seeded and minced	2-inch piece fresh gingerroot, peeled and finely chopped
3 tbsp rice wine vinegar		

1 Bury the mackerel in coarse sea salt. Set aside in a cool place for 2 hours.
2 Lift the mackerel from the salt and brush them clean.
3 To make the dressing, whisk the vinegar with the sugar, then stir in the remaining ingredients.
4 Cut two slashes in each side of all the mackerel, going right through to the bone. Season. Grill in an oiled hinged basket for about 5 minutes. Turn the fish over and cook on the other side until the flesh near the head flakes easily when tested with the point of a sharp knife and the skin is very crisp, about 5 minutes longer. Remove to plates and serve with the dressing.

087 SEARED SEA BASS WITH TOMATO, AVOCADO, AND CAPER RELISH

PREPARATION TIME *10 minutes* **COOKING TIME** *3–5 minutes* **SERVES 4**

4 sea bass fillets, skin on, about 5 oz each

virgin olive oil for brushing

salt and freshly ground black pepper

small fresh basil leaves for garnish

lime wedges for serving

RELISH

¼ cup olive oil

1 plump garlic clove, cut into 8 slices

1 shallot, quartered

bunch of fresh parsley stems

a few fresh basil stems

2 tsp salted capers, well rinsed and dried

juice of ½ lime

2 roma tomatoes, seeded and cut into thin strips

1 avocado, peeled, pitted, and diced

sugar (optional)

1 Make the relish by gently warming the oil with the garlic, shallot, parsley and basil stems, 2 tablespoons water, and some salt and pepper in a covered small saucepan for 20 minutes, so the flavors infuse the oil. Strain the oil and let cool.

2 Shortly before cooking the sea bass, add the capers, lime juice, tomatoes, and avocado to the oil. Taste and adjust the seasoning, adding a little sugar, if necessary.

3 Brush the sea bass with virgin olive oil and sprinkle with seasoning. Grill, skin-side down, on an oiled rack close to the heat for 1–2 minutes, then turn the fish over and raise the rack to about 4–6 inches from the heat. Grill until the flesh is barely cooked, 2–3 minutes longer.

4 Remove from the grill. Garnish with basil leaves and serve with the relish and lime wedges.

088 SWEET AND SHARP BROCHETTES

PREPARATION TIME *10 minutes, plus 1 hour chilling* **COOKING TIME** *6–8 minutes* **SERVES 4**

2 swordfish or tuna steaks, about 5 oz each, cut into bite-sized chunks

10 oz monkfish fillet, cut into bite-sized chunks

16 raw tiger shrimp, shelled but with the last tail section left on

1 plump garlic clove, crushed

2 tbsp teriyaki sauce

juice of ½ lime

2 tbsp chile oil

2 limes, cut into 8 wedges

1 lemon, cut into 8 wedges

fresh cilantro for garnish

1 Put the fish and shrimp into a bowl.

2 Mix together the garlic, teriyaki sauce, lime juice, and chile oil. Pour this over the fish and stir gently to ensure all the pieces are evenly coated, then cover the bowl and let marinate in a cool place for 1 hour.

3 Lift the fish and shrimp from the bowl and thread alternately on eight skewers, intermingling them with the lime and lemon wedges.

4 Grill on an oiled rack until the shrimp have turned pink and the fish is cooked through, 3–4 minutes on each side, turning the brochettes once. Garnish with cilantro.

089 MONKFISH BROCHETTES WITH ROSEMARY AND ANCHOVY SAUCE

PREPARATION TIME *10 minutes* **COOKING TIME** *6–8 minutes* **SERVES 4**

2 monkfish fillets, about 12 oz each, cut into 1¼-inch cubes	**lemon wedges for serving**	**9 salted anchovy fillets, rinsed and dried**
salt and freshly ground black pepper	ROSEMARY AND ANCHOVY SAUCE	**7 tbsp extra virgin olive oil**
olive oil for brushing	**1½ tbsp chopped fresh rosemary leaves**	**juice of 1½ lemons**

1 Make the sauce: Put the rosemary into a small blender and chop finely. Add the anchovy fillets and mix to a thick paste. With the motor running, slowly pour in the oil, then add the lemon juice. Season to taste. Set aside.
2 Thread the monkfish cubes onto skewers. Season them and brush with oil. Grill on an oiled rack until evenly browned, 6–8 minutes, turning once.
3 Serve with the sauce and lemon wedges.

090 SALMON WITH SPICED TEA MARINADE

PREPARATION TIME *10 minutes plus 2½ hours cooling and marinating* **COOKING TIME** *8 minutes*
SERVES 4

2 Assam teabags	**¼ cup sweet soy sauce**	**toasted sesame oil for brushing**
1 cup boiling water	**1 tbsp clear honey**	
2¼-inch piece fresh gingerroot	**4 pieces salmon fillet, skin on**	**scallions, sliced on the diagonal, for garnish**
1 plump garlic clove		

1 Put the teabags into a bowl, pour on the boiling water, and stir, then let infuse for 5 minutes.
2 Lift out and discard the teabags. Press the ginger through a garlic press into the tea, then repeat with the garlic. Stir in the soy sauce and honey. Leave until cold.
3 Put the salmon fillets into a dish in a single layer. Pour the tea marinade over them. Turn the salmon over, then cover and let marinate in a cool place for 2 hours, turning occasionally.
4 Lift the salmon from the marinade and pat dry. Brush with sesame oil, then grill on an oiled rack, skin-side down first, until done to your taste, about 4 minutes on each side. Remove the salmon fillets from the grill, scatter the scallions over them, and serve.

091 PROSCIUTTO-WRAPPED MONKFISH

PREPARATION TIME *10 minutes, plus 30–60 minutes marinating* **COOKING TIME** *8 minutes* **SERVES 4**

2 monkfish fillets, about
  12 oz each
olive oil for brushing
1 tsp fresh thyme leaves
1 tbsp chopped fresh
  flat-leaf parsley
freshly ground black
  pepper

1 lemon, halved
4–6 slices prosciutto

DRESSING
3 tbsp olive oil
3 tbsp peanut oil
1½ tbsp tarragon vinegar

1½ tbsp medium-dry
  white wine
2 heaped tsp chopped
  fresh dill
2 heaped tsp chopped
  fresh parsley
½ tbsp wholegrain mustard

1 Brush the monkfish with olive oil. Combine the thyme leaves and parsley on a plate. Roll the fillets in the mixture, then season with black pepper. Squeeze lemon juice evenly over the fillets. Wrap each fillet in prosciutto, securing the loose ends with soaked wooden toothpicks (see page 10). Brush with olive oil. Place in a single layer in a nonreactive dish, cover, and let marinate in a cool place for 30–60 minutes.
2 Grill the fish on an oiled rack until the fish is just opaque and the prosciutto is crisp, about 4 minutes on each side .
3 Meanwhile, make the dressing by mixing the ingredients together in a blender, or using an immersion blender, until a green emulsion is formed.
4 Serve the fish with some dressing trickled over. Serve the remaining dressing separately.

092 FISH TORTILLAS WITH TOMATO AND CILANTRO SALSA

PREPARATION TIME *15 minutes* **COOKING TIME** *6 minutes* **SERVES 4**

4 flounder fillets, skin on,
  about 6 oz each
8 flour tortillas
½ cup mayonnaise *(see
  page 179)*

BASTE
1 garlic clove, crushed
salt and freshly ground
  black pepper

½ tsp ground cumin
½ tsp dried oregano
½ tsp hot paprika
1 tbsp lime juice
2 tbsp olive oil

TOMATO AND CILANTRO SALSA
4 vine-ripened tomatoes,
  seeded and diced

1 small red onion, finely
  chopped
2 tbsp chopped fresh
  cilantro
1 fresh, hot red chile,
  seeded and finely
  chopped
1 tbsp lemon juice

1 Make the salsa by combining all the ingredients. Cover and set aside.
2 For the baste, crush the garlic to a paste with a pinch of salt. Combine with some black pepper, the spices, lime juice, and olive oil. Brush the fish with the mixture.
3 Grill the fish in an oiled hinged basket, or directly on an oiled rack, for 3 minutes on each side.
4 Meanwhile, warm the tortillas at the side of the grill rack for 30 seconds on each side. (Wrap in a napkin and keep warm, if necessary.)
5 Remove the fish from the grill, flake it coarsely with a fork, and serve in the tortillas along with the salsa and mayonnaise.

093 SALMON ROULADES WITH GREEN HERB SAUCE

PREPARATION TIME *15 minutes* **COOKING TIME** *20–25 minutes* **SERVES 6**

3 garlic cloves, unpeeled	finely grated zest of	GREEN HERB SAUCE
olive oil for brushing	3 limes	6 tbsp virgin olive oil
6 pieces salmon tail fillet,	3 tbsp chopped fresh dill	2 tbsp white wine vinegar
about 10 oz each,	salt and freshly ground	2 tbsp chopped fresh
skinned	black pepper	parsley
½ cup dry bread crumbs	lemon wedges for serving	2 tbsp chopped fresh dill
		1 tsp Dijon mustard

1   Preheat the oven to 400°F. Brush the garlic cloves with olive oil, place in a small baking dish, and roast until soft, about 10 minutes. Let cool a little.

2   Meanwhile, make the herb sauce by combining all the ingredients with some seasoning in a blender and blending until smooth. Set aside.

3   Cut each piece of salmon in half horizontally. Place each slice in turn between two sheets of plastic wrap and pound carefully with a rolling pin until increased in size by about one-quarter.

4   Peel the cooked garlic and mash the cloves, then mix with the bread crumbs, lime zest, dill, and seasoning. Divide among the salmon slices and roll up toward the narrow end. Secure with wooden toothpicks that have been soaked in water for 20 minutes.

5   Brush the salmon rolls with olive oil and grill on an oiled rack until just cooked, 10–12 minutes, turning occasionally; take care not to overcook. Serve with the herb sauce and lemon wedges.

POULTRY

When grilling poultry, remember that bone and skin add flavor. The skin also protects the meat from the fierce heat, and, when cooked to the proper crispness, adds richness. Take care, though, as fat dripping onto hot coals will cause flareups, and bone-in chicken can char on the outside before the meat near the bone is done. However, skinless, boneless pieces can cook too quickly and dry out. Even if you don't want to eat the skin, it is best to leave it on during grilling.

Take poultry out of the refrigerator 30 minutes before putting it on the grill. Making shallow cuts in chicken breasts, and deeper ones through to the bone of thighs and drumsticks, will enable flavorings to penetrate and ensure even cooking. Brush chicken, especially skinless, boneless pieces, frequently during grilling, using a marinade, baste, or oil.

Cook bone-in pieces bone-side down until no longer pink in the center. Skin-on pieces should be seared skin-side down for a couple of minutes, then turned over to continue cooking. All poultry, with the exception of duck, must be well cooked but not dried out. White breast meat usually takes less time to cook than the darker meat of thighs and drumsticks (see page 14). If you have a lot of chicken to grill, precook bone-in chicken pieces in a preheated 400°F oven for about 15 minutes, then finish the cooking immediately on the grill, reducing the usual grilling time by about 10 minutes.

CHAPTER 3

094 CHICKEN WITH CILANTRO, LIME, AND AVOCADO

PREPARATION TIME *15 minutes, plus 1–2 hours marinating* **COOKING TIME** *15 minutes* **SERVES 4**

8 chicken thighs	2 tsp ground cumin	3 tbsp chopped fresh
2 tbsp olive oil	pinch of sugar	cilantro
grated zest and juice of	salt and freshly ground	fresh cilantro leaves and
1 lime	black pepper	lime wedges for serving
2 garlic cloves, crushed	2 large avocados	

1 Using the point of a sharp knife, cut three slashes in each chicken thigh. Lay the chicken thighs in a nonreactive dish.
2 Combine the olive oil, lime zest, half the lime juice, the garlic, cumin, sugar, and seasoning. Brush this evenly over the chicken, making sure it goes into the slashes. Cover and let marinate in a cool place for 1–2 hours.
3 Lift the chicken from the dish. Grill on an oiled rack for 15–20 minutes, turning every 3 minutes.
4 Meanwhile, halve, pit, peel, and chop the avocados, then mix with the remaining lime juice and the chopped cilantro. Season.
5 Remove the chicken from the grill, garnish with cilantro leaves, and serve with the avocado and lime wedges.

095 DUCK WITH ORANGE AND MUSTARD DRESSING

PREPARATION TIME *15 minutes* **COOKING TIME** *13–15 minutes* **SERVES 2**

2 duck breasts	1 tbsp olive oil	3 tbsp hazelnuts, lightly
5 oranges	salt and freshly ground	toasted, skinned, and
1 tbsp Dijon mustard	black pepper	coarsely chopped
1 tbsp clear honey	salad leaves, including	
1 tbsp hazelnut oil	watercress, for serving	

1 Using a sharp knife, score diagonal parallel lines ½ inch apart through the skin and fat of the duck breasts to make a crisscross pattern; do not pierce the meat.
2 Squeeze the juice from four oranges. Mix 1 tablespoon of the orange juice with the mustard and honey. Spread this over the breasts.
3 Grill the breasts, skin-side down first, on an oiled rack until the skin is crisp, about 5 minutes. Turn the breasts over and cook to the desired degree of doneness, 8–10 minutes longer.
4 Meanwhile, make the dressing: Whisk together 5 tablespoons of orange juice with the hazelnut oil and olive oil. Season to taste.
5 Transfer the duck breasts to a plate, pour half the dressing over them, cover with foil, and let rest for 5 minutes.
6 Remove the peel and pith from the remaining orange and divide the orange into sections. Divide the salad leaves and orange sections between two serving plates. Slice the duck breasts diagonally and arrange on the salads. Sprinkle with the hazelnuts and pour the remaining dressing over.

096 CHICKEN WITH LEMON AND MUSTARD

PREPARATION TIME *10 minutes, plus 2 hours marinating* **COOKING TIME** *16–20 minutes* **SERVES 4**

8 bone-in chicken pieces, such as breast halves, thighs, and drumsticks	MARINADE **2 plump garlic cloves** **salt and freshly ground black pepper**	**3 tbsp Dijon mustard** **5 tbsp olive oil** **5 tbsp lemon juice** **½ tsp dried thyme**

1   Cut deep slashes in the chicken, then arrange in a single layer in a nonreactive dish.
2   Crush the garlic to a paste with a pinch of salt. Mix with the remaining ingredients. Spread evenly over the chicken and turn the pieces over to ensure they are evenly coated, then cover and let marinate in a cool place for 2 hours, turning occasionally.
3   Grill the chicken pieces, skin-side down first, on an oiled rack until the skin is golden and the juices run clear when the thickest part is pierced with a skewer, 8–10 minutes on each side, turning occasionally.

097 TANDOORI CHICKEN KABOBS

PREPARATION TIME *10 minutes, plus 2 hours marinating* **COOKING TIME** *10 minutes* **SERVES 4**

8 boneless chicken thighs, cut into 1-inch pieces MARINADE **2 garlic cloves, finely chopped**	**2 tsp grated fresh gingerroot** **½ fresh, hot red chile, finely chopped** **1 cup plain yogurt** **1 tsp ground cardamom**	**1 tsp ground coriander** **1 tsp garam masala** **1 tsp ground cumin** **salt**

1   Put the chicken in a shallow, nonreactive dish.
2   Make the marinade by stirring the ingredients together. Pour this over the chicken and turn the pieces over to ensure they are coated thoroughly and evenly. Cover and let marinate in a cool place for 2 hours, turning occasionally.
3   Drain the chicken from the marinade and thread onto skewers. Grill the chicken on an oiled rack until browned and the juices run clear when the thickest part is pierced with a skewer, about 5 minutes on each side, turning occasionally.

098 CHICKEN WITH ORANGE AND MINT

PREPARATION TIME *15 minutes, plus 1–2 hours marinating* **COOKING TIME** *12–16 minutes* **SERVES 4**

1 tbsp olive oil **1 garlic clove, finely chopped** **5 tbsp orange juice** **2 tbsp lemon juice**	**2–3 tbsp chopped fresh mint** **pinch of sugar** **salt and freshly ground black pepper**	**4 chicken breast halves** **fresh mint sprigs for garnish**

1   Combine the olive oil, garlic, orange and lemon juices, mint, sugar, and plenty of seasoning.
2   Slash the chicken with the point of a sharp knife, then lay the pieces in a nonreactive dish. Pour the marinade over the breasts and turn them over so they are evenly coated. Cover and let marinate in a cool place for 1–2 hours, turning occasionally.
3   Lift the chicken from the dish (reserve the marinade) and grill on an oiled rack for 6–8 minutes on each side, brushing occasionally with the marinade. Serve garnished with mint sprigs.

099 TUSCAN CHICKEN WITH TOMATO AND BLACK OLIVE SALAD

PREPARATION TIME *10 minutes* **COOKING TIME** *10 minutes* **SERVES 4**

4-6 garlic cloves

2 tsp salt

1 tsp freshly ground black
   pepper

3 tbsp finely chopped fresh
   rosemary

12 skinless, boneless
   chicken thighs

12 thin slices pancetta

olive oil for brushing

TOMATO AND BLACK OLIVE SALAD

4 vine-ripened tomatoes,
   sliced

1 garlic clove, finely
   chopped

⅓ cup sliced oil-cured
   black olives

salt and freshly ground
   black pepper

3 tbsp extra virgin olive oil

1 tbsp chopped fresh
   flat-leaf parsley

1. Make the salad: Put the tomatoes, garlic, and olives into a bowl. Season, then trickle the oil over. Scatter on the parsley. Set aside.
2. Pound the garlic, salt, pepper, and rosemary to a paste, using a mortar and pestle, spice grinder, or the end of a rolling pin in a small bowl. Rub the paste liberally over the underside of the thighs.
3. Reshape the thighs and wrap each one in a slice of pancetta. Brush with olive oil. Secure with wooden toothpicks that have been soaked in water for 10 minutes.
4. Grill the chicken thighs on an oiled rack until they are golden, crisp, and cooked through, about 5 minutes on each side. Remove the thighs from the grill, season with black pepper, and serve with the tomato and olive salad.

100 CHICKEN WITH GINGER, GARAM MASALA, AND COCONUT

PREPARATION TIME *10 minutes, plus 1–2 hours marinating* **COOKING TIME** *15 minutes* **SERVES 4**

8 chicken drumsticks

salt and freshly ground
   black pepper

fresh cilantro leaves for
   garnish

SPICE MIXTURE

1 onion, chopped

4 garlic cloves, crushed

1 tbsp grated fresh
   gingerroot

1 tbsp garam masala

½ cup canned coconut
   milk

3 tbsp Thai fish sauce

1 small handful fresh
   cilantro

1. Using a sharp knife, make several deep slashes in each of the drumsticks, through to the bone. Put them in a nonreactive dish.
2. Combine all the spice mixture ingredients in a blender or food processor and pulse until smooth. Pour this over the drumsticks and turn them over to coat evenly; make sure the mixture goes into the slashes. Cover and let marinate in a cool place for 1–2 hours, turning occasionally.
3. Lift the chicken from the dish. Grill on an oiled rack for 15 minutes, turning every 3 minutes.
4. Remove from the grill, sprinkle with salt and pepper, and garnish with cilantro leaves.

101 CHICKEN STRIPS WITH BASIL AND LIME

PREPARATION TIME *10 minutes, plus 1–2 hours marinating* **COOKING TIME** *10 minutes* **SERVES 4**

**4 skinless chicken breast
 halves**
7 tbsp virgin olive oil
grated zest of 1 large lime
¼ cup lime juice

**2 tbsp shredded fresh
 basil leaves**
**salt and freshly ground
 black pepper**

BASIL AND LIME MAYONNAISE
**½ cup mayonnaise (see
 page 179)**
**2 tbsp finely shredded fresh
 basil leaves**
juice of ½ lime, or to taste

1   Cut each chicken breast lengthwise into three strips and put into a shallow, nonreactive bowl.
2   Mix the oil with the lime zest and juice, basil leaves, and seasoning, adding plenty of black
    pepper. Pour this over the chicken and stir to ensure the chicken is well coated, then cover and
    let marinate in a cool place for 1–2 hours.
3   Meanwhile, make the basil and lime mayonnaise by mixing the mayonnaise with the shredded
    basil and adding lime juice and black pepper to taste.
4   Lift the chicken from the marinade and thread the strips onto skewers. Grill on an oiled rack until
    golden and cooked through, about 10 minutes, turning two or three times. Serve the chicken
    accompanied by the mayonnaise.

102 SQUAB CHICKENS WITH PERSIAN MARINADE

PREPARATION TIME *15 minutes, plus 4–6 hours marinating* **COOKING TIME** *25 minutes* **SERVES 4**

4 squab chickens,
butterflied*
⅛ tsp saffron threads
pinch of sugar
juice of 4 lemons

1 garlic clove, finely
chopped
salt and freshly ground
black pepper
¼ cup thick, plain yogurt

1 onion, coarsely grated
¾-inch piece fresh
gingerroot, grated
pinch of cayenne pepper

1   Thread two oiled metal skewers diagonally through each bird to hold them in shape during cooking. Alternatively, thread one skewer through the wings and body and another skewer through the thighs. Place the chickens in a shallow, nonreactive bowl.

2   Grind the saffron and sugar to a powder using a mortar and pestle, or the end of a rolling pin in a small bowl. Stir in the lemon juice.

3   Crush the garlic to a paste with a pinch of salt. Mix with the yogurt, onion, ginger, cayenne pepper, and some black pepper. Pour this evenly over the chickens, then cover and let marinate in a cool place for 4–6 hours, turning occasionally.

4   Lift the chickens from the marinade (reserve the marinade) and grill, bone-side down, on an oiled rack for 15 minutes. Turn them over and grill until the skin is crisp and the juices run clear when the flesh between the legs and the body is pierced with a sharp knife, about 10 minutes longer, brushing occasionally with the remaining marinade.

*   If you are unable to buy butterflied birds, do it yourself. Place each one in turn on a board, cut down either side of the backbone with poultry shears or heavy-duty kitchen scissors, and lift out the backbone. Turn the bird over, open it out, and press down firmly to open it out flat.

103 CHICKEN AND LEMON GRASS KABOBS

PREPARATION TIME *10 minutes, plus 8 hours marinating* **COOKING TIME** *10 minutes* **SERVES 4**

4 skinless, boneless
chicken breast halves,
cut into 1-inch cubes
8 lemon grass stems,
outer layers removed

MARINADE
1 tbsp finely chopped
fresh gingerroot
3 garlic cloves, finely
chopped
1 fresh, hot red chile,
seeded and minced

grated zest of 1 lime
juice of 2 limes
1 tbsp clear honey
¼ cup dark soy sauce
¼ cup rice wine vinegar
2 tbsp sweet chile sauce

1   Make the marinade by combining the ingredients in a bowl. Add the chicken and stir to ensure all the pieces are evenly coated. Cover and let marinate in a cool place for about 8 hours, stirring occasionally.

2   Lift the chicken from the bowl (reserve the remaining marinade). Pierce a hole through each cube, then thread them onto the lemon grass stems.

3   Grill the kebabs on an oiled rack for about 10 minutes, turning occasionally and brushing with the reserved marinade.

104 DUCK WITH MANGO DIP

PREPARATION TIME *15 minutes, plus 30-60 minutes marinating* **COOKING TIME** *15-20 minutes* **SERVES 4**

4 duck breasts	2 pieces of star anise	½ cup finely shredded
4 plump garlic cloves,	salt and freshly ground	scallion
sliced	black pepper	½ cup finely shredded
1 tbsp fresh tamarind, or		English cucumber
lemon juice	MANGO DIP	pinch of crushed dried
grated zest and juice of	¾ cup sugar	chiles
1 orange	1 cup white wine vinegar	
pinch of crushed dried	½ cup finely shredded	
chiles	fresh mango	

1 Using a sharp knife, score diagonal parallel lines ½ inch apart through the skin and fat of the duck breasts to make a crisscross pattern; do not pierce the meat.
2 Put the garlic, tamarind, orange zest and juice, chiles, and star anise into a blender and mix to a paste. Brush the spice paste evenly over the duck breasts. Cover and let marinate in a cool place for 30-60 minutes.
3 Meanwhile, make the mango dip: Gently heat the sugar in the vinegar until it dissolves, then increase the heat and boil for 2 minutes. Remove from the heat, add the remaining ingredients, and let cool.
4 Grill the breasts, skin-side down first, on an oiled rack until the skin is crisp, about 5 minutes. Turn the breasts over and cook to the desired degree of doneness, 8-10 minutes longer.
5 Remove the duck breasts from the grill, cover with foil, and let rest for 5 minutes. Season and serve with the mango dip.

105 GUINEA FOWL WITH RUM, ORANGE, AND MAPLE SYRUP

PREPARATION TIME *10 minutes, plus 6 hours marinating* **COOKING TIME** *35 minutes* **SERVES 4**

1 guinea fowl, about 2½ lb,	MARINADE	large pinch of ground
butterflied*	2 tbsp dark rum	allspice
	2 tbsp freshly squeezed	salt and freshly ground
	orange juice	black pepper
	2 tbsp maple syrup	1 tbsp finely chopped
	1 tbsp peanut oil	fresh gingerroot

1 Thread two oiled metal skewers diagonally through each bird to hold them in shape during cooking. Alternatively, thread one skewer through the wings and body and another skewer through the thighs. Put the guinea fowl into a nonreactive dish.
2 Combine the remaining ingredients. Brush evenly all over the guinea fowl. Pour any remaining marinade around the bird. Cover and leave in a cool place for 6 hours, basting occasionally.
3 Lift the bird from the marinade (reserve any remaining marinade) and grill, bone-side down, on an oiled rack for 20 minutes. Turn the bird over and grill until the skin is crisp and the juices run clear when the flesh between the legs and the body is pierced with a skewer, about 15 minutes longer, brushing occasionally with the remaining marinade.
* See note on recipe 102 (above left) regarding butterflying.

MOROCCAN CHICKEN WITH TABOULEH

PREPARATION TIME *15 minutes, plus 2–5 hours marinating* **COOKING TIME** *10 minutes* **SERVES 2**

6 boneless chicken thighs, cut into 1-inch pieces

2 tbsp olive oil

5 tbsp lemon juice

small handful of fresh cilantro, finely chopped

small handful of fresh flat-leaf parsley, finely chopped

1 tbsp ground cumin

1 tbsp ground cinnamon

1 tbsp ground coriander

1 plump garlic clove, finely chopped

salt and freshly ground black pepper

TABOULEH

⅓ cup bulghur wheat

2 tbsp olive oil

2 tbsp lemon juice

4 oz bottled Italian mixed peppers in oil, drained and chopped

handful of fresh flat-leaf parsley, finely chopped

4 large sprigs of mint, finely chopped

1 Thread the chicken onto skewers. Lay the skewers in a single layer in a nonreactive dish.
2 Combine the olive oil, lemon juice, herbs, spices, garlic, and seasoning. Pour this over the chicken and turn the skewers over to ensure they are well coated, then cover and let marinate in a cool place for 2–5 hours.
3 Meanwhile, make the tabouleh: Put the bulghur wheat into a bowl, pour 5 tablespoons boiling water over, and leave until the water has been absorbed, about 30 minutes, stirring occasionally.
4 Fluff up the bulghur with a fork. Fork through the remaining tabouleh ingredients and season.
5 Lift the chicken skewers from the dish (reserve the marinade) and grill on an oiled rack for 5 minutes on each side, brushing occasionally with the reserved marinade. Using a fork, slip the cooked chicken from the skewers onto the tabouleh.

107 SQUAB CHICKENS WITH GARLIC, LEMON, AND THYME

PREPARATION TIME *10 minutes, plus 4 hours marinating* **COOKING TIME** *25 minutes* **SERVES 2**

4 squab chickens, butterflied*	MARINADE	juice of 1½ large lemons
	3 garlic cloves, crushed	salt and freshly ground black pepper
	3 tbsp fresh thyme leaves	
	6 tbsp fruity olive oil	

1 Thread two metal skewers diagonally through each bird to hold them in shape during cooking. Alternatively, thread a skewer through the wings and body and another skewer through the thighs. Place the chickens in a shallow, nonreactive bowl.

2 Combine the marinade ingredients and pour this evenly over the chickens. Cover and let marinate in a cool place for 4 hours, turning occasionally.

3 Lift the chickens from the marinade (reserve the marinade) and grill, bone-side down, on an oiled rack for 15 minutes. Turn them over and grill until the skin is crisp and the juices run clear when the flesh between the legs and the body is pierced with a sharp knife, about 10 minutes longer, brushing occasionally with the remaining marinade.

* If you are unable to buy butterflied birds, do it yourself: Place each one in turn on a board, cut down either side of the backbone with poultry shears or heavy-duty kitchen scissors, and lift out the backbone. Turn the bird over, open it out, and press down firmly to open it out flat.

108 TURKEY MORSELS IN PEANUT MARINADE

PREPARATION TIME *10 minutes, plus 2 hours marinating* **COOKING TIME** *10 minutes* **SERVES 4**

1 lb turkey breast cubes	1 cup plain yogurt	1 tbsp Dijon mustard
½ cup peanut butter	½ tbsp Worcestershire sauce	salt and freshly ground black pepper
1 plump garlic clove, finely chopped	few drops of hot pepper sauce	bunch of scallions

1 Put the turkey cubes into a nonreactive bowl.

2 Mix the peanut butter and garlic with 5 tablespoons of the yogurt, then add the Worcestershire sauce, hot pepper sauce, mustard, and salt to taste. Pour this over the turkey and stir gently to ensure all the cubes are evenly coated. Cover and let marinate in a cool place for 2 hours.

3 Meanwhile, slice some of the green parts of the scallions and reserve for garnish. Finely slice the white parts and mix with the remaining yogurt. Season to taste. Cover and chill until required.

4 Lift the turkey from the marinade and thread onto skewers. Grill on an oiled rack for about 10 minutes, turning occasionally. Remove from the grill. Sprinkle the sliced scallion greens over the yogurt mixture and serve with the turkey kabobs.

109 SPRING CHICKENS GLAZED WITH HONEY AND SPICES

PREPARATION TIME *10 minutes, plus 4–6 hours marinating* **COOKING TIME** *25 minutes* **SERVES 6**

3 broiler-fryer chickens, split in half down the backbone*	2 tbsp white wine vinegar	1½ tbsp finely chopped fresh rosemary
	3 tbsp soy sauce	
	3 garlic cloves, crushed	2 tbsp light brown sugar
	2 tbsp clear honey	1 tbsp Dijon mustard
MARINADE	1-inch piece fresh	salt and freshly ground
2 tbsp toasted sesame oil	gingerroot, grated	black pepper

1 Make the marinade by stirring all the ingredients together until the sugar has dissolved.
2 Put the chickens in a single layer in a nonreactive dish. Pour the marinade over them and turn the birds over to ensure they are evenly coated. Cover and let marinate in a cool place for 4–6 hours, turning occasionally.
3 Drain the marinade from the chickens into a saucepan and bring to a boil on the grill rack.
4 Grill the chickens, bone-side down, on the oiled rack for 15 minutes. Turn them over and grill until the skin is crisp and the juices run clear when the flesh between the legs and the body is pierced with a skewer, about 10 minutes longer, brushing occasionally with the marinade.
* If preferred, you can use 6 butterflied squab chickens. To butterfly them yourself, place each one in turn on a board, cut down either side of the backbone with poultry shears or heavy-duty kitchen scissors, and lift out the backbone. Turn the bird over, open it out, and press down firmly to open it out flat.

110 TURKEY CUTLETS WITH COCONUT AND CILANTRO

PREPARATION TIME *10 minutes, plus 4–6 hours marinating* **COOKING TIME** *12 minutes* **SERVES 4**

4 turkey cutlets	large handful of fresh cilantro	1 tbsp garam masala
		½ cup canned coconut
MARINADE	1 tbsp finely chopped fresh gingerroot	milk
3 garlic cloves, chopped		freshly ground black
½ fresh, hot red chile, seeded and chopped	1 onion, chopped	pepper
	3 tbsp Thai fish sauce	

1 Using the point of a sharp knife, make cuts in the surfaces of the turkey cutlets. Lay the cutlets in a single layer in a nonreactive dish.
2 Make the marinade by putting all the ingredients into a blender or food processor and pulsing until the mixture is smooth.
3 Pour the marinade over the cutlets, then turn them over to coat thoroughly. Cover and let marinate in a cool place for 4–6 hours, turning occasionally.
4 Lift the turkey cutlets from the dish and grill on an oiled rack for about 6 minutes on each side, turning once.

111 GUINEA FOWL WITH MUSTARD AND BALSAMIC VINEGAR

PREPARATION TIME *10 minutes, plus 6–8 hours marinating* **COOKING TIME** *35 minutes* **SERVES 4**

1 guinea fowl, about 2½ lb, butterflied*	MARINADE **2 garlic cloves, peeled** **salt and freshly ground** **black pepper**	**1 tbsp Dijon mustard** **1 tsp herbes de Provence** **1 tbsp olive oil** **¼ cup balsamic vinegar**

1 Thread two oiled metal skewers diagonally through the bird to hold it in shape during cooking. Alternatively, thread one skewer through the wings and body and another skewer through the thighs. Put the guinea fowl in a nonreactive dish.

2 Make the marinade: Crush the garlic to a paste with a pinch of salt. Combine with the remaining ingredients. Pour evenly over the guinea fowl and turn the bird so that it is well coated. Cover and let marinate in a cool place for 6–8 hours, turning occasionally.

3 Lift the bird from the marinade (reserve the marinade) and grill, bone-side down, on an oiled rack for 20 minutes. Turn the bird over and grill until the skin is crisp and the juices run clear when the flesh between the legs and the body is pierced with a skewer, about 15 minutes longer, brushing occasionally with the remaining marinade.

* If you are unable to buy a butterflied bird, do it yourself. Place it on a board, cut down either side of the backbone with poultry shears or heavy-duty kitchen scissors, and lift out the backbone. Turn the bird over, open it out, and press down firmly to open it out flat.

112 PEPPERED CHICKEN BROCHETTES

PREPARATION TIME *10 minutes, plus 1–2 hours marinating* **COOKING TIME** *10–12 minutes* **SERVES 4**

1 lb skinless, boneless chicken breast halves, cut into 1¼-inch cubes **2 tbsp olive oil** **½ tbsp coarsely ground black peppercorns**	**1 fresh, hot red chile, seeded and thinly sliced** **1 garlic clove, finely chopped** **grated zest and juice of 2 small lemons** **1½ tbsp clear honey**	**8 button mushrooms** **olive oil for brushing** **salt and freshly ground black pepper** **chopped fresh flat-leaf parsley for garnish**

1 Put the chicken cubes in a nonreactive bowl.

2 Mix together the oil,. peppercorns, chile, garlic, lemon zest and juice, and honey. Pour over the chicken and stir gently to ensure the chicken is evenly coated. Cover and let marinate in a cool place for 1–2 hours.

3 Brush the mushrooms with olive oil and sprinkle them with seasoning. Thread one mushroom onto each of four skewers.

4 Lift the chicken from the marinade and thread the cubes onto the skewers, then finish each with another mushroom.

5 Grill on an oiled rack for 10–12 minutes, turning occasionally. Remove from the grill, sprinkle with parsley, and serve.

113 CHICKEN WITH CHILE JAM

PREPARATION TIME *10 minutes, plus 2 hours marinating* **COOKING TIME** *45 minutes* **SERVES 4**

4 chicken leg quarters	**7 oz fresh, hot red chiles,**	**1 tsp soy sauce**
	seeded and chopped	**1 tbsp chopped fresh**
CHILE JAM	**2 garlic cloves, chopped**	**cilantro leaves**
⅓ cup packed brown sugar	**2 shallots, chopped**	**5 tbsp plain yogurt**
7 tbsp rice wine vinegar	**½ tsp grated fresh**	
½ cup raisins	**gingerroot**	

1   Make the jam: Gently heat the sugar in the vinegar, stirring, until the sugar has dissolved, then bring to a boil. Add the raisins and cook until the liquid is syrupy and a light caramel color. Stir in the chiles, garlic, shallots, ginger, and soy sauce. Transfer to a blender and pulse until coarse-fine. Let cool. Mix with the cilantro leaves and yogurt.
2   Cut deep slashes in the chicken legs and place in a nonreactive bowl. Rub the chile jam into the legs, making sure it goes well into the slashes. Cover and leave in a cool place for 2 hours.
3   Grill the chicken legs on an oiled rack until cooked through, crisp, and slightly charred, 25–30 minutes .

114 CHICKEN AND SAUSAGE KABOBS

PREPARATION TIME *10 minutes* **COOKING TIME** *10 minutes* **SERVES 4**

1 lb skinless, boneless	**4 herbed pork link**	**16 small fresh sage or bay**
chicken (preferably	**sausages, cut into**	**leaves (optional)**
thighs and/or	**1-inch lengths**	**olive oil for brushing**
drumsticks), cut into	**4-oz piece pancetta or**	**salt and freshly ground**
1¼-inch cubes	**slab bacon , cut into**	**black pepper**
	¾-inch cubes	

1   Thread the chicken, sausage, and pancetta or bacon onto long skewers, inserting the sage or bay leaves at intervals, if using. Brush with olive oil.
2   Grill the kabobs on an oiled rack until the chicken and sausage are cooked through and browned, about 10 minutes, turning occasionally. Remove the kabobs from the grill and sprinkle with seasoning before serving.

115 PERSIAN-STYLE CHICKEN KABOBS

PREPARATION TIME *10 minutes, plus 2 hours marinating* **COOKING TIME** *10 minutes* **SERVES 4**

1 lb boneless chicken	MARINADE	**salt and freshly ground**
thighs, cut into	**1 cup thick, plain yogurt**	**black pepper**
1¼-inch cubes	**3-4 saffron threads,**	
chopped fresh cilantro	**crushed**	
leaves for garnish	**1 tbsp chopped fresh mint**	
lemon wedges for serving	**2 tbsp olive oil**	

1   Put the chicken in a nonreactive dish.
2   Make the marinade by combining the ingredients. Add to the chicken and stir to ensure the chicken is well coated. Cover and let marinate in a cool place for 2 hours, stirring occasionally.
3   Lift the chicken from the marinade and thread the pieces onto skewers. Grill on an oiled rack until cooked through and browned, about 10 minutes, turning occasionally. Remove from the grill, sprinkle with cilantro, and serve with lemon wedges.

116 DUCK WITH GINGERED PLUMS

PREPARATION TIME *15 minutes* **COOKING TIME** *20-25 minutes* **SERVES 4**

4 duck breasts	6 purple-skinned plums,	2 tbsp cider vinegar
clear honey for brushing	pitted and sliced	2 tbsp sugar
Chinese five-spice powder	1 small garlic clove, finely	2 tsp grated fresh
for sprinkling	chopped	gingerroot
	4 tsp soy sauce	

1 Using a sharp knife, score diagonal parallel lines ½ inch apart through the skin and fat of the duck breasts to make a crisscross pattern; do not pierce the meat. Brush the breasts with honey, then sprinkle with five-spice powder.
2 Grill the breasts, skin-side down first, on an oiled rack until the skin is crisp, about 5 minutes . Turn the breasts over and grill to the desired degree of doneness, 8-10 minutes longer.
3 Remove from the grill, cover with foil, and let rest for 5 minutes.
4 Meanwhile, put the remaining ingredients into a saucepan. Set on the side of the grill rack and bring to a boil, then let simmer for 5 minutes.
5 Sprinkle the duck with seasoning and serve with the plums and juices.

117 ITALIAN CHICKEN BURGERS

PREPARATION TIME *10 minutes, plus 2–4 hours chilling* **COOKING TIME** *10–12 minutes* **SERVES 4**

1 lb ground chicken	salt and freshly ground	mixed salad leaves
1½ tbsp finely chopped	black pepper	mayonnaise *(see page 179)*
sun-dried tomatoes in oil	olive oil for brushing	sun-dried tomato strips
1½ tbsp chopped fresh basil		fresh basil leaves
3 tbsp freshly grated	FOR SERVING	
Parmesan cheese	4 ciabatta rolls, halved	
	horizontally	

1 Combine the ground chicken with the sun-dried tomatoes, basil, Parmesan, and seasoning until thoroughly mixed. With wet hands, form the mixture into four ¾-inch-thick patties. If possible, cover and leave in a cool place for 2–4 hours.
2 Brush the burgers with oil and grill on an oiled rack until browned and the juices run clear, 5–6 minutes on each side .
3 Meanwhile, warm the rolls at the side of the grill rack for 20–30 seconds. To serve, put a few salad leaves on the bottom half of each roll. Add a burger, then some mayonnaise, and top with sun-dried tomato strips and basil leaves.

118 ASH-BAKED CHICKEN THIGHS

PREPARATION TIME *10 minutes* **COOKING TIME** *35 minutes* **SERVES 3–6**

6 chicken thighs	5 garlic cloves, thinly	salt and freshly ground
¼ cup finely chopped	sliced	black pepper
fresh parsley	1 lemon, very thinly sliced	

1 Wrap two chicken thighs with one-third of the parsley, garlic, lemon, and seasoning in a loose packet of double-thickness, heavy-duty foil. Twist the edges together to seal tightly. Wrap securely in a third piece of foil. Repeat with the remaining chicken to make two more packets.
2 Push the hot coals to one side of the fire, add the chicken packets in a single layer, and scatter hot coals in an even layer on the top. Cook for 35 minutes, then carefully remove the packets and let stand for 5–10 minutes before opening.

119 SICHUAN CHICKEN

PREPARATION TIME *10 minutes, plus 1–2 hours marinating* **COOKING TIME** *14–16 minutes* **SERVES 4**

4 chicken breast halves	1 tbsp Sichuan	1 tbsp garam masala
	peppercorns, lightly	1 tsp ground ginger
MARINADE	toasted and crushed	1 tsp toasted sesame oil
2 tbsp sake	1 tsp crushed coriander	1–2 dashes of hot pepper
1 tbsp clear honey	seeds	sauce

1 Using the point of a sharp knife, score each chicken breast three times on both sides. Place in a nonreactive dish.
2 Make the marinade by mixing all the ingredients together. Pour evenly over the chicken, then cover and let marinate in a cool place for 1–2 hours.
3 Lift the chicken from the dish and grill on an oiled rack for 7–8 minutes on each side.

120 CHICKEN WITH INDIAN SPICES

PREPARATION TIME *10 minutes, plus 1–2 hours marinating* **COOKING TIME** *15 minutes* **SERVES 4**

	SPICE MIXTURE	
8 chicken drumsticks	**1 onion, chopped**	**3 tbsp Thai fish sauce**
naan bread for serving	**4 garlic cloves, crushed**	**1 tbsp garam masala**
fresh cilantro leaves	**1 tbsp grated fresh**	**small handful of fresh**
for garnish	**gingerroot**	**cilantro**
	½ cup canned coconut	**salt and freshly ground**
	milk	**black pepper**

1 Cut deep slashes in each chicken drumstick and place in a nonreactive dish.
2 Make the spice mixture by putting all the ingredients in a blender or food processor and pulsing until smooth. Pour over the chicken and turn the drumsticks over so the pieces are evenly coated. Cover and let marinate in a cool place for 1–2 hours, turning occasionally.
3 Lift the chicken from the dish and grill on an oiled rack until cooked through, about 15 minutes, turning every 3 minutes, .
4 Meanwhile, warm the naan bread at the side of the grill rack for 30 seconds on each side. Remove the drumsticks from the grill, sprinkle them with salt, and garnish with cilantro leaves. Serve with the naan bread.

121 CHICKEN WITH PESTO AND LEMON

PREPARATION TIME *10 minutes, plus 2 hours marinating* **COOKING TIME** *14–16 minutes* **SERVES 4**

5 tbsp Pesto *(see page 172)*	**freshly ground black**
juice of 1 small lemon	**pepper**
1½ tbsp extra virgin	**4 chicken breast halves**
olive oil	**basil sprigs for garnish**

1 Mix the pesto sauce with the lemon juice, extra virgin olive oil, and black pepper.
2 Place the chicken in a nonreactive dish. Spread the pesto mixture evenly over the chicken, then cover and let marinate in a cool place for at least 2 hours.
3 Grill the chicken on an oiled rack for 7–8 minutes on each side. Remove from the grill, garnish with basil sprigs, and serve.

122 TURKEY BROCHETTES WITH LEMON AND TERIYAKI SAUCE

PREPARATION TIME *10 minutes, plus 2 hours marinating* **COOKING TIME** *9–10 minutes* **SERVES 4**

1¼ lb turkey breast cubes	**4 tsp lemon juice**	**¼ cup peanut oil**
	4 tsp teriyaki sauce	**freshly ground black**
MARINADE	**1 tbsp clear honey**	**pepper**
1 garlic clove, finely	**1½ tbsp chopped fresh**	
chopped	**cilantro**	

1 Put the turkey into a nonreactive bowl.
2 Make the marinade by combining all the ingredients. Stir into the turkey, making sure all the pieces are evenly coated. Cover and leave in a cool place for 2 hours, stirring occasionally.
3 Lift the turkey from the bowl (reserve any remaining marinade) and thread onto skewers. Grill on an oiled rack for 9–10 minutes, turning occasionally and brushing with reserved marinade.

123 INDONESIAN BURGERS

PREPARATION TIME *10 minutes, plus 2 hours marinating* **COOKING TIME** *10-15 minutes* **SERVES 4**

1 tbsp peanut oil
1 onion, finely chopped
2 plump garlic cloves, finely chopped
1 lb ground chicken
1 tsp ground cumin
1 tsp ground coriander
½ tsp turmeric
salt and freshly ground black pepper

8 freshly cut slices of firm bread
Fresh Pineapple and Mango Salsa *(see page 175)* for serving

PEANUT SAUCE
1 tbsp peanut oil
1 small onion, finely chopped

1 plump garlic clove, finely chopped
½ tsp hot chile powder
½ cup crunchy peanut butter
2 tbsp lime juice
2 tsp dark soy sauce
¼ tsp dark brown sugar

1 Heat the oil in a frying pan and fry the onion and garlic until softened. Let cool.
2 Mix the ground chicken with the cumin, coriander, turmeric, onion, and garlic. Season with black pepper. With floured hands, form the mixture into four or six ¾-inch-thick patties. Leave in a cool place for at least 2 hours.
3 Meanwhile, make the peanut sauce: Heat the oil in a frying pan, add the onion, and fry gently until very soft and lightly browned, adding the garlic about halfway through. Stir in the chile powder for 10 seconds, then stir in the peanut butter, lime juice, soy sauce, and 1 cup water. When the sauce is evenly blended and thick, season with salt and sugar. Set aside until required.
4 Grill the burgers on an oiled rack until browned and crisp and cooked through, about 5 minutes on each side. Meanwhile, warm the sauce at the side of the grill rack. Serve the burgers in the bread slices, with the warm sauce and the salsa.

124 CHICKEN AND TARRAGON BURGERS

PREPARATION TIME *15 minutes, plus 2 hours chilling* **COOKING TIME** *10 minutes* **SERVES 4-6**

1 tbsp olive oil
1 onion, finely chopped
2 garlic cloves, finely chopped
1½ lb ground chicken
4 oz prosciutto, chopped
2 tbsp chopped fresh tarragon leaves

freshly ground black pepper
4-6 ciabatta rolls, split in half horizonally
lettuce leaves and sliced pitted green olives for serving

TOMATO MAYONNAISE
2-3 tsp sun-dried tomato paste, to taste
½ cup mayonnaise *(see page 179)*

1 Heat the oil in a frying pan and fry the onion and garlic until softened. Let cool.
2 Mix the ground chicken with the prosciutto, tarragon, onion, and garlic. Season with black pepper. With floured hands form the mixture into four or six ¾-inch-thick patties. Leave in a cool place for at least 2 hours.
3 Meanwhile, make the mayonnaise by stirring the sun-dried tomato paste into the mayonnaise until evenly blended. Season with black pepper, if necessary.
4 Grill the burgers on an oiled rack until browned and crisp and cooked through, about 5 minutes on each side.
5 While the burgers are cooking, toast the cut sides of the rolls at the side of the grill rack.
6 Cover the toasted sides of the bottom halves of the rolls with lettuce leaves, put the burgers on top, add a spoonful of the tomato mayonnaise, and finish with green olive slices. Cover with the tops of the rolls and serve.

125 TURKISH CHICKEN WRAPS

PREPARATION TIME *10 minutes, plus 1–3 hours marinating* **COOKING TIME** *14–16 minutes* **SERVES 4**

**4 skinless, boneless
  chicken breast halves**
2 garlic cloves
**salt and freshly ground
  black pepper**
½ tsp ground cinnamon
½ tsp ground allspice
¼ cup thick, plain yogurt

3 tbsp lemon juice
1 tbsp olive oil
4 pita breads
**shredded iceberg lettuce
  and sliced tomatoes
  for serving**

CILANTRO AIOLI
3 garlic cloves
2 egg yolks
juice of 1 lime, or to taste
1¼ cups peanut oil
**small handful of fresh
  cilantro leaves,
  chopped**

1 Put the chicken into a nonreactive dish.
2 Crush the garlic with a pinch of salt, then mix with the spices, yogurt, lemon juice, oil, and black pepper. Coat the chicken evenly with the mixture. Cover and let marinate in a cool place for 1–3 hours, turning occasionally.
3 To make the aïoli, put the garlic, egg yolks, and lime juice into a blender and mix briefly. With the motor running, slowly pour in the oil until the mixture becomes thick and creamy. Season and transfer to a bowl. Cover and chill, if desired. Stir in the cilantro and serve within 30 minutes.
4 Lift the chicken from the marinade. Grill on an oiled rack for 7–8 minutes on each side, turning once. Remove from the grill, cover, and let rest for 5–10 minutes before slicing.
5 Meanwhile, warm the pita breads at the side of the grill rack for 30 seconds per side. Split each pita open and stack the two halves, cut-side up, on top of each other. Divide the lettuce and tomatoes among the pita stacks. Lay the chicken on top, then add some cilantro aïoli. Roll up the pita breads around the filling.

126 PEKING-STYLE CHICKEN

PREPARATION TIME *15 minutes, plus 4–6 hours marinating* **COOKING TIME** *30 minutes* **SERVES 4**

3½ lb chicken breast quarters	GLAZE	DIPPING SAUCE
Chinese pancakes for serving	2 tbsp hoisin sauce	2 tsp toasted sesame oil
1 bunch of scallions, sliced	2 tbsp white wine vinegar	1-inch piece fresh gingerroot, peeled and grated
	2 tbsp clear honey	
	2 tbsp mango chutney	½ cup hoisin sauce
	1 tbsp soy sauce	
	juice of 1 lemon	

1 Make the glaze by stirring the ingredients together. Brush evenly and thoroughly over the chicken, then place in a single layer in a shallow, nonreactive dish. Cover and let marinate in a cool place for 4–6 hours, brushing occasionally with any remaining glaze.

2 Meanwhile, make the dipping sauce: Heat the sesame oil in a small pan, add the ginger, and cook gently for 5 minutes. Strain the oil into the hoisin sauce and stir to combine. Pour into a small dish. Set aside.

3 Lift the chicken from the dish (reserve any remaining glaze) and grill on an oiled rack for 25 minutes, brushing with any remaining glaze and turning regularly. Remove from the grill, cover, and let rest for about 5 minutes before slicing the meat.

4 Meanwhile, warm the pancakes. Serve the sliced chicken, scallions, pancakes, and dipping sauce separately so that everyone can assemble their own.

127 GRILLED CHICKEN DRUMSTICKS

PREPARATION TIME *10 minutes, plus 4–6 hours marinating* **COOKING TIME** *20–25 minutes* **SERVES 4**

8 chicken drumsticks	MARINADE	2 tbsp Worcestershire sauce
8 baby onions	1 plump garlic clove, finely chopped	1 tbsp Dijon mustard
	½ cup ketchup *(see recipe page 184)*	2 tbsp dark brown sugar

1 Cut a couple of deep slashes in each chicken drumstick and lay them in a large, shallow, nonreactive dish.

2 Make the marinade by combining the ingredients. Pour evenly over the chicken, then stir the drumsticks around to ensure they are evenly coated. Cover and let marinate in a cool place for 4–6 hours, turning occasionally.

3 Meanwhile, blanch the onions for 5 minutes. Drain and dry well. Thread onto skewers.

4 Lift the drumsticks from the marinade (reserving any remaining marinade). Brush the onions with some of the reserved marinade.

5 Grill the drumsticks and onions on an oiled rack for 15–20 minutes, turning regularly and brushing occasionally with the reserved marinade. Serve the drumsticks with the onions.

128 CHICKEN WITH CAPER AND ANCHOVY VINAIGRETTE

PREPARATION TIME *10 minutes* **COOKING TIME** *14–16 minutes* **SERVES 4**

1 tbsp small capers, crushed	5 tbsp virgin olive oil, plus extra for brushing	4 boneless chicken breast halves
6 anchovy fillets, pounded	1 tsp freshly ground black pepper	shredded fresh flat-leaf parsley for garnish
2 tbsp lemon juice		

1 Combine the capers, anchovy fillets, lemon juice, oil, and black pepper.
2 Brush the chicken with oil and season with black pepper. Grill on an oiled rack for 7–8 minutes on each side.
3 Remove the chicken from the grill, cover, and let rest for 5–10 minutes. Carve the chicken into slices. Stir the vinaigrette and pour over the slices. Sprinkle with the parsley and serve.

129 SPICED GRILLED QUAIL

PREPARATION TIME *15 minutes, plus 1–2 hours marinating* **COOKING TIME** *15 minutes* **SERVES 4-8**

8 quails, butterflied	juice of 1½ lemons	salt and freshly ground black pepper
1 tsp fennel seeds, finely crushed	3 tbsp virgin olive oil	
	½ tbsp paprika	

1 Thread a skewer through the wings and body of each quail. Thread another skewer through the thighs. Place the quails in a shallow, nonreactive bowl.
2 Mix the fennel seeds, lemon juice, olive oil, paprika, and seasoning. Rub thoroughly over the birds, then cover and let marinate in a cool place for 1–2 hours.
3 Grill the quails on an oiled rack, bone-side down, for 8 minutes. Turn them over and grill until the skin is crisp and browned and the juices run clear when the thickest part is pierced with a fine skewer, about 5–7 minutes longer.

130 JERK CHICKEN

PREPARATION TIME *10 minutes, plus 2 hours marinating* **COOKING TIME** *20–25 minutes* **SERVES 6**

6 chicken leg quarters	3 tbsp coarsely chopped fresh gingerroot	leaves from a small bunch of fresh thyme sprigs
JERK SAUCE	1–2 fresh, hot red chiles, seeded and finely chopped	freshly ground black pepper
1 onion, coarsely chopped		
½ cup white wine vinegar		
½ cup dark soy sauce	½ tsp ground allspice	

1 Put the chicken in a large, shallow, nonreactive dish.
2 Make the jerk sauce by combining the ingredients in a blender until smooth. Pour evenly over the chicken and turn the pieces over to ensure they are evenly coated, then cover and let marinate in a cool place for 2 hours, turning occasionally.
3 Lift the chicken legs from the marinade (reserve any remaining marinade) and grill, skin-side down first, on an oiled rack until the skin is golden and the juices run clear when the thickest part is pierced with a skewer, 20–25 minutes, turning and brushing occasionally with the reserved marinade.

131 CHICKEN, MANGO, AND MINT KABOBS

PREPARATION TIME *10 minutes, plus 1–2 hours marinating* **COOKING TIME** *10 minutes* **SERVES 4**

4 skinless, boneless
  chicken breast halves,
  cut into bite-sized pieces
1 ripe mango
lime wedges and mint
  sprigs for serving

MARINADE
juice of 2 limes
¼ cup olive oil
2 tbsp chopped fresh mint
1 tsp brown sugar

salt and freshly ground
  black pepper

1 Put the chicken in a nonreactive bowl.
2 Mix together the marinade ingredients. Pour over the chicken and stir gently to ensure that it is evenly coated. Cover and let marinate in a cool place for 1–2 hours.
3 Meanwhile, peel the mango and cut the flesh into pieces the same size as the chicken.
4 Lift the chicken from the bowl (reserve any remaining marinade) and thread alternately with the mango onto four skewers. Brush with the remaining marinade and grill on an oiled rack until golden and cooked through, about 10 minutes, turning two or three times. Serve the kabobs with lime wedges and mint sprigs.

132 CHICKEN WITH EASTERN GREMOLATA

PREPARATION TIME *10 minutes, plus 2 hours marinating* **COOKING TIME** *15-20 minutes* **SERVES 4**

4 chicken thighs	GREMOLATA	**2 tbsp finely chopped**
4 chicken drumsticks	**¼ cup chopped fresh**	**garlic**
salt and freshly ground	**cilantro**	**1 tbsp grated orange zest**
black pepper	**¼ cup chopped fresh**	**¼ cup olive oil**
	flat-leaf parsley	

1 Make the gremolata: Combine the herbs, garlic, and orange zest in a small blender. Add the oil and seasoning, and blend to a paste.
2 Cut deep slashes in the chicken and place in a nonreactive bowl. Spread the paste over the chicken thighs and drumsticks, making sure it goes into the slashes. Cover and let marinate in a cool place for about 2 hours.
3 Grill the chicken on an oiled rack for 15-20 minutes, turning frequently.

133 TURKEY CUTLETS WITH GARLIC, GINGER, AND SESAME

PREPARATION TIME *10 minutes, plus 4-6 hours marinating* **COOKING TIME** *12 minutes* **SERVES 4**

4 turkey cutlets	**2 tbsp grated fresh**	**1 tbsp toasted sesame**
	gingerroot	**oil**
MARINADE	**½ cup dark soy sauce**	**2 tsp sesame seeds**
3 garlic cloves, finely	**1 tbsp rice wine or medium**	**2 tbsp dark brown sugar**
chopped	**sherry**	

1 Using the point of a sharp knife, make cuts in the surfaces of the turkey cutlets. Lay the cutlets in a single layer in a nonreactive dish.
2 Combine the marinade ingredients. Pour evenly over the cutlets, then turn them over to coat thoroughly. Cover and let marinate in a cool place for 4-6 hours, turning occasionally.
3 Lift the turkey cutlets from the marinade and grill on an oiled rack for about 6 minutes on each side, turning once.

134 BASIL-FLAVORED CHICKEN

PREPARATION TIME *10 minutes* **COOKING TIME** *14-16 minutes* **SERVES 4**

4 chicken breast halves	**¾ cup virgin olive oil, plus**	**1 tbsp balsamic vinegar**
leaves from a 2-oz bunch	**extra for brushing**	
of fresh basil	**4 tsp wholegrain mustard**	
freshly ground black	**6 anchovy fillets, drained**	
pepper	**2 tbsp red wine vinegar**	

1 Carefully loosen the skin on each chicken breast and insert 2 or 3 basil leaves under it to lie flat on the breast meat. Smooth the skin back into place. Season the skin with black pepper. Brush the other side of the breasts with oil and season with black pepper.
2 Put the remaining basil leaves in a small blender with the mustard, anchovies, and vinegars. Blend until smooth. With the motor running, slowly pour in the oil until evenly combined. Transfer to a serving bowl and set aside.
3 Grill the chicken on an oiled rack until cooked through, 7-8 minutes on each side, turning once. Serve with the basil sauce.

135 CHICKEN WITH GINGER, LIME, AND YOGURT

PREPARATION TIME *15 minutes, plus 2-3 hours marinating* **COOKING TIME** *14-16 minutes* **SERVES 4**

1¼ lb chicken breast halves
naan bread for serving
chopped fresh cilantro
   for garnish

MARINADE
2 garlic cloves
salt and freshly ground
   black pepper
½ cup thick, plain yogurt
1-inch piece fresh
   gingerroot, grated

1 tbsp ground coriander
1 tsp garam masala
pinch of crushed dried
   chiles
grated zest of 1 lime
1 tbsp lime juice

1 Put the chicken breasts in a nonreactive dish.
2 Make the marinade: Crush the garlic to a paste with a pinch of salt. Combine the yogurt with the garlic paste, the ginger, coriander, garam masala, chiles, lime zest, and juice. Season with black pepper. Pour over the chicken and turn it over so each piece is evenly coated. Cover and let marinate in a cool place for 2-3 hours, turning occasionally.
3 Lift the chicken from the dish (reserve any remaining marinade) and grill on an oiled rack for 7-8 minutes on each side, turning once and brushing with any remaining marinade.
4 Meanwhile, warm the naan at the side of the grill rack.
5 Remove the cooked chicken from the grill, sprinkle with some chopped cilantro, and serve with the warm naan bread.

136 CHICKEN WITH LEMON, MINT, AND CHILE

PREPARATION TIME *10 minutes, plus 1-2 hours marinating* **COOKING TIME** *15 minutes* **SERVES 2**

4 chicken drumsticks
¼ cup olive oil
handful of mint leaves
   (about 20)

juice of 2 large or 1 small
   lemon
2 garlic cloves, chopped
1 fresh, hot red chile,
   seeded and chopped

2 pinches of saffron threads
salt and freshly ground
   black pepper
lemon wedges for serving

1 Cut deep slashes in the drumsticks and put them in a nonreactive dish.
2 Put the oil, most of the mint and lemon juice, the garlic, chile, saffron, and black pepper into a blender and blend to a soft purée. Pour this over the chicken and turn the chicken over so the pieces are evenly coated. Cover and let marinate in a cool place for 1-2 hours.
3 Lift the chicken from the dish and grill on an oiled rack until cooked through, about 15 minutes, turning every 3 minutes. Remove from the grill and sprinkle with salt and the remaining lemon juice and mint. Serve with lemon wedges.

137 ITALIAN-STUFFED CHICKEN BREASTS

PREPARATION TIME *15 minutes* **COOKING TIME** *20 minutes* **SERVES 4**

⅛ cup pine nuts

4 tbsp unsalted butter,
  softened

1 tsp chopped fresh parsley

1 tsp snipped fresh chives

1 tsp chopped fresh
  tarragon

salt and freshly ground
  black pepper

4 skinless, boneless
  chicken breast halves

12 sun-dried tomatoes
  in oil, drained

4 large slices prosciutto

olive oil for brushing

1 Toast the pine nuts in a dry, heavy-based frying pan, shaking the pan frequently, until lightly
   and evenly colored. Reserve 1 tablespoon. Grind the remaining nuts.
2 Beat the butter with the herbs and seasoning until smooth, then add the ground pine nuts.
3 Cut three slits in the top of each chicken breast, going about halfway through them. Tuck
   a sun-dried tomato in each slit, then press a heaped teaspoon of the herb butter into each slit
   and reform the breasts.
4 Wrap a slice of prosciutto around each chicken breast, overlapping at the ends. Secure with
   wooden toothpicks that have been soaked in water for 20 minutes. Brush with olive oil and
   season with black pepper.
5 Grill on an oiled rack until the chicken juices run clear when the breasts are pierced with a fine
   skewer, about 20 minutes, turning once.

138 CHICKEN WITH MUSTARD AND HERBS

PREPARATION TIME *10 minutes, plus 2–3 hours marinating* **COOKING TIME** *15 minutes* **SERVES 4**

8 large chicken thighs	1 tbsp dried tarragon	1½ tbsp Dijon mustard
¼ cup olive oil	1 heaped tbsp chopped	salt and freshly ground
2 tbsp red wine vinegar	fresh parsley	black pepper

1 Cut deep slashes in the chicken thighs, then lay them in a nonreactive dish.
2 Combine the olive oil, vinegar, tarragon, parsley, mustard, and seasoning. Pour this over the chicken, making sure it goes into the slashes and that the pieces are evenly coated. Cover and let marinate in a cool place for 2–3 hours, turning occasionally.
3 Lift the chicken from the dish and grill on an oiled rack for 15 minutes or so, turning once and brushing with any remaining marinade.

139 TURKEY TIKKA BURGERS

PREPARATION TIME *10 minutes, plus 4 hours chilling* **COOKING TIME** *12–16 minutes* **SERVES 4**

olive oil for frying	3 tbsp chopped fresh	salt and freshly ground
1 onion, finely chopped	cilantro	black pepper
1¼lb ground turkey	2 tbsp plain yogurt	4 small naan breads and
¼ cup tikka masala	1 tbsp mango chutney	Raita *(see page 62)*
paste		for serving

1 Heat a little oil in a frying pan, add the onion, and fry until softened. Remove from the heat and let cool.
2 Mix the onion with the remaining ingredients until thoroughly combined. With wet hands, form the mixture into four ¾-inch-thick patties. If possible, cover and leave in a cool place for 4 hours or overnight to let the flavors develop.
3 Grill the burgers on an oiled rack until the juices run clear, 6–8 minutes on each side.
4 Meanwhile, warm the naan breads at the side of the grill rack for 20–30 seconds. Serve the burgers with the raita and naan breads.

140 CHICKEN BREASTS WITH GINGER, HONEY, AND ORANGE

PREPARATION TIME *10 minutes, plus 1–2 hours marinating* **COOKING TIME** *15–20 minutes* **SERVES 4**

4 part-boned chicken	2 tbsp clear honey	salt and freshly ground
breast halves	finely grated zest and juice	black pepper
1-inch piece fresh	of 1 large orange	
gingerroot, grated		

1 Cut three deep slashes in each chicken breast. Place the chicken in a single layer in a nonreactive dish.
2 Combine the ginger, honey, orange zest and juice, and seasoning, then spread over the chicken, working it well into the slashes. Cover and let marinate in a cool place for 1–2 hours.
3 Lift the chicken from the dish and grill on an oiled rack until cooked through, 15–20 minutes, turning once or twice.

141 JAPANESE CHICKEN SKEWERS

PREPARATION TIME *10 minutes, plus 1 hour chilling* **COOKING TIME** *10 minutes* **SERVES 4**

¼ cup Japanese soy sauce
¼ cup sake
2 tbsp mirin
1 tbsp sugar
8 skinless, boneless
   chicken thighs, cut into
   bite-sized cubes

CUCUMBER SALAD

1 small English cucumber
pinch of salt
2 tbsp rice wine vinegar
pinch of sugar, or to taste
1-inch piece of fresh
   gingerroot

1 Gently heat the soy sauce, sake, mirin and sugar in a small saucepan, stirring frequently, until the sugar has dissolved. Simmer until thickened and syrupy. Let cool.
2 Put the chicken in a nonreactive bowl and stir in half the soy sauce mixture. Cover and let marinate in a cool place for 1 hour, stirring once or twice. Reserve the remaining soy mixture.
3 Make the salad: Slice the cucumber lengthwise using a potato peeler. Sprinkle with salt and leave for 30 minutes. Rinse well and dry thoroughly on paper towels. Put into a bowl.
4 Stir the rice wine vinegar and sugar together. Using a garlic crusher, squeeze the piece of ginger to extract as much juice as possible into the mixture. Pour this dressing over the cucumber and toss together. Set aside.
5 Lift the chicken from the marinade and thread onto skewers. Grill on an oiled rack for about 10 minutes, turning occasionally. Remove the skewers from the grill, trickle the reserved soy mixture over them, and serve with the salad.

142 THAI-STYLE CHICKEN

PREPARATION TIME *10 minutes, plus 2-3 hours marinating* **COOKING TIME** *15 minutes* **SERVES 6**

3 boneless chicken breast
   halves
6 chicken drumsticks
lime wedges for serving

MARINADE
¾-inch piece fresh
   gingerroot, grated

2 shallots, finely chopped
1 lemon grass stem, peeled
   and finely chopped
2 garlic cloves, finely
   chopped
1 fresh, hot red chile,
   seeded and finely
   chopped

3 tbsp chopped fresh
   cilantro
6 tbsp lime juice
1 tsp sugar
1 tbsp toasted sesame oil
few drops of Thai fish
   sauce, to taste

1 Cut deep slashes in the chicken pieces, then place in a single layer in a shallow, nonreactive dish.
2 Mix together all the marinade ingredients, pour over the chicken, and turn the pieces so they are evenly coated. Cover and let marinate in a cool place for 2-3 hours, turning occasionally.
3 Lift the chicken from the dish and grill on an oiled rack until browned and cooked through, 6-7 minutes on each side for the breasts and 15 minutes for the drumsticks, turning every 3 minutes. Cut the cooked chicken breasts in half. Serve with lime wedges.

143 DEVILED CHICKEN

PREPARATION TIME *10 minutes, plus 2–4 hours marinating* **COOKING TIME** *15 minutes* **SERVES 6**

12 chicken thighs
freshly ground black
  pepper
	SAUCE
	1 plump garlic clove,
	  crushed
	3 tbsp ketchup *(see
	  page 184)*
	1½ tbsp apricot jam
		1 tbsp Worcestershire
		  sauce
		1 tsp German mustard
		pinch of cayenne pepper
		1 tbsp Thai fish sauce

1. Cut lengthwise slashes in the chicken thighs with a sharp knife, then place them in a large, shallow, nonreactive dish.
2. Make the sauce by stirring the garlic, ketchup, jam, and Worcestershire sauce together until smooth, then mix in the remaining ingredients. Spread over the thighs, working it into the slashes. Cover and let marinate in a cool place for 2–4 hours.
3. Lift the thighs from the dish and grill on an oiled rack until they are browned and cooked through, about 15 minutes, turning every 3 minutes.

144 CHICKEN WITH GARLIC AND LEMON OIL

PREPARATION TIME *10 minutes* **COOKING TIME** *25 minutes* **SERVES 4**

¼ cup olive oil
1 small garlic clove, finely
  chopped
3 tbsp lemon juice
	3–4 tbsp chopped mixed
	  fresh herbs, such as flat-
	  leaf parsley, cilantro,
	  thyme, and oregano
		salt
		4 chicken breast quarters

1. Mix together the olive oil, garlic, lemon juice, herbs, and a small pinch of salt. Set aside.
2. Grill the chicken on an oiled rack until the juices run clear when the thickest part is pierced with a fine skewer, about 25 minutes, turning once. Lift onto plates, spoon the garlic and lemon oil over the breasts, and serve.

145 CHICKEN KALAMATA OLIVADE

PREPARATION TIME *10 minutes, plus 2 hours marinating* **COOKING TIME** *25 minutes* **SERVES 4**

4 chicken leg quarters
24 Kalamata olives, pitted
  and finely chopped, plus
  ¼ cup oil from the jar
2 garlic cloves, finely
  chopped
	2 tbsp sun-dried tomato
	  paste
	2 tsp finely chopped fresh
	  oregano leaves
	freshly ground black
	  pepper
		fresh cilantro and lime
		  wedges for serving

1. Cut four deep slashes on both sides of each chicken leg quarter.
2. Mix the olives with the oil, garlic, tomato paste, oregano, and black pepper to make a paste. Spread the paste over the chicken, making sure it goes into the slashes. Cover and let marinate in a cool place for 2 hours.
3. Grill the chicken on an oiled rack until the skin is crisp and the juices run clear when the thickest part of the legs is pierced with a skewer, about 25 minutes, turning once. Lift onto plates, garnish with cilantro, and serve with lime wedges.

ASIAN CHICKEN WITH FRUITED
NOODLE SALAD

PREPARATION TIME *15 minutes, plus 4–6 hours marinating* **COOKING TIME** *15 minutes* **SERVES 4**

8 chicken drumsticks
¼ cup hoisin sauce
2 tbsp clear honey
2 tbsp ketchup *(see page 184)*
1 tbsp Chinese five-spice powder
dash of hot pepper sauce
1 garlic clove
salt and freshly ground black pepper

FRUITED NOODLE SALAD
6 tbsp virgin olive oil
2 tbsp balsamic vinegar
1 tsp sun-dried tomato paste
8 oz fine egg noodles
2 ripe peaches or nectarines, pitted and chopped
4 ripe purple-skinned plums, pitted and sliced

2 tbsp chopped fresh mint
2 tbsp chopped fresh cilantro
¼ cup lightly toasted cashew nuts

1 Slash each drumstick several times with the point of a sharp knife, then lay them in a shallow, nonreactive dish.
2 Combine the hoisin sauce, honey, ketchup, five-spice powder, and pepper sauce. Crush the garlic to a paste with a pinch of salt, then add to the other ingredients along with some black pepper. Spoon evenly over the chicken, making sure it goes well into the slashes. Cover and let marinate in a cool place for 4–6 hours, turning occasionally.
3 Lift the chicken from the dish (reserve any remaining marinade) and grill on an oiled rack until cooked through, about 15 minutes, turning once and brushing with any remaining marinade.
4 Meanwhile, make the salad. Whisk the oil, vinegar, tomato paste, and seasoning together. Cook the noodles according to the package directions. Drain well and toss with the dressing. Let cool, then mix with the remaining salad ingredients. Serve the chicken with the salad.

147 CAJUN CHICKEN WITH TOMATO SALSA

PREPARATION TIME *10 minutes, plus 2–3 hours marinating* **COOKING TIME** *15 minutes* **SERVES 6**

2 tsp dried thyme
2 tsp dried oregano
2 tsp paprika
1 tsp ground cumin
1 tsp cayenne pepper
salt and freshly ground
   black pepper

6 boneless chicken breast
   halves
peanut oil for brushing
lime quarters for serving

TOMATO SALSA
1½ lb firm but ripe roma
   tomatoes, diced

1 red onion, finely chopped
1 fresh, hot red chile,
   seeded and finely
   chopped
1½ tbsp chopped fresh
   cilantro
1½ tbsp balsamic vinegar
3 tbsp olive oil

1   Mix together the herbs, spices, and seasoning. Brush the chicken lightly with oil, then rub in the spice mixture. Cover and let marinate in a cool place for 2–3 hours.
2   Meanwhile, make the salsa by combining the ingredients. Add salt to taste. Cover and chill.
3   Thread the lime quarters onto skewers.
4   Grill the chicken on an oiled rack until browned and cooked through, 12–15 minutes, turning once. Grill the lime skewers alongside until caramelized. Serve the chicken with the lime quarters and accompanied by the salsa.

148 BRONZED CHICKEN THIGHS

PREPARATION TIME *5 minutes* **COOKING TIME** *15 minutes* **SERVES 4**

2 tbsp olive oil, plus extra
  for brushing
1 tsp pimenton (smoked
  Spanish paprika), or
  sweet paprika

1 tbsp sun-dried tomato
  paste
juice of ½ lemon
1 garlic clove, crushed
½ tbsp sweet chile sauce
8 chicken thighs

salt and freshly ground
  black pepper
fresh thyme leaves
  for garnish

1   Mix together the olive oil, pimenton, tomato paste, lemon juice, garlic, and sweet chile sauce to form a thick paste.
2   Brush the thighs with oil and grill on an oiled rack for 7 minutes, turning once. Brush generously with the paste and grill until the juices run clear when the thickest part is pierced with a skewer, about 7 minutes longer.
3   Remove from the grill, sprinkle with seasoning and thyme leaves, and serve.

149 CHICKEN SUPREMES WITH TAPENADE

PREPARATION TIME *15 minutes* **COOKING TIME** *25 minutes* **SERVES 4**

4 chicken supremes
  (chicken breast halves
  with wing attached)
6 tbsp ricotta cheese
¼ cup black olive tapenade

1 tbsp capers, drained and
  chopped
4 sun-dried tomatoes in oil,
  drained and chopped

salt and freshly ground
  black pepper
olive oil for brushing

1   Loosen the skin covering each chicken breast and cut three or four deep slits in the top of each breast, going about halfway through the meat.
2   Break up the ricotta with a fork, then beat in the tapenade, capers, sun-dried tomatoes, and seasoning. Divide into four portions. Spread the stuffing over the meat of each breast, carefully pressing it into the slits. Smooth the skin back in place to reform the breasts.
3   Brush the skin with olive oil and sprinkle with seasoning. Grill on an oiled rack, skin-side up first, until cooked through, about 25 minutes, turning once.

150 MUSHROOM-STUFFED CHICKEN THIGHS

PREPARATION TIME *10 minutes* **COOKING TIME** *8–10 minutes* **SERVES 4**

1 cup finely chopped
  mushrooms
1 tbsp unsalted butter
2 tbsp cream cheese

1 tbsp chopped fresh
  parsley
salt and freshly ground
  black pepper

8 boneless chicken thighs
olive oil for brushing

1   Fry the mushrooms in the butter until tender. Using a slotted spoon, transfer them onto paper towels to drain.
2   Mix the mushrooms with the cheese, parsley, and seasoning and use to stuff the chicken thighs. Secure the thighs closed with wooden toothpicks that have been soaked in water for 20 minutes. Brush the thighs with oil and season them.
3   Grill on an oiled rack until browned and cooked through, 8–10 minutes, turning once.

MEAT

When choosing meat for the grill, select only lean, tender cuts, such as thick sirloin steaks, lamb chops, or kabobs made from leg of pork. There is no better treatment for a thick, naturally tender steak than to toss it onto the grill. The high heat delivers a crisp, lightly charred exterior and a juicy interior. Best cuts are sirloin, filet mignon, and T-bone.

Look for steaks at least ¾ inch thick—or preferably 2 inches—as thinner steaks tend to dry out and toughen. Move cuts thicker than 1 inch to a cooler part of the grill once both sides are well seared, so that they continue cooking inside. Add or subtract about 1 minute for every ½-inch difference in thickness. Cook over a medium-hot fire, with the grill rack 4–6 inches above the heat.

Fat dripping onto hot coals can cause flareups, so trim off any excess (although a little is necessary to give flavor and keep the meat moist) and snip the remainder at 1-inch intervals to prevent it from curling. Fat dripping from sausages can also flare up, and there is a risk of undercooking the center, so you may want to precook sausages and simply reheat them on the grill. A simple way of testing meat for readiness is to press it lightly with your finger—rare: the meat will give easily and no juices will appear on the surface; medium: the meat will still be slightly springy but a few juices will appear on the surface; well done: the meat will be very firm to the touch and the surface will be covered with juices.

151 HAM STEAKS WITH PAPRIKA SPICE RUB AND MANGO SALSA

PREPARATION TIME *15 minutes, plus 2 hours marinating* **COOKING TIME** *10–12 minutes* **SERVES 4**

4 ham steaks, about 6 oz each	MANGO SALSA	⅛ tsp dark brown sugar
2 tsp ground cumin	2 large, ripe mangoes	salt and freshly ground
2 tsp paprika	juice of 2 limes	black pepper
4 tsp dark brown sugar	½ red onion, finely chopped	
¼ cup olive oil	3 tbsp finely chopped fresh cilantro	

1 Trim any surplus fat from the steaks, leaving enough to keep them moist. Snip the remaining fat at 1-inch intervals.
2 Mix the cumin, paprika, sugar, and oil together. Rub this all over the ham steaks, then cover and let marinate in a cool place for 2 hours.
3 Meanwhile, make the salsa: Dice one-quarter of the mango flesh. Purée the remaining mango flesh with the lime juice, then stir in the chopped onion, cilantro, and diced mango. Add the sugar and seasoning to taste.
4 Grill the ham steaks on an oiled rack until the juices run clear when the thickest part is pierced with a fine skewer, 5–6 minutes on each side. Serve with the salsa.

152 LAMB TENDERLOIN WITH CORIANDER, CUMIN, AND GARLIC

PREPARATION TIME *10 minutes, plus 4–8 hours marinating* **COOKING TIME** *10–15 minutes* **SERVES 6**

1 tbsp coriander seeds	leaves from a fresh rosemary sprig	1 tbsp sun-dried tomato paste
1 tsp cumin seeds	2 tbsp balsamic vinegar	salt and freshly ground
4 fresh bay leaves, coarsely torn	2 tbsp olive oil	black pepper
2 plump garlic cloves	3 tbsp thick, plain yogurt	1½–1¾ lb lamb tenderloins

1 Heat a small, heavy-based frying pan, add the coriander and cumin seeds, and toast them, shaking the pan occasionally, until they become fragrant. Add the bay leaves just before the end of cooking. Tip into a spice grinder and grind finely.
2 Chop the garlic and rosemary together finely. Combine with the vinegar, oil, yogurt, tomato paste, ground spices, and seasoning. Smear thoroughly and evenly over the lamb, then cover and let marinate in a cool place for 4–8 hours.
3 Grill the lamb on an oiled rack until well browned and cooked to the desired degree of doneness, 8–12 minutes, turning occasionally. Remove the lamb from the grill and let rest for about 5 minutes before slicing and serving.

153 PORK, PANCETTA, AND PARMESAN BURGERS

PREPARATION TIME *10 minutes, plus 1 hour chilling* **COOKING TIME** *12 minutes* **SERVES 4**

1 lb ground pork	freshly ground black	Grilled Tomato Salsa *(see*
½ cup coarsely chopped	pepper	*page 175)* or Red Pepper,
pancetta	4 squares of focaccia,	Black Olive, and Caper
½ cup freshly grated	halved horizontally	Relish *(see page 185)*
Parmesan cheese	salad leaves, such as	for serving
1½ tbsp finely chopped	arugula, mâche, frisée,	
fresh sage	and radicchio	
1 large egg, beaten	for serving	

1   Using a fork or your hands, combine the pork, pancetta, Parmesan, sage, egg, and black pepper in a large bowl. With damp hands, form into four 1-inch-thick patties. Leave in a cool place for at least 1 hour.
2   Grill the burgers on an oiled rack until the juices run clear, about 6 minutes on each side, turning once.
3   Meanwhile, warm the focaccia at the side of the grill rack. Cover the bottom halves of the focaccia with salad leaves, add the burgers, and top with a spoonful of the salsa or relish.

154 SPANISH BURGERS

PREPARATION TIME *15 minutes, plus 4–8 hours chilling* **COOKING TIME** *15–20 minutes* **SERVES 4**

1 onion, finely chopped	salt and freshly ground	MARINADE
1 tbsp olive oil	black pepper	⅔ cup olive oil
1¼ lb coarsely ground	4 ciabatta or sourdough	2 garlic cloves, crushed
pork	rolls, split in half	1 tbsp sun-dried tomato
3 oz smoked Spanish	mayonnaise *(see page 179)*,	paste
chorizo, finely chopped	lettuce, chopped	1 tbsp chopped fresh
3 tbsp chopped fresh	tomatoes and scallions	thyme
oregano	for serving	2 tsp chopped fresh parsley

1   Fry the onion in the oil until softened. Let cool, then mix with the pork, chorizo, oregano, and seasoning. With floured hands, form into four 1-inch-thick patties. Place in a single layer in a shallow dish.
2   Make the marinade by mixing all the ingredients together. Pour over the burgers and turn them over so they are evenly coated, then cover and let marinate in a cool place for 4–8 hours.
3   Lift the burgers from the marinade; reserve the marinade. Grill the burgers on an oiled rack for 6–7 minutes on each side, brushing occasionally with the marinade.
4   Meanwhile, toast the cut sides of the rolls at the side of the grill rack. Serve the burgers in the rolls, with mayonnaise, lettuce, tomato, and scallions.

155 INDIAN-STYLE LAMB BURGERS

PREPARATION TIME *15 minutes, plus 1 hour chilling* **COOKING TIME**: *10–12 minutes* **SERVES 6**

3 scallions, finely chopped
1 peppadew (bottled mild
    pepper piquante), finely
    chopped
2 garlic cloves, crushed and
    finely chopped
1 tsp grated fresh
    gingerroot

seeds from 6 cardamom
    pods, finely crushed
½ tsp ground cumin
leaves from a small bunch
    of fresh cilantro, finely
    chopped
salt and freshly ground
    black pepper

1½ lb lean ground lamb

FOR SERVING
mini naan or pita breads
thick, plain yogurt mixed
    with chopped fresh mint

1 Combine the scallions, peppadew, garlic, ginger, spices, cilantro, and some seasoning, then mix
   in the lamb. With floured hands, form the mixture into four 4-inch-diameter patties. Chill for at
   least 1 hour.
2 Grill on an oiled rack until cooked through and the juices run clear when the burgers are pierced
   with a fine skewer, 5–6 minutes on each side, turning carefully.
3 Meanwhile, warm the breads at the side of the grill rack for 30 seconds on each side. Serve the
   burgers with the breads and minted yogurt sauce.

156 KOFTAS

PREPARATION TIME *15 minutes, plus 4 hours marinating* **COOKING TIME** *10–12 minutes* **SERVES 4**

1 small onion, quartered
2 garlic cloves, chopped
1-inch piece fresh
    gingerroot, chopped
1 tsp ground cumin
1 tsp ground coriander
1 tbsp olive oil, plus extra
    for brushing

1 lb ground lamb
3 tbsp chopped fresh
    cilantro
1 extra large egg, beaten
salt and freshly ground
    black pepper

FOR SERVING
Raita *(see page 62)*
    sprinkled with toasted
    and crushed cumin
    seeds
lemon wedges

1 Put the onion, garlic, and ginger in a small blender or food processor and blend until finely
   chopped. Add the spices and blend again until evenly combined.
2 Heat the oil in a frying pan, add the onion mixture, and fry for 2–3 minutes, stirring. Let cool.
3 Put the lamb into a bowl and break it up with a fork. Add the onion mixture, cilantro, and
   seasoning. Mix in enough just enough egg to bind. If time permits, cover and keep in a cool place
   for up to 4 hours, or overnight in the refrigerator.
4 Divide the mixture into eight equal portions. With wet hands, mold each portion into a long
   sausage around a skewer.
5 Brush the koftas with oil and grill on an oiled rack until nicely browned and cooked to the desired
   degree of doneness, 8–10 minutes, turning occasionally.
6 Serve the koftas with the raita and lemon wedges.

157 BEEF AND MUSHROOM BURGERS WITH ROASTED RED PEPPER DRESSING

PREPARATION TIME *15 minutes, plus 20 minutes soaking and 1 hour chilling*
COOKING TIME *13–15 minutes* **SERVES 4**

2 heaped tbsp dried porcini mushrooms	4 tsp wholegrain mustard	ROASTED RED PEPPER DRESSING
2 tsp unsalted butter	2 tbsp chopped fresh herbs	1 red bell pepper
2 cups chopped cremini mushrooms	salt and freshly ground black pepper	2 tbsp balsamic vinegar
1 garlic clove, finely chopped	4 crisp bread rolls or buns, split horizontally	1 tsp fresh thyme
1 lb lean ground beef	salad leaves for serving	1 tsp chopped garlic
		6 tbsp olive oil

1 Place the dried porcini in a bowl and just cover with boiling water. Let soak for 20 minutes, then drain, pat dry, and mince.

2 Heat the butter in a frying pan, add the cremini mushrooms and garlic, and fry until the liquid has evaporated and the mushrooms are tender. Stir in the minced dried porcini just before the end of cooking. Let cool.

3 Mix the beef with the mushroom mixture, mustard, herbs, and seasoning until thoroughly combined. Divide the mixture into four equal portions. With wet hands, form each portion into a 1-inch-thick patty. If time permits, cover and leave in a cool place for 1 hour, or more, to allow the flavors to develop.

4 To make the dressing, roast the red pepper (see page 20). Leave until cool enough to handle, then peel off the skin and discard, along with the seeds. Put into a blender with the vinegar, thyme, and garlic. Pulse to mix, then, with the motor running, slowly pour in the olive oil until smooth. Season to taste.

5 Grill the burgers on an oiled rack, turning once, for 4–5 minutes on each side for medium-rare; cook longer if you prefer them more well done.

6 Meanwhile, toast the rolls on the grill rack. Mix the salad leaves with a little dressing, then put them on the bottom half of each roll. Top with the burgers and spoon a little more dressing over them. Cover with the top halves of the rolls and serve.

158 STEAK AND MUSHROOM KABOBS

PREPARATION TIME *15 minutes, plus 8 hours marinating* **COOKING TIME** *6–8 minutes* **SERVES 6-8**

2 lb boneless sirloin steak,
cut into 1¼-inch cubes
8 oz sliced bacon
4 button cremini
mushrooms

MARINADE
5 tbsp soft red wine
2½ tbsp olive oil, plus extra
for brushing
2 shallots, finely chopped
2 garlic cloves, crushed

1 tbsp tomato paste
2 tbsp chopped fresh
parsley
sprig of fresh thyme
salt and freshly ground
black pepper

1 Put the steak cubes into a nonreactive dish.
2 Make the marinade by combining the ingredients. Stir into the steak to ensure all the pieces are evenly coated, then cover and let marinate in a cool place for 8 hours, stirring occasionally.
3 Lay the bacon slices on a board and stretch with the back of a knife. Cut each slice in half, then roll up each half tightly.
4 Brush the mushrooms with oil and season with black pepper.
5 Lift the steak from the marinade and thread onto skewers, alternating with the mushrooms and bacon rolls. Grill over medium-hot coals on an oiled rack until cooked to the desired degree of doneness, 6–8 minutes, turning occasionally.

159 GREEK LAMB BROCHETTES

PREPARATION TIME *10 minutes, plus 2 hours marinating* **COOKING TIME** *6–8 minutes* **SERVES 4**

1 lb lean, boneless lamb,
cut into 1¼-inch cubes
4 small pita breads
for serving

MARINADE
1 tbsp chopped fresh mint
3-4 saffron strands,
crushed
2 tbsp olive oil

salt and freshly ground
black pepper
1 cup thick, plain yogurt

1 Put the lamb into a nonreactive bowl.
2 Stir the mint, saffron, oil, and seasoning into the yogurt until evenly mixed. Pour over the lamb and stir to ensure it is evenly coated, then cover and let marinate in a cool place for 2 hours, stirring occasionally.
3 Lift the lamb from the bowl and thread the cubes onto skewers. Grill on an oiled rack until well browned but still juicy inside, 6–8 minutes, turning regularly so that the lamb cooks evenly.
4 Meanwhile, warm the pita breads at the side of the grill rack for 30 seconds on each side. Remove the brochettes from the grill, sprinkle with salt, and serve with the breads.

160 LAMB KABOBS WITH FIGS AND APRICOTS

PREPARATION TIME *10 minutes, plus 8 hours marinating* **COOKING TIME** *8–10 minutes* **SERVES 4**

1 lb boned leg of lamb, cut
   into 1¼-inch cubes
1 large orange, sliced
1 onion, quartered
4 dried figs
8 dried apricot halves

MARINADE
2½ tbsp smooth peanut
   butter
1½ tbsp olive oil
3 tbsp thick, plain yogurt
juice of 1 lemon
1 garlic clove, finely
   chopped
2 scallions, chopped

1 tsp ground cumin
1 tsp coriander seeds
½ tsp ground fenugreek
pinch of hot chile powder,
   or to taste
salt and freshly ground
   black pepper

1 Put the lamb into a nonreactive bowl.
2 Mix together the peanut butter, olive oil, yogurt, lemon juice, garlic, scallions, spices, and seasoning. Pour over the lamb. Stir to ensure all the cubes are evenly coated, then cover and let marinate in a cool place for 8 hours, stirring occasionally.
3 Cut the orange slices in half. Separate the onion quarters into leaves. Lift the lamb from the bowl and thread onto skewers, alternating with the halved orange slices, figs, apricots, and onions.
4 Grill on an oiled rack until the lamb is browned but still pink in the center, 8–10 minutes, turning regularly.

161 PORK BROCHETTES WITH LEMON AND GINGER

PREPARATION TIME *10 minutes, plus 2½ hours marinating* **COOKING TIME** *12–15 minutes* **SERVES 4**

1¼ lb boneless pork, cut
   into 1¼-inch cubes
juice of 1 lemon
salt and freshly ground
   black pepper

3 garlic cloves
¼ cup thick, plain yogurt
1 tbsp grated fresh
   gingerroot
1 tsp ground cardamom

½ tsp ground cumin
½ tsp grated nutmeg
drop of hot pepper sauce
1½ lemons

1 Put the pork into a nonreactive bowl. Stir in the lemon juice and plenty of black pepper. Cover and let marinate in a cool place for 30 minutes.
2 Meanwhile, crush the garlic with a pinch of salt, then combine with the yogurt, ginger, cardamom, cumin, nutmeg, and pepper sauce.
3 Drain the lemon juice from the pork. Stir in the ginger mixture to coat the cubes evenly and thoroughly. Cover and let marinate in a cool place for 2 hours.
4 Meanwhile, cut the lemons into thick slices, then cut the slices in half.
5 Lift the pork from the ginger mixture, shaking off the excess, and thread onto skewers, alternating with the lemon pieces. Grill on an oiled rack until well browned and cooked through, 12–15 minutes, turning regularly.

162 PEPPERED STEAKS WITH AÏOLI

PREPARATION TIME *15 minutes, plus 3–4 hours marinating* **COOKING TIME** *6–10 minutes* **SERVES 4**

**4 boneless sirloin steaks,
6–7 oz each**
**2 plump garlic cloves,
halved lengthwise**
olive oil for brushing
**2 tbsp mixed black and
white peppercorns,
lightly crushed**

AÏOLI
**6 plump garlic cloves,
crushed**
**2 egg yolks, at room
temperature**
**juice of 1 small lemon, plus
extra to taste**
2 cups olive oil

**3 tbsp wholegrain mustard
freshly ground black
pepper**

1   Rub the steaks with the cut sides of the garlic, then brush the steaks with oil.
2   Spread the peppercorns close together on a plate. Press one side of each steak firmly onto the
    peppercorns; turn the steaks over and repeat on the other side. Cover the steaks and let marinate
    in a cool place for 3–4 hours.
3   Meanwhile, make the aïoli: Put the garlic, egg yolks, and lemon juice in a blender and blend
    briefly. With the motor running, slowly pour in the olive oil in a thin, steady stream until the
    mixture becomes the consistency of thick cream. Transfer to a bowl, stir in the mustard, and
    season to taste. Add more lemon juice, if necessary.
4   Grill the steaks on a lightly oiled rack, turning once, to the desired degree of doneness: about
    3 minutes for rare or 4 minutes for medium. Serve the steaks with the aïoli.

163 LAMB BROCHETTES WITH APRICOT AND MINT SALSA

PREPARATION TIME *15 minutes, plus 4 hours marinating* **COOKING TIME** *8–10 minutes* **SERVES 4**

**1¼ lb lean, boneless lamb,
cut into 1¼-inch cubes**
2 tbsp orange marmalade
2 tbsp soy sauce
1 tsp wholegrain mustard

APRICOT AND MINT SALSA
**1 cup dried apricots,
finely chopped**
**1 red bell pepper, seeded
and finely chopped**
¼ cup chopped fresh mint

juice of 2 limes
1 red onion, finely chopped
**salt and freshly ground
black pepper**

1   Put the lamb into a nonreactive bowl.
2   Mix together the marmalade, soy sauce, mustard, and seasoning. Pour over the lamb. Stir to
    ensure all the cubes are evenly coated, then cover and let marinate in a cool place for 4 hours,
    stirring occasionally.
3   Make the salsa by combining all the ingredients.
4   Lift the lamb from the bowl (reserve the marinade) and thread onto skewers. Grill on an oiled rack
    until the lamb is nicely browned and cooked to the desired degree of doneness, 8–10 minutes,
    turning regularly and brushing with any remaining marinade. Serve with the salsa.

164 PORK AND APPLE SKEWERS

PREPARATION TIME *10 minutes, plus 3–4 hours marinating* **COOKING TIME** *12–15 minutes* **SERVES 4**

1 lb pork tenderloin, cut
   into 1¼-inch cubes
fresh sage leaves
¼ cup sharp apple juice
grated zest and juice of
   ½ lemon

2 tbsp wholegrain mustard
4 tbsp grapeseed oil
salt and freshly ground
   black pepper
2 crisp, red apples

1 Put the pork into a nonreactive bowl.
2 Chop 1 tablespoon sage and mix with the apple juice, lemon zest and juice, mustard, oil, and seasoning. Stir into the pork to ensure the cubes are evenly coated, then cover and let marinate in a cool place for 3–4 hours.
3 Meanwhile, core the apples and cut into wedges.
4 Lift the pork from the bowl, reserving the marinade. Thread the pork and apple alternately onto skewers, interspersing the pieces with sage leaves.
5 Grill on an oiled rack until the pork is cooked through, 12–15 minutes, turning regularly and brushing with the remaining marinade.

165 PORK WITH CILANTRO AND LIME

PREPARATION TIME *10 minutes, plus 1–2 hours marinating* **COOKING TIME** *14–16 minutes* **SERVES 4**

4 pork steaks, ¾–1 inch thick
small bunch of fresh
 chives, finely snipped
2 tbsp chopped fresh
 cilantro
lime quarters for serving

MARINADE
2 tbsp dry white vermouth
3½ tbsp olive oil
2 garlic cloves, finely
 chopped
3 tbsp chopped fresh
 cilantro

grated zest and juice
 of 2 limes
1 tsp sugar
salt and freshly ground
 black pepper

1 Lay the pork in a shallow, nonreactive dish.
2 Make the marinade by combining all the ingredients. Pour over the pork and turn the steaks to ensure they are evenly coated, then cover and let marinate in a cool place for 1–2 hours, turning once or twice.
3 Lift the pork from the marinade (reserve the marinade) and grill on an oiled rack over medium-hot coals until the juices run clear when the thickest parts of the steaks are pierced with a fine skewer, 7–8 minutes on each side, turning occasionally and basting with the remaining marinade.
4 Meanwhile, combine the chives and cilantro.
5 Remove the pork from the grill, sprinkle with the herbs, and serve with lime quarters.

166 LAMB KABOBS WITH SUN-DRIED TOMATOES AND THYME

PREPARATION TIME *10 minutes, plus 2 hours marinating* **COOKING TIME** *8–10 minutes* **SERVES 4**

1 lb boned leg of lamb, cut
 into 1¼-inch cubes

MARINADE
⅔ cup plain yogurt
3 garlic cloves, finely
 chopped
¼ cup red wine

2 tbsp olive oil
2 tbsp sun-dried
 tomato paste
1 tsp dried thyme

1 Put the lamb into a nonreactive bowl.
2 Make the marinade by combining the ingredients. Stir into the lamb to coat the pieces evenly. Cover and let marinate in a cool place for 2 hours.
3 Lift the lamb from the bowl (reserve any remaining marinade) and thread onto skewers. Grill on an oiled rack until well browned, but still juicy inside, 8–10 minutes, turning regularly and brushing with the reserved marinade.

167 BEEF AND RED PEPPER KABOBS

PREPARATION TIME *15 minutes, plus 4 hours marinating* **COOKING TIME** *5-10 minutes* **SERVES 6**

2 lb boneless sirloin steak, cut into 1¼-inch cubes
1 small onion, cut lengthwise into 9 wedges, keeping the root end intact
1 red bell pepper, cut into 1-inch pieces

MARINADE
3 tbsp olive oil
1 garlic clove, finely chopped
1½ tbsp lemon juice
½ tbsp pimenton (smoked paprika)

1 tsp harissa sauce
1 tsp ground coriander
1 tsp ground cumin
salt and freshly ground black pepper

1   Place the steak in a nonreactive bowl.
2   Make the marinade by combining all the ingredients. Pour over the steak and stir to ensure all the pieces are evenly coated, then cover and let marinate in a cool place for 4 hours, stirring occasionally.
3   Lift the meat from the marinade and thread onto skewers, alternating with the onion wedges and pepper pieces. Grill on an oiled rack until well browned and cooked to the desired degree of doneness, 5-10 minutes.

168 SOUVLAKIA

PREPARATION TIME *10 minutes, plus 3-4 hours marinating* **COOKING TIME** *8-10 minutes* **SERVES 6**

1½ lb lean, boneless lamb, cut into 1¼-inch cubes
5 tbsp olive oil
1 large onion
4 garlic cloves
½ tsp ground cumin

½ tsp cayenne pepper
salt and freshly ground black pepper

FOR SERVING
pita breads

lemon wedges
thick, plain yogurt, seasoned with salt, freshly ground black pepper, and some chopped fresh cilantro

1   Put the lamb into a nonreactive bowl.
2   Combine the olive oil, onion, garlic, cumin, cayenne, and plenty of black pepper in a food processor or blender and blend until mushy. Pour over the lamb and stir to coat the cubes evenly, then cover and let marinate in a cool place for 3-4 hours, stirring occasionally.
3   Lift the lamb from the bowl (reserve the remaining marinade) and thread onto skewers. Grill on an oiled rack until the lamb is nicely browned and cooked to the desired degree of doneness, 8-10 minutes, turning regularly and brushing with the remaining marinade.
4   Meanwhile, warm the pita breads at the side of the grill rack for 30 seconds on each side. Remove the kabobs from the grill, sprinkle with salt and a little lemon juice, and tuck into the pita breads with a spoonful of cilantro yogurt.

169 BACON-WRAPPED SAUSAGES WITH MUSTARD DIP

PREPARATION TIME *10 minutes* **COOKING TIME** *12–14 minutes* **SERVES 4–6**

12 large, fresh pork link
   sausages, or frankfurters
12 bacon slices

2 tbsp fresh thyme leaves
   (optional)

MUSTARD DIP
¼ cup wholegrain mustard
½ cup mayonnaise *(see
   page 179)*

1   Make the mustard dip by beating the mustard into the mayonnaise.
2   Add the sausages to a pan of boiling water and quickly return to a boil, then simmer gently
   for 3 minutes. Drain and rinse under cold running water to speed cooling. Pat dry.
3   Stretch each bacon slice with the back of a knife. Sprinkle the optional thyme over one side of
   each slice. Place a sausage diagonally across one end of each bacon slice and roll up to enclose
   the sausage completely. Secure with soaked wooden toothpicks (see page 10).
4   Grill the bacon-wrapped sausages on an oiled rack until well browned and cooked through,
   7–8 minutes, turning regularly.

170 HONEY AND MUSTARD-GLAZED SAUSAGES

PREPARATION TIME *5 minutes* **COOKING TIME** *13–15 minutes* **SERVES 4**

2 tbsp clear honey
2 tbsp wholegrain mustard
juice of 1 small lemon

2 garlic cloves, finely
   chopped (optional)

8 large, fresh pork link
   sausages, or frankfurters

1 Mix together the honey, mustard, lemon juice, and optional garlic, and season lightly.
2 Add the sausages to a pan of boiling water and quickly return to a boil, then simmer gently for 3 minutes. Drain and rinse under cold running water to speed cooling. Pat dry.
3 Brush the sausages with some of the honey mixture, then grill on an oiled rack until evenly browned and cooked through, 8–10 minutes, turning occasionally and brushing with the honey mixture to glaze.

171 LAMB WITH YOGURT, MINT, AND LIME

PREPARATION TIME *10 minutes, plus 2 hours marinating* **COOKING TIME** *8–10 minutes* **SERVES 6**

1½ lb boneless lamb,
   cut into 1¼-inch cubes

MARINADE
1 cup thick, plain yogurt
2 tbsp virgin olive oil
1 garlic clove, finely
   chopped
4 saffron strands, crushed

1 tbsp chopped fresh mint
grated zest and juice of
   ½ lime
salt and freshly ground
   black pepper

1 Put the lamb into a nonreactive bowl.
2 Make the marinade by combining the ingredients. Add to the lamb and stir to coat evenly. Cover and let marinate in a cool place for 2 hours.
3 Thread the lamb onto skewers. Grill on an oiled rack until well browned, but still juicy inside, 8–10 minutes, turning regularly.

172 FRAGRANT LAMB KABOBS

PREPARATION TIME *10 minutes, plus 4–6 hours marinating* **COOKING TIME** *8–10 minutes* **SERVES 6–8**

2 lb lean, boneless lamb,
   cut into 1½-inch cubes
1 lemon, cut into 12
   wedges
12 fresh bay leaves

MARINADE
¼ cup olive oil
2½ tsp dried oregano
1 tsp paprika
1 tsp ground cumin

grated zest and juice of
   ½ large lemon
salt and freshly ground
   black pepper

1 Put the lamb into a nonreactive dish.
2 Make the marinade by combining all the ingredients. Mix with the lamb so the cubes are evenly coated, then cover and let marinate in cool place for 4–6 hours.
3 Thread the lamb cubes onto skewers, alternating with the lemon wedges and bay leaves. Grill the kabobs on an oiled rack until well browned, but still juicy inside, 8–10 minutes, turning regularly.

173 SURPRISE HAMBURGERS

PREPARATION TIME *10 minutes, plus 2 hours chilling* **COOKING TIME** *10-15 minutes* **SERVES 4**

1 onion, finely chopped	2 tsp chopped fresh parsley	salad leaves and ketchup
1 tbsp olive oil	salt and freshly ground	*(see page 184)* for
1 plump garlic clove, finely	black pepper	serving
chopped	2 oz feta cheese	
1 lb lean ground beef	4 sesame hamburger buns	

1   Cook the onion in the oil until softened and lightly colored. Stir in the garlic toward the end of cooking. Remove from the heat and let cool.
2   Mix the onion and garlic with the beef, parsley, and seasoning. Divide the mixture into four equal portions and form into 4-inch-diameter patties, enclosing one-quarter of the cheese in each one. Leave in a cool place for 2 hours.
3   Grill the hamburgers on an oiled rack for 3–4 minutes on each side for medium-rare, or longer if you prefer the burgers more well done.
4   Meanwhile, warm the buns at the side of the rack. Split in half, place salad leaves on the bottom, top with a burger and ketchup, and close with the top of the bun.

174 VENISON SAUSAGES WITH RED ONION MARMALADE

PREPARATION TIME *5 minutes* **COOKING TIME** *35-40 minutes* **SERVES 4**

8 large, fresh venison or	12 oz red onions, thinly	¼ cup red wine vinegar
pork link sausages	sliced	salt and freshly ground
	⅛ tsp brown sugar	black pepper
RED ONION MARMALADE	1 tsp fresh thyme leaves	
2 tbsp olive oil	1 cup red wine	

1   First make the marmalade. Heat the oil in a pan, add the onions and sugar, and cook gently until the onions are golden and softened, about 10 minutes. Add the thyme. Pour in the wine and vinegar and bring to a simmer, then season and let simmer gently until the liquid has almost evaporated. Check the seasoning and adjust the sweetness/sharpness with more sugar or vinegar, as necessary.
2   Grill the sausages on an oiled rack until cooked through, 8–10 minutes, turning occasionally. Serve with the marmalade.

175 BUTTERFLIED LEG OF LAMB

PREPARATION TIME *10 minutes, plus 1 hour marinating* **COOKING TIME** *30–40 minutes* **SERVES 6**

1 leg of lamb, about 4–4½ lb, boned and butterflied	handful of mixed fresh mint and parsley	freshly ground black pepper
3 plump garlic cloves, cut into thin slivers	6 anchovy fillets	small handful of rosemary sprigs for cooking
	2 oz pancetta	lemon wedges for serving
	1 tbsp lemon juice	

1 Lay the lamb flat, skin-side down. With a sharp knife, cut ½-inch-deep slashes across the lamb at 2-inch intervals.
2 Put the garlic, herbs, anchovy fillets, pancetta, lemon juice, and black pepper into a food processor or blender and pulse until mixed to a smooth paste. Push this well into the incisions in the lamb. Season the outside of the lamb with black pepper.
3 Push in skewers diagonally from opposite corners of the lamb to keep it flat during cooking. Cover the lamb and leave in a cool place for 1 hour.
4 Just before putting the lamb on the grill, scatter the rosemary sprigs over the hot coals. Grill the lamb on an oiled rack to the desired degree of doneness: 15 minutes on each side for medium rare, or 20 minutes on each side for well done.
5 Remove the lamb from the grill, cover, and let rest for about 10 minutes before carving.

176 INDONESIAN PORK BURGERS

PREPARATION TIME *10 minutes, plus 10 minutes soaking and 1 hour chilling* **COOKING TIME** *12 minutes*
SERVES 4

¼ cup canned coconut milk	2 tbsp chopped fresh basil	1 tbsp lime juice
1 cup fresh bread crumbs		pinch of sugar
1 lb ground pork	1 tbsp chopped fresh cilantro	peanut oil for brushing
1 garlic clove, finely chopped	1 tbsp Thai fish sauce	
2 tbsp Thai red curry paste	grated zest of 1 lime	

1 Pour the coconut milk over the bread crumbs and let soak for 10 minutes.
2 Combine the soaked bread crumbs with the remaining ingredients, mixing thoroughly until well combined. With wet hands, form the mixture into eight ¾- to 1-inch-thick patties. Chill for 1 hour or more.
3 Brush the burgers with peanut oil and grill on an oiled rack until golden and the juices run clear, about 6 minutes on each side, turning once.

177 RACK OF LAMB WITH SESAME AND MUSTARD

PREPARATION TIME *10 minutes, plus 2 hours marinating* **COOKING TIME** *15–25 minutes* **SERVES 4**

2 racks of lamb, 1½ lb each, trimmed of excess fat	MARINADE	**1½ tbsp sugar**
large sprigs of fresh sage for cooking	**3 tbsp soy sauce**	**1 plump garlic clove, finely chopped**
	2 tbsp Dijon mustard	**1 tbsp coarse sea salt**
	2 tbsp lightly toasted sesame seeds	**2 tsp freshly ground black pepper**
	1½ tbsp toasted sesame oil	

1 Make the marinade by stirring all the ingredients together. Rub over the lamb, then let marinate in a cool place for 2 hours.
2 Just before putting the lamb on the grill, scatter the sage over the hot coals.
3 Cover the lamb bones with foil to prevent them from burning. Grill on an oiled rack, turning once, to the desired degree of doneness: 15 minutes for rare lamb, 20 minutes for medium rare, and 25 minutes for well done.
4 Remove from the grill and let rest, covered, for 10 minutes before dividing into chops.

178 AROMATIC LAMB TENDERLOIN

PREPARATION TIME *10 minutes, plus 4–8 hours marinating* **COOKING TIME** *8–12 minutes* **SERVES 6**

1½–1¾ lb lamb tenderloins	MARINADE	**juice of 1 lemon**
	2 tbsp olive oil	**2 tsp ground cardamom**
	2 plump garlic cloves, crushed	**2 tsp ground cinnamon**
	1½ tbsp sun-dried tomato paste	**⅛ tsp cayenne pepper**
		handful of fresh mint leaves, finely chopped

1 Lay the lamb tenderloins in a nonreactive dish.
2 Make the marinade by combining all the ingredients. Rub thoroughly over the lamb, then cover and let marinate in cool place for 4–8 hours.
3 Grill the lamb on an oiled rack until well browned and cooked to the desired degree of doneness, 8–12 minutes, turning regularly.
4 Remove from the grill and let rest, covered, for about 5 minutes before slicing.

179 HAM STEAKS WITH APRICOT GLAZE

PREPARATION TIME *10 minutes* **COOKING TIME** *10–12 minutes* **SERVES 4**

4 ham steaks	APRICOT GLAZE	**2 tsp Worcestershire sauce**
	3 tbsp apricot jam, warmed slightly	**freshly ground black pepper**
	1 tbsp Dijon mustard	

1 Trim any surplus fat from the steaks, leaving enough to keep them moist. Snip the remaining fat at 1-inch intervals.
2 Make the glaze by combining all the ingredients.
3 Brush the glaze over the ham steaks, then grill on an oiled rack for 5–6 minutes on each side, turning once.

180 SPICED LAMB CHOPS

PREPARATION TIME *15 minutes, plus 4 hours marinating* **COOKING TIME** *12–18 minutes* **SERVES 4**

olive oil for frying	1 tbsp mustard seeds,	salt and freshly ground
1 large onion, finely	lightly crushed	black pepper
chopped	2 tsp cumin seeds,	8 lamb loin chops
1 plump garlic clove, finely	lightly crushed	chopped fresh cilantro
chopped	1 tsp paprika	Pineapple and Macadamia
1 tbsp coriander seeds,	⅔ cup thick, plain yogurt	Nut Salsa *(see page 178)*
lightly crushed		for serving

1   Heat the oil in a frying pan, add the onion, and cook until softened and lightly colored; stir in the garlic toward the end of cooking. Add all the seeds and cook, stirring, for 1–2 minutes. Transfer the onion mixture to a bowl and stir in the paprika, yogurt, and seasoning. Let cool.

2   Coil the "tail" end of the chops around the eye of the meat and secure with wooden toothpicks. Put the chops in a single layer in a shallow, nonreactive dish. Pour the yogurt mixture over them and turn the chops over. Cover and leave in a cool place for about 4 hours, turning occasionally.

3   Lift the chops from the dish (reserve the marinade). Grill on an oiled rack, turning once, for 3 minutes on each side for medium rare, or for 5 minutes on each side for well done.

4   Remove the chops from the grill and sprinkle with chopped cilantro. Serve with the salsa.

181 PORK WITH PLUM SAUCE

PREPARATION TIME *15 minutes* **COOKING TIME** *30–35 minutes* **SERVES 4**

6 pork sirloin chops,
  1 inch thick
peanut oil for brushing
salt and freshly ground
  black pepper

PLUM SAUCE
1 tbsp peanut oil
2 shallots, finely chopped
1 tbsp finely chopped fresh
  gingerroot
½ tbsp Sichuan
  peppercorns, finely
  crushed

8 oz plums, quartered and
  pitted
1 tbsp light soy sauce
5 tbsp sweet sherry
½ tbsp clear honey
lime juice to taste

1   Make the plum sauce: Heat the oil in a frying pan, add the shallots, and fry until softened. Add the ginger and peppercorns toward the end of cooking and stir until they smell fragrant. Add the plums, soy sauce, sherry, and honey. Bring to a boil, then cover and simmer until the plums are tender. Add lime juice to taste. Set aside.
2   Trim any excess fat from the chops and snip the remaining fat at 1-inch intervals. Brush the chops with peanut oil and season them.
3   Grill the chops on an oiled rack until lightly charred and the juices run clear when the thickest part is pierced with a skewer, 8–10 minutes on each side. Meanwhile, warm the sauce at the side of the grill rack. Serve the chops with the warm sauce.

182 THAI-STYLE LAMB BURGERS

PREPARATION TIME *15 minutes, plus 4 hours chilling* **COOKING TIME** *15–18 minutes* **SERVES 4**

olive oil for frying
1 small onion, finely
  chopped
2 garlic cloves, finely
  chopped
1¼ lb ground lamb
1 tbsp red Thai curry paste

1 tbsp Thai fish sauce
1 tbsp lime juice
1 tbsp chopped fresh mint
1 tsp grated lime zest
1 tsp finely chopped
  lemon grass

FOR SERVING
4 small pita breads
lightly dressed mixed salad
  leaves with fresh cilantro
lime slices

1   Heat a little oil in a frying pan, add the onion, and fry until softened, adding the garlic toward the end of the cooking. Remove with a slotted spoon and drain on paper towels. Let cool.
2   Mix the onion with the remaining ingredients until thoroughly combined. With wet hands, shape the mixture into eight 1-inch-thick patties. If time permits, cover and leave in a cool place for at least 4 hours or overnight.
3   Grill on an oiled rack until cooked through and the juices run clear when the burgers are pierced with a fine skewer, 5–6 minutes on each side, turning once.
4   Meanwhile, warm the pita breads at the side of the grill rack for 30 seconds on each side. Split the pitas open to form a pocket and fill with salad. Add two burgers to each pita bread, and serve with lime slices.

183 VEAL CHOPS WITH GREEN HERB SAUCE

PREPARATION TIME *10 minutes, plus 2 hours marinating* **COOKING TIME** *12-15 minutes* **SERVES 4**

4 veal rib chops,
   1-1½ inches thick
2 tbsp virgin olive oil
1 tbsp lemon juice
coarse sea salt and freshly
   ground black pepper

GREEN HERB SAUCE
1 tsp Dijon mustard
½ cup extra virgin olive oil
½ tbsp lemon juice
3 tbsp chopped fresh
   flat-leaf parsley
3 tbsp chopped fresh basil

1-2 garlic cloves, crushed
2 tsp small salted capers,
   well rinsed and dried

1 Put the veal chops into a nonreactive dish.
2 Stir the oil, lemon juice, and black pepper together. Pour over the veal and turn the chops over
   to ensure they are coated thoroughly and evenly. Cover and let marinate in a cool place
   for 2 hours, turning occasionally.
3 Meanwhile, make the green herb sauce: Whisk the mustard, olive oil, and lemon juice together
   until emulsified. Stir in the herbs, garlic, and capers, and season to taste. Add more lemon juice,
   if necessary.
4 Lift the veal chops from the dish and grill on an oiled rack until well browned, but still moist and
   slightly pink inside, 12-15 minutes, turning once. Remove from the grill, sprinkle with sea salt,
   and serve with the sauce.

184 STEAK SANDWICHES WITH ONION RELISH

PREPARATION TIME *10 minutes* **COOKING TIME** *45-50 minutes* **SERVES 4**

4 boneless sirloin steaks
olive oil for brushing
4 small baguettes, about
   8 inches long
butter for spreading
Dijon or wholegrain
   mustard for spreading

ONION RELISH
2 tbsp olive oil
1 lb large onions, sliced
   thinly into rings
1 tbsp balsamic vinegar
1 tbsp Worcestershire
   sauce

⅛ tsp brown sugar
salt and freshly ground
   black pepper

1 First make the onion relish. Heat the oil in a large, heavy frying pan, add the onions, and cook
   very gently, stirring occasionally, until they are soft and tinged with brown. Stir in the vinegar,
   Worcestershire sauce, sugar, and seasoning. Continue to cook until the liquid has evaporated.
   Check the sweetness and seasoning. Set aside to cool.
2 Brush the steaks with olive oil, then grill on an oiled rack until cooked to the desired degree of
   doneness: about 3 minutes on each side for rare, 4 minutes on each side for medium.
3 Meanwhile, split the baguettes lengthwise and warm them at the side of the grill rack. Spread the
   inside of each bottom half with butter and a little mustard. Lay a steak in each baguette and top
   with onion relish. Close the baguettes and eat.

185 CARIBBEAN PORK AND PINEAPPLE SKEWERS

PREPARATION TIME *10 minutes, plus 3-4 hours marinating* **COOKING TIME** *12-15 minutes* **SERVES 4-6**

1½ lb boneless pork, cut into 1¼-inch cubes	MARINADE	1½ tbsp peanut oil
½ small fresh pineapple, peeled, cored, and cubed	2 garlic cloves, crushed	2 tbsp pineapple juice
	1-inch piece fresh gingerroot, grated	2 tbsp dark rum
	¼ tsp ground allspice	salt and freshly ground black pepper
	2 tbsp dark brown sugar	

1   Put the pork into a nonreactive bowl.
2   Make the marinade by combining all the ingredients. Stir into the pork, ensuring the cubes are evenly coated, then cover and let marinate in a cool place for 3-4 hours.
3   Lift the pork from the bowl, reserving the marinade. Thread the pork and pineapple cubes alternately onto skewers. Grill on an oiled rack until the pork is browned and cooked through, 12-15 minutes, turning regularly and brushing with the remaining marinade.

186 STEAKS WITH MUSTARD AND SOY

PREPARATION TIME *10 minutes, plus 4 hours marinating* **COOKING TIME** *6-10 minutes* **SERVES 4**

3 tbsp Dijon mustard	1 tbsp olive oil	4 boneless sirloin steaks, 1 inch thick
1 tbsp soy sauce	3 tbsp chopped fresh cilantro	
1 tbsp grated fresh gingerroot		

1   Mix together the mustard, soy sauce, ginger, olive oil, and cilantro. Smooth this over the steaks, then cover and let marinate in a cool place for about 4 hours.
2   Grill the steaks on an oiled rack, turning once, to the desired degree of doneness: about 3 minutes on each side for rare steaks, 5 minutes on each side for medium steaks.

187 RIB OF BEEF WITH MUSTARD AÏOLI

PREPARATION TIME *10 minutes* **COOKING TIME** *8 minutes* **SERVES 8**

4-lb bone-in beef rib roast, cut into individual ribs	MUSTARD AÏOLI	juice of 1 small lemon, plus extra to taste (optional)
salt and freshly ground black pepper	6 plump garlic cloves, crushed	2 cups olive oil
	2 egg yolks, at room temperature	3 tbsp wholegrain mustard

1   Make the mustard aïoli: Put the garlic, egg yolks, and lemon juice in a blender and blend briefly to mix. With the motor running, slowly pour in the olive oil in a thin, steady stream until the mixture becomes the consistency of thick cream. Transfer to a bowl, stir in the mustard, and season to taste; add more lemon juice, if necessary.
2   Grill the ribs on an oiled rack for about 4 minutes, giving them a quarter turn halfway through, to create a crisscross charred pattern. Turn the ribs over and repeat on the other side. Cook for longer if you prefer them well done.
3   Move the ribs from the grill and sprinkle with seasoning, then cover with foil and let rest for 5-10 minutes.
4   Cut away the bones, then cut the meat into thick slices. Serve the beef with the aïoli.

188 STEAK FAJITAS

PREPARATION TIME *10 minutes, plus 8–24 hours marinating* **COOKING TIME** *20 minutes* **SERVES 6-8**

2-lb thick piece of skirt, flank, or rump steak

MARINADE
2 tbsp olive oil
3 garlic cloves, finely chopped
juice of 1½ limes

½–1 tsp crushed dried chiles
1 tbsp paprika
1 tsp dried oregano
1 tsp ground cumin
salt and freshly ground black pepper

FOR SERVING
12–16 flour tortillas
Grilled Tomato Salsa
  (see page 175)
1 small head iceberg lettuce, finely shredded
1 cup sour cream

1   Lay the steak in a nonreactive dish.
2   Make the marinade by mixing all the ingredients in a blender. Pour over the beef, then cover and let marinate in a cool place for 8–24 hours, turning occasionally.
3   Lift the beef from the marinade (reserve the marinade) and grill on an oiled rack for about 20 minutes for medium rare, basting frequently with the remaining marinade. Remove the beef from the grill, cover, and let rest for about 5 minutes.
4   Meanwhile, wrap the tortillas in foil and put at the side of the grill rack to warm for 5 minutes.
5   To serve, slice the beef thinly and serve with the salsa, lettuce, sour cream, and tortillas so that each person can assemble and roll their own fajita.

189 LAMB CHOPS WITH SAFFRON AND LEMON

PREPARATION TIME *10 minutes, plus 2 hours marinating* **COOKING TIME** *8–10 minutes* **SERVES 6**

6 lamb chops,	**2 tbsp virgin olive oil**	**1½ tsp lemon zest**
1 inch thick	**1 garlic clove, finely**	**1½ tsp lemon juice**
	chopped	**salt and freshly ground**
MARINADE	**4 saffron strands, crushed**	**black pepper**
1 cup thick, plain yogurt	**1 tbsp chopped fresh mint**	

1 Put the lamb into a nonreactive bowl.
2 Make the marinade by combining the ingredients. Add to the lamb and stir to coat evenly. Cover and let marinate in a cool place for 2 hours.
3 Grill the chops on an oiled rack until well browned, but still juicy inside, 8–10 minutes, turning regularly.

190 TURKISH LAMB BROCHETTES

PREPARATION TIME *10 minutes, plus 3–4 hours marinating* **COOKING TIME** *10 minutes* **SERVES 4**

1¼ lb lean, boneless lamb,	**2 tbsp olive oil, plus extra**	**salt and freshly ground**
cut into bite-sized cubes	**for brushing**	**black pepper**
¼ cup lemon juice	**1 tsp ground cumin**	**12 cubes of eggplant**
1 garlic clove, finely	**1 tsp ground cardamom**	**8 bay leaves**
chopped		

1 Put the lamb into a nonreactive bowl.
2 Combine the lemon juice, garlic, olive oil, cumin, cardamom, and seasoning. Stir into the lamb to coat the pieces evenly, then cover and let marinate in a cool place for 3–4 hours.
3 Brush the eggplant cubes with olive oil, and season them.
4 Lift the lamb from the marinade (reserve any remaining marinade) and thread onto skewers, alternating with the eggplant and inserting the bay leaves at intervals.
5 Grill on an oiled rack until browned and cooked to the desired degree of doneness, about 10 minutes, turning frequently and brushing with the reserved marinade.

191 BUTTERFLIED CHINESE LAMB

PREPARATION TIME *15 minutes, plus 8 hours marinating* **COOKING TIME** *30–35 minutes* **SERVES 8**

2½-lb boned shoulder	MARINADE	**1 tbsp clear honey**
of lamb	**¼ cup soy sauce**	**3 star anise**
4 garlic cloves, cut into	**¼ cup Madeira or medium**	**3 tbsp chopped fresh**
thin slivers	**dry sherry**	**cilantro**
	1-inch piece fresh	**freshly ground black**
	gingerroot, grated	**pepper**

1 Make the marinade by mixing all the ingredients in a blender.
2 Open out the lamb and cut a few slits all over the surface. Insert the garlic slivers into the slits. Put the lamb into a nonreactive dish, pour the marinade over, and cover. Let marinate in a cool place for 8 hours, or overnight, turning occasionally.
3 Lift the lamb from the marinade (reserving the marinade) and grill on an oiled rack over medium heat for 30–35 minutes for medium rare, basting frequently with the remaining marinade.

192 STEAK WITH ROASTED GARLIC AND MUSHROOMS

PREPARATION TIME *10 minutes* **COOKING TIME** *35-40 minutes* **SERVES 6-8**

6-8 small, whole garlic
   bulbs, outer papery
   skins removed
olive oil for sprinkling
   and brushing
3-lb rib steak
coarse sea salt and freshly
   ground black pepper

12-16 medium-sized
   portobello mushrooms

FOR SERVING (OPTIONAL)
Tomatoes with Tapenade
   and Parsley Topping *(see
   page 160)*

Herb Damper Breads *(see
   page 161)*
bottled or homemade
   béarnaise or hollandaise
   sauce

1   Place each garlic bulb on a piece of heavy-duty foil and sprinkle with a little oil. Fold the foil loosely around the bulbs, then twist the edges together tightly to seal. Cook on the grill rack for 20 minutes, turning frequently.
2   Season the steak generously with black pepper and brush with oil. Brush the mushrooms with oil and season them.
3   Grill the steak on an oiled rack, turning frequently, until well browned and cooked to the desired degree of doneness: 10-15 minutes for medium rare.
4   Remove the steak from the grill, cover, and let rest for 5-10 minutes before sprinkling with sea salt and slicing thickly.
5   Meanwhile, grill the mushrooms, gill-side up, for 4-6 minutes.
6   Unwrap the garlic and squeeze out the soft cloves onto the steaks. Serve with the mushrooms, as well as with the optional tomatoes with tapenade and parsley topping, damper bread, and béarnaise or hollandaise sauce.
*   Put some hickory or mesquite chips on the hot coals for a smoky flavor.

193 KENTUCKY-STYLE BEEF TENDERLOIN

PREPARATION TIME *10 minutes, plus 4 hours marinating* **COOKING TIME** *10-14 minutes* **SERVES 6**

2 beef tenderloins,
   about 12 oz each
6 slices sourdough bread
Aïoli *(see page 106)*,
   lettuce, and tomatoes
   for serving

KENTUCKY RUB
1 tbsp paprika
½ tbsp freshly ground
   black pepper
½ tsp English mustard
   powder

½ tsp garlic granules
½ tsp dried sage
½ tsp dried oregano
½ tsp ground chiles
salt

1   Using a large, sharp knife held horizontally, cut into one side of each tenderloin and almost but not quite through to the opposite side. Open out flat, like a book.
2   Make the Kentucky rub by combining all the ingredients. Rub thoroughly all over the tenderloins. Cover and let marinate in a cool place for about 4 hours.
3   Reform each tenderloin and grill on an oiled rack until well browned, but still pink in the center, 5-7 minutes on each side.
4   Remove the beef from the grill, cover with foil, and let rest for 5-10 minutes.
5   Carve the beef into thin slices and serve with the bread, aïoli, lettuce, and tomatoes.

194 SPICED BEEF KABOBS

PREPARATION TIME *15 minutes, plus 8 hours marinating* **COOKING TIME** *6–8 minutes* **SERVES 4**

1¼ lb boneless sirloin steak,
    cut into 1¼-inch cubes
1 red bell pepper
1 yellow bell pepper
16 cherry tomatoes
olive oil for brushing

salt and freshly ground
    black pepper

MARINADE
½ cup ketchup *(see
    page 184)*

¼ cup red wine
2 tbsp soy sauce
1 tbsp chile sauce
2 tsp Jamaican Jerk
    Seasoning *(see
    page 189)*

1   Put the beef into a nonreactive bowl.
2   Make the marinade by combining all the ingredients. Stir into the beef to coat the cubes evenly and thoroughly. Cover and let marinate in a cool place for 8 hours, stirring occasionally.
3   Meanwhile, cut the peppers into 1-inch squares. Stack in pairs of one each color. Brush the pepper stacks and the tomatoes with oil and season them.
4   Lift the beef from the marinade (reserve any remaining marinade) and thread onto skewers, alternating with the pepper stacks and tomatoes.
5   Grill on an oiled rack to the desired degree of doneness, 6–8 minutes, turning regularly and brushing with any remaining marinade.

195 GREEK LAMB STEAKS WITH EGGPLANT SALSA

PREPARATION TIME *10 minutes, plus 3 hours marinating* **COOKING TIME** *18–25 minutes* **SERVES 4**

4 lamb leg steaks	EGGPLANT SALSA	2 tbsp chopped fresh mint
2 garlic cloves, finely	1 lb eggplants, diced	2 tbsp lemon juice
chopped	1 small onion, chopped	4 oz feta cheese, crumbled
2 tbsp chopped fresh mint	1 garlic clove, crushed and	
2 tsp lemon juice	chopped	
3 tbsp olive oil	olive oil for frying	
salt and freshly ground	2 tbsp chopped fresh	
black pepper	flat-leaf parsley	

1 Score the lamb steaks on each side and place in a nonreactive dish.

2 Combine the garlic, mint, lemon juice, olive oil, and seasoning. Pour over the lamb and turn to coat the steaks, then cover and let marinate in a cool place for 3 hours, turning occasionally.

3 Meanwhile, make the salsa: Fry the eggplant, onion, and garlic in a little olive oil until the eggplant is golden brown, about 10 minutes, stirring occasionally. Remove from the heat and stir in the herbs, lemon juice, cheese, and seasoning. Set aside.

4 Lift the lamb from the dish and grill on an oiled rack to the desired degree of doneness: 4–5 minutes on each side for medium, 6–7 minutes for well done. Remove from the grill and serve with the salsa.

196 LAMB WITH MEDITERRANEAN FLAVORS

PREPARATION TIME *10 minutes, plus 8 hours marinating* **COOKING TIME** *15 minutes* **SERVES 6**

3½-lb bone-in shoulder of	3 tbsp chopped fresh	½ tsp saffron threads,
lamb, cut into large	cilantro	lightly toasted and
pieces	2 tbsp sun-dried tomato	pounded
	paste	salt and freshly ground
MARINADE	1 tbsp clear honey	black pepper
¼ cup olive oil	2 tsp Dijon mustard	
3 garlic cloves, finely	2 tsp paprika	
chopped	2 tsp ground cumin	

1 Put the lamb into a nonreactive bowl.

2 Combine all the marinade ingredients. Pour over the lamb and stir to ensure all the pieces are evenly coated. Cover and let marinate in a cool place for 8 hours, stirring occasionally.

3 Lift the lamb from the bowl. Grill on an oiled rack until the lamb is well browned and cooked through, about 15 minutes, turning regularly.

197 LAMB STEAKS WITH ROSEMARY AND LEMON

PREPARATION TIME *5 minutes, plus 3 hours marinating* **COOKING TIME** *8–12 minutes* **SERVES 4**

4 lamb leg steaks, about 5 oz each	grated zest and juice of 1 lemon	leaves from 3 rosemary sprigs, finely chopped
3 tbsp virgin olive oil	2 garlic cloves, crushed	2 lemons, halved

1   Lay the lamb steaks in a single layer in a shallow, nonreactive dish.
2   Combine the oil, lemon zest and juice, garlic, and rosemary. Pour over the lamb and turn the steaks over, then cover and let marinate in a cool place for 3 hours, turning a couple of times.
3   Lift the lamb from the dish (reserve the marinade) and grill on an oiled rack, turning once, to the desired degree of doneness: 4 minutes on each side for medium, 6 minutes for well done.
4   Meanwhile, brush the halved lemons with the remaining marinade and grill, cut side down, on the rack for 4–5 minutes on each side. Squeeze the juice from the caramelizeded lemons over the lamb steaks before serving.

198 PASTRAMI-STYLE LAMB

PREPARATION TIME *10 minutes, plus 8 hours marinating* **COOKING TIME** *10–12 minutes* **SERVES 6**

2 lamb tenderloins, about 12 oz each	RUB	½ tbsp English mustard powder
light rye bread, sliced tomatoes, and red onions for serving	1 plump garlic clove	½ tbsp dried thyme
	1 tbsp coarse sea salt	½ tbsp ground sage
	½ tbsp freshly ground black pepper	½ tsp ground allspice

1   Make the rub: Mash the garlic to a paste with the salt, then add the remaining ingredients. Rub thoroughly all over the lamb, then cover and let marinate in a cool place for 8 hours.
2   Grill the lamb on an oiled rack, turning regularly, until well browned and cooked to the desired degree of doneness: 10–12 minutes for medium rare.
3   Remove the lamb from the grill and let rest for 5–10 minutes, then slice thinly. Serve on light rye bread with sliced tomatoes and red onions.

199 SPICED PORK STEAKS

PREPARATION TIME *10 minutes, plus 4 hours marinating* **COOKING TIME** *15 minutes* **SERVES 4**

4 pork steaks	½ tsp ground coriander	pinch of sugar
	2 tbsp sun-dried tomato paste	salt and freshly ground black pepper
MARINADE	1 tbsp olive oil	
1 tsp ground cumin	4 garlic cloves, crushed	
1 tsp dried oregano	grated zest of 1 lime	
½ tsp ground cardamom	3 tbsp lime juice	
½ tsp harissa sauce		

1   Using the point of a sharp knife, cut three or four slashes in each pork steak. Place in a shallow, nonreactive dish.
2   Combine all the marinade ingredients and spread evenly all over the pork. Cover and let marinate in a cool place for 4 hours.
3   Grill on an oiled rack over medium-hot coals for 7–8 minutes on each side, turning once.

200 CHINESE PORK TENDERLOIN

PREPARATION TIME *10 minutes, plus 4–6 hours marinating* **COOKING TIME** *20 minutes* **SERVES 6**

2 pork tenderloins, about 1 lb each	1 fresh, hot red chile, seeded and chopped	1 tsp Chinese five-spice powder
2 plump garlic cloves, cut into thin slivers	⅔ cup Chinese plum sauce	fine strips of scallion and thinly sliced
1-inch piece fresh gingerroot, grated	2 tbsp peanut oil	cucumber for serving
	1 tbsp dark soy sauce	

1 Using the point of a thin, sharp knife, make slits in the pork. Insert the garlic slivers in the slits. Place in a nonreactive dish.

2 Mix together the ginger, chile, plum sauce, peanut oil, soy sauce, and Chinese five-spice powder. Pour over the pork and turn the tenderloins to ensure they are evenly coated, then cover and let marinate in a cool place for 4–6 hours.

3 Lift the tenderloins from the marinade and grill on an oiled rack over medium-hot coals until the juices run clear when the thickest parts of the tenderloins are pierced with a skewer, about 20 minutes, turning occasionally and basting with the remaining marinade. Serve with scallion strips and cucumber slices.

201 KOREAN SPICED PORK

PREPARATION TIME *10 minutes, plus 4–6 hours marinating* **COOKING TIME** *18 minutes* **SERVES 4**

2 pork tenderloins, about 12 oz each	MARINADE	2 garlic cloves, crushed
1 tbsp lime juice	⅔ cup soy sauce	1-inch piece fresh gingerroot, grated
1 cup fresh cilantro leaves	6 tbsp medium-dry sherry	pinch of crushed dried chiles
	1 tbsp toasted sesame oil	
	1 tbsp light brown sugar	

1 Put all the marinade ingredients in a small saucepan and bring to a boil. Remove from the heat and let cool.

2 Lay the tenderloins in a shallow, nonreactive dish. Pour the marinade over them and turn them to ensure they are completely coated, then cover and let marinate in a cool place for at least 4–6 hours, turning occasionally.

3 Lift the pork from the marinade (reserve the remaining marinade) and grill on an oiled rack until they are caramelized all over and the juices run clear when the thickest part of a tenderloin is pierced with a skewer, about 18 minutes, turning regularly and basting with the marinade.

4 Pour the remaining marinade into a pan, put on the grill rack, and bring to a boil. Add the lime juice and boil for 2 minutes. Remove from the heat and add the cilantro. Slice the pork and serve with the sauce.

202 CHAR SUI PORK

PREPARATION TIME *10 minutes, plus 4–6 hours marinating* **COOKING TIME** *14–16 minutes* **SERVES 4**

4 pork steaks

MARINADE
1 tbsp sunflower oil
1 tbsp toasted sesame oil
2 tbsp hoisin sauce
2 tbsp clear honey
2 tbsp soy sauce

1 tsp Chinese five-spice powder
freshly ground black pepper
2 garlic cloves, finely chopped
2-inch piece fresh gingerroot, grated

FOR SERVING
6 scallions, sliced lengthwise into shreds
½ English cucumber, seeded and cut into long, thin strips
Chinese plum sauce
lime wedges

1   Lay the pork steaks in a single layer in a shallow, nonreactive dish.
2   Make the marinade by stirring together all the ingredients except the ginger. Using a garlic press, squeeze the juice from the ginger into the other ingredients, then stir in. Pour this over the pork and turn the steaks to ensure they are completely coated, then cover and let marinate in a cool place for at least 4–6 hours, turning occasionally.
3   Lift the pork from the marinade (reserve the remaining marinade) and grill on an oiled rack until the juices run clear when the thickest part of a steak is pierced with a skewer, 7–8 minutes on each side, turning once and basting with any remaining marinade. Serve the steaks with the scallions, cucumber, plum sauce, and lime wedges.

203 BARBECUED SHREDDED PORK SANDWICH

PREPARATION TIME *10 minutes, plus up to 24 hours marinating* **COOKING TIME** *2½–3 hours* **SERVES 8**

4½-lb boneless pork shoulder roast	**3 tbsp mixed granulated and light soft brown sugar**	FOR SERVING
		16 hamburger buns or bread rolls
SOUTHERN SPICE RUB	**2 tbsp paprika**	**Barbecue Sauce (see page 179)**
1 tbsp cumin seeds	**2 tsp hot chile powder**	
½ tbsp black peppercorns	**salt**	**coleslaw**

1 Make the spice rub: Heat a small, heavy-based frying pan, add the cumin seeds, and toast over medium heat until fragrant. Grind the cumin seeds. Add the peppercorns to the pan and toast until fragrant, then coarsely grind. Mix the ground cumin and peppercorns with the remaining rub ingredients.

2 Rub the spice mixture thoroughly into the pork. Re-roll the roast and tie tightly with string at regular intervals. Cover and let marinate in a cool place for up to 24 hours.

3 Grill the pork on an oiled rack over indirect medium heat (see page 8) until very tender and cooked through (see page 14), 2½–3 hours, turning regularly.

4 Remove from the grill, cover, and let rest for about 10 minutes.

5 Using two forks, pull or shred the pork into pieces. Mix with the barbecue sauce and serve in the buns or rolls, with coleslaw.

204 PORK WITH GINGER AND CHILE

PREPARATION TIME *10 minutes, plus 4 hours marinating* **COOKING TIME** *20 minutes* **SERVES 4**

2 pork tenderloins, about 12 oz each	**2-inch piece fresh gingerroot, grated**	**freshly ground black pepper**
	1½ tbsp lemon juice	
MARINADE	**3 tbsp soy sauce**	DIPPING SAUCE
3 garlic cloves, finely chopped	**2 tbsp clear honey**	**¼ cup Thai sweet chile sauce**
	½ tbsp toasted sesame oil	
½ fresh, hot red chile, seeded and thinly sliced	**½ tbsp peanut oil**	**2 tbsp lime or lemon juice**

1 Make the marinade: Pound the garlic, chile, and ginger together in a bowl using the end of a rolling pin. Stir in the remaining marinade ingredients.

2 Prick the pork all over with a fork, then rub with the marinade. Lay the pork in a nonreactive dish and pour any remaining marinade over. Cover and let marinate in a cool place for 4 hours, turning occasionally.

3 Make the dipping sauce by mixing the chile sauce with the lime or lemon juice in a small bowl.

4 Lift the pork from the marinade (reserve any remaining marinade) and grill on an oiled rack for about 20 minutes, turning twice and brushing with the reserved marinade.

5 Remove the pork from the grill, cover, and let rest for 5–10 minutes before slicing and serving with the dipping sauce.

205 SWEET AND STICKY SPARERIBS

PREPARATION TIME *5 minutes* **COOKING TIME** *55 minutes* **SERVES 4**

3 lb meaty pork spareribs or baby back ribs	3-inch piece fresh gingerroot, grated	6 tbsp clear honey
5 garlic cloves, crushed and finely chopped	6 tbsp soy sauce	2 tsp chile sauce
	6 tbsp dry sherry	lemon wedges for serving

1   Preheat the oven to 375ºF. Lay the ribs in a large, foil-lined roasting pan and cook in the oven until tender, 35–40 minutes .

2   Combine the garlic, ginger, soy sauce, sherry, honey, and chile sauce to make the baste.

3   When cooked, brush the ribs liberally and evenly with the baste. Reserve the remaining baste.

4   Grill the ribs on an oiled rack until well browned and glazed, 10–15 minutes, turning occasionally and brushing with the baste. Brush once more, then remove from the grill.

5   Transfer to a board and divide into individual ribs. Serve with lemon wedges.

206 VENISON WITH FRESH FIG CHUTNEY

PREPARATION TIME *15 minutes, plus 2 hours marinating* **COOKING TIME** *12–15 minutes* **SERVES 4**

4 venison steaks, about 6 oz each	2 tbsp balsamic vinegar	pinch of cayenne pepper
freshly ground black pepper	½ tbsp clear honey	2 tbsp port wine
		1 tbsp red-currant jelly
	FRESH FIG CHUTNEY	6 ripe figs, quartered
½ tsp Chinese five-spice powder	2 tsp olive oil	salt
	4 shallots, quartered	

1   Season the venison liberally with black pepper, then rub in the five-spice powder. Mix the balsamic vinegar with the honey and brush liberally over the steaks. Cover and let marinate in a cool place for 2 hours.

2   Meanwhile, make the chutney: Heat the oil in a pan, add the shallots, and cook gently until softened but not colored. Stir in the cayenne, then add the port and red-currant jelly. Bring to a boil, then simmer gently until syrupy. Add the figs and season to taste. Heat through. Remove from the heat and let cool.

3   Grill the venison steaks on an oiled rack until cooked to the desired degree of doneness: about 4 minutes on each side. Serve with the fig chutney.

207 WARM BEEF SALAD

PREPARATION TIME *15 minutes, plus 6–8 hours marinating* **COOKING TIME** *12–20 minutes* **SERVES 6**

2-inch piece fresh
  gingerroot
2 garlic cloves, chopped
⅔ cup rice wine
  or dry sherry
2 tbsp Chinese fermented
  black beans, crushed
1-lb beef tenderloin tip

2 tbsp finely chopped
  fresh cilantro leaves
1 tbsp rice vinegar or
  sherry vinegar
1 tbsp peanut oil
1 tbsp toasted sesame oil
4 handfuls of small spinach
  leaves, coarsely torn

1 bunch of watercress,
  coarsely torn
1 small head radicchio,
  coarsely torn
lightly toasted sesame
  seeds for garnish

1 Thinly slice half of the ginger and cut the slices into shreds; set aside. Grate the remaining ginger.
2 Combine the grated ginger with the garlic, rice wine, and black beans.
3 Put the beef into a nonreactive bowl and pour the ginger mixture over, then cover and let marinate in a cool place for 6–8 hours, turning occasionally.
4 Lift the beef from the marinade (reserve the marinade) and dry it thoroughly. Flatten the thicker end with a rolling pin. Pour the marinade into a pan and bring to a boil at the side of the grill rack; boil until slightly reduced.
5 Grill the beef on the oiled rack until cooked to the desired degree of doneness, 4–8 minutes on each side, turning and brushing with the marinade occasionally.
6 Remove the beef from the grill, cover, and let rest for 5–8 minutes. Meanwhile, strain the marinade and stir in the cilantro, rice vinegar, oils, and shredded ginger.
7 Mix the salad leaves in a serving bowl or deep plate. Slice the beef thinly and mix with the sauce, then toss with the salad. Sprinkle with the sesame seeds and serve.

208 CHINESE-STYLE RIBS

PREPARATION TIME *10 minutes* **COOKING TIME** *1 hour* **SERVES 4-6**

4 lb meaty pork spareribs
  or baby back ribs
½ tbsp Sichuan peppercorns
⅔ cup clear honey
3 garlic cloves, crushed
2 tbsp rice wine or dry
  sherry

2 tbsp Chinese plum sauce
2 tbsp ginger juice
  (produced by squeezing
  fresh gingerroot in a
  garlic press)
2–3 tsp chile sauce

1 tbsp Chinese five-spice
  powder
lime wedges for serving

1   Preheat the oven to 375°F. Lay the ribs in a large, foil-lined roasting pan and cook in the oven until tender, about 45 minutes.
2   Meanwhile, heat a heavy-based frying pan. Add the Sichuan peppercorns and toast until they smell fragrant. Grind in a spice grinder or in a small bowl using the end of a rolling pin. Combine with the remaining ingredients (except the lime wedges).
3   Brush this mixture liberally all over the cooked ribs, making sure they are evenly coated. Reserve the remaining mixture.
4   Grill the ribs on an oiled rack until well browned and glazed, 10–15 minutes, turning occasionally and brushing with the remaining mixture. Brush once more, then remove the ribs from the grill.
5   Transfer to a board and divide into individual ribs. Serve with lime wedges.

209 ITALIAN HAMBURGERS

PREPARATION TIME *15 minutes, plus 4 hours chilling* **COOKING TIME** *10–15 minutes* **SERVES 4**

1 small onion, finely
  chopped
olive oil for cooking
1 garlic clove, finely
  chopped
1¼ lb ground beef

¼ cup Pesto *(see page 172)*
2 tbsp chopped black olives
4 oz mozzarella cheese,
  coarsely chopped
salt and freshly ground
  black pepper

4 ciabatta rolls, split open
sliced tomato and arugula,
  lightly dressed with
  vinaigrette, for serving

1   Fry the onion in a little oil until softened, adding the garlic toward the end of the cooking. Remove with a slotted spoon and drain on paper towels. Let cool.
2   Mix the beef with the onion, garlic, and pesto, using your hands. Then knead in the olives, mozzarella, and seasoning.
3   Divide the mixture into four equal portions. With wet hands, form each portion into a 1-inch-thick patty. If time permits, cover and leave the burgers in a cool place for at least 4 hours.
4   Grill on an oiled rack until well browned and the juices run clear when a burger is pierced with a fine skewer, 4–5 minutes on each side, turning once.
5   Meanwhile, toast the rolls at the side of grill rack. Serve the burgers in the rolls with the sliced tomato and arugula.

210 STEAK WITH RICH TOMATO SAUCE

PREPARATION TIME *10 minutes* **COOKING TIME** *20-25 minutes* **SERVES 4**

4 boneless sirloin steaks	3 garlic cloves, finely	1 lb vine-ripened tomatoes,
salt and freshly ground	chopped	chopped
black pepper	3 fresh sage leaves, finely	⅔ cup chopped black olives
	shredded	⅛ cup capers, drained
RICH TOMATO SAUCE	1 fresh, hot red chile,	1 tbsp chopped fresh
2-oz can anchovy fillets	seeded and finely	oregano
in oil	chopped	2 tbsp chopped fresh
3 tbsp extra virgin olive oil		flat-leaf parsley

1 Drain and reserve the oil from the anchovies. Chop the anchovies finely. Brush the steaks with some of the anchovy oil, then season them. Set aside in a cool place while preparing the sauce.

2 Heat the extra virgin olive oil in a pan, add the garlic and sage, and cook until the garlic begins to color. Stir in the chile and cook briefly, then add the tomatoes, olives, capers, anchovies, and oregano. Simmer for 10 minutes. Season with black pepper.

3 Grill the steaks on a lightly oiled rack, turning once, until cooked to the desired degree of doneness: about 3 minutes for rare steaks, 5 minutes for medium.

4 Meanwhile, add the parsley to the sauce and warm through at the side of the grill rack. Serve the steaks with the sauce.

211 SAUSAGES WITH PLUM SAUCE

PREPARATION TIME *10 minutes* **COOKING TIME** *25-30 minutes* **SERVES 6**

12 large, fresh pork link	1 tbsp finely chopped fresh	1 tbsp light soy sauce
sausages, or frankfurters	gingerroot	5 tbsp sweet sherry
	½ tbsp Sichuan	½ tbsp clear honey
PLUM SAUCE	peppercorns, finely	lime juice to taste
1 tbsp peanut oil	crushed	
2 shallots, finely chopped	8 oz plums, quartered	
	and pitted	

1 Make the plum sauce: Heat the oil in a frying pan, add the shallots, and fry until softened. Add the ginger and peppercorns toward the end of cooking and stir until they smell fragrant. Add the plums, soy sauce, sherry, and honey. Bring to a boil, then cover and simmer until the plums are tender. Add lime juice to taste. Set aside.

2 Add the sausages to a pan of boiling water and quickly return to a boil, then simmer gently for 3 minutes. Drain and rinse under cold running water to speed cooling. Pat dry.

3 Grill the sausages on an oiled rack until evenly browned and cooked through, 8-10 minutes, turning occasionally. Serve the sausages with the plum sauce either poured over or as a dipping sauce.

VEGETARIAN DISHES

A selection of grilled vegetable dishes works well as a main course. Add an interesting dressing or sauce, some cheese, and bread—cooked or warmed on the grill rack—or a grilled potato dish to make a delicious spread.

Many vegetables respond well to being grilled, but some take a surprisingly long time to cook. Precook firm vegetables such as carrots, cauliflower, baby onions, and broccoli in boiling water, to reduce the cooking time and to prevent the outside from becoming overdone before the inside is tender. Drain and dry them well before grilling. Coat cut surfaces with oil or dressing to prevent them from drying out and to promote browning. Sweet potatoes and baby squash can be cooked in the embers of the fire—wrap them in a double thickness of heavy-duty foil to keep them clean and help them to cook evenly.

When choosing vegetables for brochettes, bear in mind cooking times, because all the items must grill in the same time (after any precooking for items such as new potatoes and baby fennel bulbs). If grilling a selection of vegetables, put those that require the longest cooking on first. Use an oiled hinged basket to make turning and lifting vegetables easier. Or, for small vegetables, such as button mushrooms and shallots, try an oiled fine-mesh grill rack, which will prevent them from falling onto the coals. Vegetables can also be enclosed in foil packets and cooked on the grill rack for maximum flavor.

212 VEGETABLE SATAY

PREPARATION TIME *15 minutes* **COOKING TIME** *30 minutes* **SERVES 4**

2 leeks, cut into chunks

1 yellow crookneck squash, cut into chunks

1 zucchini, cut into chunks

4 oz mushrooms, halved

3 tbsp dark soy sauce

2 tsp toasted sesame oil

8-12 fresh bay leaves

SATAY SAUCE

1 tbsp peanut oil

1 shallot, finely chopped

2 garlic cloves, crushed

1-inch piece fresh gingerroot, grated

1 lemon grass stem

1 fresh, hot red chile, seeded and minced

1 tsp curry powder

⅔ cup crunchy peanut butter

3 tbsp chopped fresh cilantro

sugar to taste

salt and freshly ground black pepper

1. To make the sauce, heat the oil and fry the shallot, garlic, ginger, and lemon grass until softened. Stir in the chile and curry powder for a couple of minutes. Then stir in the peanut butter and 1 cup boiling water. Bring to a boil. Add the cilantro and season with sugar, salt, and pepper. Remove from the heat.
2. Cook the leeks in a pan of boiling water for 4 minutes. Add the crookneck squash and zucchini and cook for 1 minute longer. Drain and cool under running cold water. Put into a bowl with the mushrooms.
3. Combine the soy sauce, sesame oil, and black pepper. Trickle this over the vegetables and stir gently to coat them.
4. Thread the vegetables alternately onto skewers, adding bay leaves along the way. Grill on an oiled rack for about 8 minutes, turning occasionally.
5. Meanwhile, warm the satay sauce at the side of the grill rack. Serve with the vegetables.

213 MUSHROOM AND MOZZARELLA BROCHETTES

PREPARATION TIME *10 minutes, plus 1-2 hours marinating* **COOKING TIME** *8 minutes* **SERVES 4**

12 oz mozzarella cheese cut into 1-inch cubes

8 cremini mushrooms, halved lengthwise

1 red bell pepper, cut into 1-inch pieces

6 oz zucchini, cut diagonally into 8 chunks

MARINADE

½ cup virgin olive oil

1 tbsp balsamic vinegar

2 tbsp fresh thyme leaves

salt and freshly ground black pepper

1. Put the cheese and vegetables into a nonreactive dish.
2. Make the marinade by combining all the ingredients. Pour over the vegetables and cheese and stir gently so everything is evenly coated. Cover and leave in a cool place for 1-2 hours.
3. Lift the cheese and vegetables from the marinade (reserve any remaining marinade) and thread alternately onto eight skewers.
4. Grill on an oiled rack until the cheese is golden and the vegetables are tender, about 8 minutes, turning occasionally and brushing with the remaining marinade.

214 STUFFED ONIONS

PREPARATION TIME *15 minutes* **COOKING TIME** *20–25 minutes* **SERVES 4**

4 large onions, about 10 oz each, peeled	2 tbsp chopped fresh parsley	2 egg yolks
2 tsp unsalted butter	4 oz feta cheese, crumbled	freshly ground black pepper
1 large leek, chopped	8 sun-dried tomatoes in oil, drained and sliced	
leaves from 4 fresh thyme sprigs	6 oil-cured black olives, pitted and chopped	

1   Trim the root ends of the onions, but do not cut them off completely as they hold the layers together. Cut each onion in half from top to bottom. Remove the inner layers of each onion half, leaving a shell two layers thick. Chop the removed layers.

2   Add the onion shells to a saucepan of boiling water, lower the heat, and simmer for 10 minutes. Lift from the water with a slotted spoon and let drain upside-down.

3   Meanwhile, melt the butter in a heavy frying pan. Add the chopped onion and cook over a very low heat until soft and golden. Add the leek about three-quarters of the way through the cooking. Stir in the thyme and parsley. Let cool slightly, then add the cheese, sun-dried tomatoes, olives, and egg yolks. Season with plenty of black pepper.

4   Turn each onion shell upright and pile the stuffing into the shells.

5   Grill the stuffed onions near the side of the rack until the shells are tender and the stuffing is warmed through, 10–15 minutes.

215 HALLOUMI, SQUASH, AND CHERRY TOMATO SKEWERS

PREPARATION TIME *5 minutes, plus 2–24 hours marinating* **COOKING TIME** *10 minutes* **SERVES 4**

12 oz halloumi cheese, cut into 1-inch cubes	MARINADE	freshly ground black pepper
16 small pattypan squashes	6 tbsp extra virgin olive oil	
16 cherry tomatoes	2 tbsp mixed chopped fresh oregano, thyme, mint, rosemary, and parsley	
	juice of 1 lemon	

1   Put the cheese and vegetables into a shallow, nonreactive dish.

2   Make the marinade by mixing all the ingredients together. Pour over the cheese and vegetable mixture, then stir to make sure everything is coated. Cover and let marinate in a cool place for at least 2 hours, or up to 24 hours.

3   Lift the cheese and vegetables from the marinade (reserve any remaining marinade) and thread alternately onto skewers, beginning and ending with a pattypan squash and pushing all the ingredients quite close together.

4   Grill on an oiled rack until tender and flecked with brown at the edges, about 10 minutes, turning frequently and brushing with any remaining marinade.

216 MEDITERRANEAN VEGETABLES WITH GARLIC TOASTS

PREPARATION TIME *15 minutes, plus 1 hour marinating* **COOKING TIME** *10–16 minutes* **SERVES 4**

3 baby eggplants, halved
    lengthwise, or 2 small
    eggplants, cut
    lengthwise into
    ½-inch-thick slices
1 red and 1 yellow bell
    pepper, cut into wedges
4 baby zucchini
1 small fennel bulb, thinly
    sliced, with the root end
    kept intact

4 scallions
4 portobello mushrooms
6–7 tbsp virgin olive oil
2 tbsp chopped mixed fresh
    herbs, such as thyme,
    oregano, and rosemary
salt and freshly ground
    black pepper
6 ripe, but not soft roma
    tomatoes, halved
1 garlic clove, crushed

1 French loaf, sliced
    diagonally
balsamic vinegar for
    sprinkling
10 black olives, halved
    and pitted

1. Put the eggplants, peppers, zucchini, fennel, scallions, and mushrooms into a large dish. Mix 4–5 tablespoons of the oil with the herbs and seasoning. Brush the tomatoes with some of the mixture and carefully stir the rest into the vegetables in the dish. Cover and let marinate in a cool place for 1 hour.
2. Mix the garlic with the remaining oil and brush over one side of each slice of bread. Sprinkle with salt. Grill at the side of an oiled rack until golden.
3. Meanwhile, lift the mixed vegetables from the dish and grill in the center of the oiled rack until tender and lightly charred, 5–8 minutes on each side. Grill the tomatoes until lightly charred but still firm, 3 minutes on each side.
4. Transfer the toasted bread to a large platter. Put the vegetables as they are done onto the toasts. Sprinkle with a little balsamic vinegar and scatter the olives over.

217 FENNEL WEDGES WITH PARMESAN DRESSING

PREPARATION TIME *10 minutes* **COOKING TIME** *8–10 minutes* **SERVES 4**

4 small fennel bulbs
olive oil for brushing
salt and freshly ground
    black pepper

PARMESAN DRESSING
1 tbsp lemon juice
1 tbsp grated lemon zest
1 tbsp white wine vinegar
½ cup virgin olive oil

1 tsp Dijon mustard
2 tbsp freshly grated
    Parmesan cheese

1. Trim the fennel bulbs (reserve the feathery leaves), then cut into thick wedges, each with some of the core. Brush with olive oil and thread onto oiled skewers. Sprinkle with seasoning.
2. Grill on an oiled rack until slightly soft and lightly charred, 8–10 minutes, turning occasionally. For softer fennel, cook for a little longer, farther from the heat.
3. Meanwhile, make the dressing by whisking all the ingredients together. Season to taste.
4. Serve the fennel with the dressing poured over and sprinkled with the reserved feathery tops. (If the fennel bulbs don't have their feathery tops, you can substitute herb fennel.)

218 VEGETABLE BROCHETTES

PREPARATION TIME *20 minutes, plus 1 hour marinating* **COOKING TIME** *10 minutes* **SERVES 6**

1 large eggplant, cut into 12 slices	6 oz halloumi cheese, cut into 1- by ½-inch pieces	MARINADE
3 red bell peppers, quartered	2 tbsp extra virgin olive oil	3 tbsp soy sauce
24 large button mushrooms	juice of 1 lime	1½ tbsp olive oil
3 zucchini, scored and cut diagonally into ¾-inch pieces	leaves from a small bunch of fresh cilantro, chopped	2 garlic cloves, crushed
		1 tbsp paprika
		1 tbsp ground cumin
		dash of hot pepper sauce

1 Make the marinade by combining all the ingredients with 3 tablespoons water. Brush the eggplant slices with some of the marinade.

2 Put the remaining vegetables in a dish and stir in the remaining marinade. Cover and let marinate in a cool place for an hour or so.

3 Meanwhile, preheat the broiler. Broil the eggplant slices until browned, 3–4 minutes, turning once. Broil the halloumi until golden but not melting, about 2 minutes . Wrap the eggplant slices around the pieces of halloumi.

4 Remove the vegetables from the marinade. Beginning and ending with a mushroom, thread the vegetables, including the eggplant and halloumi rolls, alternately onto oiled skewers.

5 Grill on an oiled rack for about 4 minutes, turning to ensure even cooking and browning.

6 Meanwhile, combine the olive oil, lime juice, cilantro, and seasoning. Remove the brochettes from the grill and trickle the dressing over them.

219 BABY BOK CHOY WITH BALSAMIC DRESSING

PREPARATION TIME *5 minutes* **COOKING TIME** *8 minutes* **SERVES 4**

8 heads baby bok choy	1 tbsp balsamic vinegar,	salt and freshly ground
1 tbsp peanut oil, plus	plus extra for sprinkling	black pepper
extra for brushing		

1   Brush the bok choy with peanut oil and sprinkle with balsamic vinegar. Grill on an oiled rack until softened and marked with charred lines, about 4 minutes on each side.
2   Meanwhile, make the dressing by combining 1 tablespoon of peanut oil with 1 tablespoon of balsamic vinegar and seasoning.
3   Remove the bok choy from the grill and trickle the dressing over them. Serve.

220 EGGPLANT SLICES WITH MINT DRESSING

PREPARATION TIME *10 minutes, plus 15–30 minutes marinating* **COOKING TIME** *10 minutes* **SERVES 4**

2 eggplants, cut into	MINT DRESSING	3–4 tbsp chopped
½-inch-thick slices	1 garlic clove, chopped	fresh mint
olive oil for brushing	5 tbsp extra virgin olive oil	
salt and freshly ground	juice of 1 lemon	
black pepper		

1   Make the dressing by mixing the garlic, olive oil, and lemon juice in a blender. Pour into a bowl and add the mint and seasoning. Set aside.
2   Brush both sides of the eggplant slices with oil. Grill on an oiled rack until softened and lightly charred, 5 minutes on each side.
3   Transfer to a plate, season, and pour the dressing over. Let marinate for 15–30 minutes.

221 SPICED SWEET POTATO WEDGES

PREPARATION TIME *15 minutes* **COOKING TIME** *20–30 minutes* **SERVES 4**

2 large, orange-fleshed	2 tsp mustard seeds	1 tsp black peppercorns
sweet potatoes,	2 tsp cumin seeds	2 tbsp olive oil
1¼ lb total weight	1 tsp coriander seeds	salt

1   Cook the whole, unpeeled potatoes in a covered pan of simmering water until crisp-tender, 15–20 minutes . Drain and leave until cool enough to handle, then cut into large wedges.
2   Heat a small, heavy-based frying pan, add the seeds and peppercorns, and toast over a low heat for 3 minutes. Tip into a spice grinder and grind.
3   Pour the oil into a large bowl and stir in the spices. Add the sweet potatoes and toss to coat.
4   Grill on an oiled rack until softened and marked with charred lines, 4–5 minutes on each side. Remove from the grill, sprinkle with salt, and serve.

222 HONEY-GLAZED SQUASH WEDGES WITH SESAME SEEDS

PREPARATION TIME *10 minutes* **COOKING TIME** *20–30 minutes* **SERVES 4**

1 large butternut squash, peeled and cut into wedges	7 tbsp clear honey 2 tbsp pumpkin seed oil 2 tbsp sesame seeds	salt and freshly ground black pepper

1   Place the squash wedges on a double layer of heavy-duty foil and drizzle the honey and oil over them. Sprinkle with the sesame seeds and season generously. Fold over the sides of the foil and twist the edges together to seal tightly.

2   Cook the packet at the side of the grill rack for 20–30 minutes, turning it over a couple of times so that the squash cooks evenly.

223 SQUASH WEDGES WITH THYME AND GARLIC

PREPARATION TIME *10 minutes* **COOKING TIME** *15–18 minutes* **SERVES 4**

2 lb acorn squash or pumpkin, seeded and cut into wedges 2 plump garlic cloves, finely chopped	leaves from 2 sprigs of fresh thyme 2 tbsp olive oil salt and freshly ground black pepper	Tomato Tartar Sauce *(see page 179)* for serving

1   Parboil the squash wedges for 5 minutes. Drain and pat dry. While still warm, toss with the garlic, thyme, olive oil, and seasoning.

2   Grill on an oiled rack until softened and lightly charred, 5–6 minutes on each side. Serve with the tomato tartar sauce.

224 GRILLED LEEKS NICOISE

PREPARATION TIME *10 minutes* **COOKING TIME** *5 minutes* **SERVES 2**

8 oz baby leeks ⅔ cup virgin olive oil, plus extra for brushing grated zest and juice of 1 lemon salt and freshly ground black pepper	4 vine-ripened tomatoes, seeded and chopped 1 tbsp capers 6 black olives, halved and pitted 2–4 salted anchovy fillets, rinsed and chopped	handful of fresh parsley and basil, chopped

1   Brush the leeks with oil and grill on an oiled rack until softened and marked with charred lines, about 5 minutes, turning once.

2   Meanwhile, whisk the oil with the lemon juice and seasoning until emulsified, or shake them together in a lidded jar.

3   Transfer the leeks to a plate, or plates, and pour the dressing over. Scatter the remaining ingredients over the leeks. Serve warm or at room temperature.

225 ARTICHOKES WITH PARSLEY AND LEMON BUTTER

PREPARATION TIME *20 minutes, plus 1 hour marinating* **COOKING TIME** *25–30 minutes* **SERVES 4**

4 globe artichokes	PARSLEY AND LEMON BUTTER	1–1½ tbsp lemon juice
lemon juice	1 garlic clove	
5 tbsp olive oil	4 tbsp unsalted butter	
salt and freshly ground	1 tbsp finely chopped fresh	
black pepper	flat-leaf parsley	

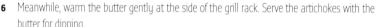

1. Make the butter: Blanch the garlic in simmering water for 5 minutes. Drain well, then mash to a paste. Beat the butter with a fork or wooden spoon until softened. Gradually work in the garlic paste, then the parsley, lemon juice, and seasoning. Leave in a cool place for several hours so the flavors can blend.
2. Snap off the artichoke stems near the base. Boil the artichokes in water acidulated with the juice of half a lemon for 10 minutes. Drain and leave until cool enough to handle, then trim off the outer layer of leaves.
3. Cut the artichokes from top to bottom into quarters and brush the cut surfaces with lemon juice. Scrape out the hairy choke and halve the quarters.
4. Lay the artichokes in a single layer in a shallow, nonreactive dish. Whisk together the olive oil, 2 tablespoons of lemon juice, and seasoning. Pour this over the artichokes and turn them over to make sure they are evenly coated, then cover and leave for an hour or so, or until needed.
5. Lift the artichokes from the dish and grill, flat-side down, on an oiled rack until well patched with brown, 5–8 minutes (don't worry if the leaves start to char). Turn the artichokes over and grill until just tender, 5–8 minutes longer.
6. Meanwhile, warm the butter gently at the side of the grill rack. Serve the artichokes with the butter for dipping.

226 SWEET AND SPICY EGGPLANT AND RED ONION KABOBS

PREPARATION TIME *15 minutes, plus 2–8 hours marinating* **COOKING TIME** *5–10 minutes* **SERVES 6**

3 small eggplants, cut
 into cubes
salt
6 red onions, quartered
3 tbsp medium sherry
1 tbsp Dijon mustard

salt and freshly ground
 black pepper
chopped fresh cilantro
 for garnish

MARINADE
6 tbsp balsamic vinegar

3 tbsp clear honey
4 tbsp toasted sesame oil
juice of 1 lemon
¼ tsp ground cumin
¼ tsp ground cardamom
pinch of cayenne pepper

1 Sprinkle the eggplant cubes with salt, then let drain in a colander for 30 minutes. Rinse thoroughly and dry on paper towels. Put into a nonreactive bowl. Separate each onion quarter into two pieces, and add to the bowl.

2 Make the marinade by combining all the ingredients. Add to the bowl and stir to coat the pieces of vegetable evenly. Cover and let marinate in a cool place for 2–8 hours.

3 Lift the vegetables from the marinade (reserve the marinade). Thread the eggplant cubes and onions alternately onto skewers. Grill on an oiled rack until beginning to caramelize, about 5 minutes, turning regularly.

4 Meanwhile, put the reserved marinade, sherry, and mustard into a small saucepan and boil on the grill rack until syrupy. Season to taste. Transfer the kabobs to plates, pour the sauce over them, and sprinkled with cilantro.

227 GREEK VEGETABLE SALAD

PREPARATION TIME *15 minutes, plus 1 hour marinating* **COOKING TIME** *20–30 minutes* **SERVES 4**

8 oz feta cheese, cut
 into ½-inch-thick
 slices
½ cup virgin olive oil
grated zest and juice of
 1½ lemons
1 tbsp balsamic vinegar

2 garlic cloves, finely
 chopped
2–3 tbsp fresh thyme
 leaves
freshly ground black
 pepper

3 lb mixed zucchini,
 eggplant, and ripe but
 not soft tomatoes
1 red onion
¾ cup pitted Kalamata
 olives

1 Put the cheese into a shallow, nonreactive dish. Combine 2 tablespoons of the olive oil with the lemon zest and juice, balsamic vinegar, garlic, 1 tablespoon of the thyme, and black pepper. Pour this over the cheese and let marinate in a cool place for 1 hour.

2 Meanwhile, cut the zucchini and eggplant diagonally into ½-inch-thick slices. Halve the tomatoes. Cut the red onion into ½-inch slices from top to bottom. Put the eggplant, zucchini, and red onion into a bowl, pour the remaining oil over them, and add black pepper. Stir to coat the vegetables well.

3 Lift the vegetables from the bowl with a slotted spoon and grill on an oiled rack until tender and lightly charred, 5–6 minutes on each side.

4 Brush the tomatoes with oil and grill for 3 minutes on each side.

5 Transfer the vegetables as they are done to a bowl or platter and cover with plastic wrap.

6 Lift the cheese from the marinade and grill on the rack until golden, about 3 minutes on each side (the cheese is easier to turn over if it is grilled in an oiled hinged basket).

7 Scatter the olives and remaining thyme over the vegetables and top with the cheese. Serve immediately, while the cheese is still warm.

228 MUSHROOMS WITH EGGPLANT AND RED PEPPER RELISH

PREPARATION TIME *10 minutes* **COOKING TIME** *40–45 minutes* **SERVES 4**

6-8 small portobello
  mushrooms, about
  2½ inches in diameter,
  stems removed
olive oil for brushing
salt and freshly ground
  black pepper
cottage cheese or ricotta
  cheese for serving

EGGPLANT AND RED PEPPER
RELISH
1 eggplant, halved
  lengthwise
1 red bell pepper, halved
  lengthwise
1-2 plump garlic cloves,
  unpeeled

¾ cup Kalamata
  olives, pitted
2 tsp capers
6 large, fresh basil leaves,
  chopped
1 tsp lemon juice, or
  to taste

1   Preheat the oven to 400°F. Make the relish: Brush the cut surfaces of the eggplant lightly
    with oil. Put the eggplant, cut-side down, on an oiled baking sheet and roast for 35–45 minutes.
    Roast the red pepper in the same way for 15–20 minutes, and roast the garlic cloves for
    10–15 minutes.
2   Chop the roasted pepper and eggplant and put into a blender or food processor. Squeeze the
    garlic from its skin and add it to the blender, along with the olives and capers. Blend until the
    ingredients are coarse-fine.
3   Scrape the relish into a saucepan and stir in the basil, lemon juice, some salt, and plenty of black
    pepper. Put to warm at the side of the grill rack.
4   Brush the mushrooms with olive oil and sprinkle with seasoning. Grill, stem-side down, in the
    center of the oiled rack for 1–2 minutes, then turn them over, fill the cavity with the relish, and
    grill for 1–2 minutes longer.
5   Carefully lift the mushrooms from the grill and top each with a small spoonful of cottage cheese
    or ricotta cheese.

229 GRILLED BABY VEGETABLES WITH BALSAMIC VINEGAR

PREPARATION TIME *15 minutes* **COOKING TIME** *6 minutes* **SERVES 6**

8 oz baby zucchini, scored
  lengthwise with a fork
4 oz baby leeks
6 baby corn
8 oz ripe, but not too soft,
  vine-ripened tomatoes,
  halved

2 oz snow peas
½ cup chile oil
2 plump garlic cloves
¼ cup balsamic vinegar
salt and freshly ground
  black pepper

⅔ cup sun-dried tomatoes
  in oil, drained
leaves from several sprigs
  of fresh thyme
grated zest of 1 small
  lemon

1   Brush the vegetables with chile oil and grill on an oiled rack until softened and lightly charred:
    about 6 minutes for the zucchini and leeks, 4–6 minutes for the baby corn, 3–5 minutes for the
    tomatoes, and 2–4 minutes for the snow peas, turning occasionally. Remove the vegetables as
    soon as they are done, put into a bowl, and cover with plastic wrap.
2   Meanwhile, press the garlic through a garlic press into the balsamic vinegar. Season.
3   Toss the cooked vegetables with the garlicky vinegar and sun-dried tomatoes. Sprinkle with the
    thyme leaves and lemon zest, and serve.

230 ROASTED VEGETABLE SALAD WITH MUSTARD AND CAPER SAUCE

PREPARATION TIME *15 minutes, plus 2 hours marinating* **COOKING TIME** *15-20 minutes* **SERVES 4**

2 lb mixed vegetables, such as baby turnips, baby carrots, baby parsnips, zucchini, eggplant, Belgian endive, bulb fennel, red onion, and baby leeks (or small leeks, halved lengthwise)

8 garlic cloves, unpeeled
4 sprigs of fresh rosemary
5 tbsp virgin olive oil
½ tbsp balsamic vinegar
salt and freshly ground black pepper

MUSTARD AND CAPER SAUCE
¾ cup mayonnaise *(see page 179)*
½ tbsp Dijon mustard
½ tbsp capers, drained and chopped
3 tbsp chopped fresh flat-leaf parsley

1   Prepare the vegetables: Blanch baby turnips, carrots, and parsnips separately in boiling water for 5 minutes, then drain and dry well. Slice zucchini and eggplant diagonally. Quarter endive lengthwise and remove the core, but leave enough to keep the leaves attached. Cut fennel lengthwise into wedges. Cut red onion into wedges, leaving them attached at the root end.

2   Place all the vegetables and the garlic in a large bowl and add the rosemary, olive oil, balsamic vinegar, and seasoning. Stir everything around, then cover and let marinate in a cool place for a couple of hours.

3   Meanwhile, make the sauce by stirring the ingredients together. Set aside.

4   Thread the garlic onto soaked wooden toothpicks (see page 10) and grill on an oiled rack until soft, about 3 minutes, turning occasionally. Grill the vegetables until they are tender and lightly charred, turning as necessary for even cooking.

5   As the vegetables are cooked, transfer them to a bowl and cover with plastic wrap. When all the vegetables are done, serve them with the sauce.

231 FIRE-COOKED EGGPLANT WITH GARLIC, CILANTRO, AND LEMON

PREPARATION TIME *5 minutes* **COOKING TIME** *10 minutes* **SERVES 4**

4 small, long, thin Asian eggplants
2 plump garlic cloves, chopped

leaves from a small bunch of fresh cilantro
2 tbsp lemon juice, or to taste

4-6 tbsp virgin olive oil
salt and freshly ground black pepper

1   Grill the whole eggplants on an oiled rack until evenly charred and softened, about 10 minutes, turning occasionally.

2   Meanwhile, put the garlic, cilantro, lemon juice, and olive oil into a small blender and blend together. Season to taste, and adjust the amounts of lemon juice and olive oil, if necessary.

3   Remove the eggplants from the grill and cut a deep slash along the center of each one. Spoon the garlic, cilantro, and lemon mixture into the eggplants and serve.

232 GRILLED VEGETABLES WITH THAI DRESSING

PREPARATION TIME *15 minutes, plus 2 hours marinating* **COOKING TIME** *25–30 minutes* **SERVES 4**

1 lb orange-fleshed sweet
  potatoes
4 baby fennel bulbs
8 oz slim asparagus spears
1 bunch of scallions
1 lemon grass stem,
  crushed
fresh cilantro for garnish

THAI DRESSING
1 tbsp coarsely chopped
  fresh gingerroot
2 garlic cloves, crushed
1–2 fresh, hot red chiles,
  seeded and chopped
1¾ cups canned coconut
  milk

1 tbsp Thai fish sauce
grated zest and juice
  of 1 lime
1 tbsp peanut butter
1 tsp brown sugar

1. Put the whole sweet potatoes into a saucepan of cold water. Bring to a boil, then lower the heat and simmer until just tender, 15–20 minutes. Drain and leave until cool enough to handle, then cut into wedges.
2. Blanch the fennel in boiling water for 2–3 minutes; cool under running cold water, drain, and leave until cold. Blanch the asparagus for 1–2 minutes in the same way.
3. Put the sweet potato wedges, fennel, asparagus, scallions, and crushed lemon grass into a large, nonreactive dish.
4. Put the dressing ingredients into a blender and blend until smooth. Pour over the vegetables and stir so the vegetables are evenly coated, then cover and leave in a cool place for 2 hours.
5. Lift the vegetables from the dressing and discard the lemon grass. Grill the vegetables on an oiled rack, turning them occasionally, until tender and marked with charred lines: 5–6 minutes for asparagus and sweet potatoes, 5 minutes for fennel, and about 3 minutes for scallions. Serve garnished with fresh cilantro.

233 ENDIVE WITH STILTON AND WALNUTS

PREPARATION TIME *10 minutes* **COOKING TIME** *7–12 minutes* **SERVES 4**

2 large or 4 small heads of
  Belgian endive, halved
  lengthwise and cored
1 tbsp mild olive oil,
  plus extra for brushing

2 ripe but firm pears,
  thickly sliced
2 tbsp walnut oil
juice of 1 small lemon
salt and freshly ground
  black pepper

6 oz Stilton or other blue
  cheese, crumbled
½ tbsp fresh thyme leaves
½ cup chopped walnuts

1. Brush the endive with olive oil and grill on an oiled rack, turning and brushing regularly, until softened and charred: 7–9 minutes for smaller heads, 10–12 minutes for larger ones.
2. Meanwhile, grill the pear slices on the rack until softened.
3. Whisk the tablespoon of olive oil with the walnut oil and lemon juice.
4. Transfer the endive to warmed plates and season. Place the pears on the endive and scatter the cheese and thyme leaves over. Trickle the walnut oil mixture over the top, sprinkle with the walnuts, and serve.

234 VEGETABLE FAJITAS WITH AVOCADO AND TOMATO SALSA

PREPARATION TIME *10 minutes, plus 4 hours marinating* **COOKING TIME** *12–15 minutes* **SERVES 6**

2 red and 2 yellow bell
  peppers, quartered
3 zucchini, sliced
  diagonally
2 eggplants, sliced
  diagonally
6 oz baby corn, halved
  lengthwise
3 fresh, mild red chiles,
  quartered
6 tbsp olive oil
juice of 1 lime

2 tbsp chopped mixed
  fresh parsley, oregano,
  and thyme
freshly ground black
  pepper

AVOCADO AND TOMATO SALSA
1 large avocado, pitted
  and finely chopped
3 tbsp lime juice
½ fresh, hot red chile,
  seeded and minced

1 vine-ripened roma
  tomato, seeded
  and diced
½ red onion, finely diced
handful of fresh cilantro
  leaves, chopped

FOR SERVING
18 small flour tortillas
sour cream
fresh cilantro
lime wedges

1 Put all the vegetables, including the chiles, into a large bowl. Mix together the olive oil, lime juice, herbs, and black pepper. Stir into the vegetables, then cover and let marinate for about 4 hours, stirring occasionally.
2 Meanwhile, make the salsa by tossing the ingredients together. Cover and chill for 30 minutes.
3 Lift the vegetables from the marinade and grill on an oiled rack until softened and lightly charred. Remove the vegetables as soon as they are done, put into a bowl, and cover with plastic wrap.
4 Meanwhile, warm the tortillas at the side of the grill rack for 30 seconds on each side.
5 When the chiles are cool enough to handle, chop them.
6 Divide the vegetables and chiles among the tortillas. Top with the avocado salsa, spoon on some sour cream, and fold over. Serve with cilantro and lime wedges.

235 GRILLED MIXED VEGETABLE PLATTER

PREPARATION TIME *15 minutes, plus 2–24 hours marinating* **COOKING TIME** *15 minutes* **SERVES 8**

	MARINADE	FOR SERVING
1 papaya	⅔ cup virgin olive oil	finely chopped fresh
8 baby eggplants (leave	juice of 1½ limes	cilantro
the stem ends on)	2 garlic cloves, crushed	thick, plain yogurt flavored
8 baby pattypan squashes	½ fresh, hot chile, seeded	with garlic, chopped
1 red bell pepper, cut into	and finely chopped	fresh herbs, and
6 large strips	¼ cup dark soy sauce	seasoning
2 heads Belgian endive,	1 tbsp wholegrain mustard	
quartered lengthwise	1 tbsp paprika	
8 baby leeks, trimmed	½ tbsp ground cumin	
to about 8 inches		
4 oz oyster mushrooms		
8 vine-ripened cherry or		
baby roma tomatoes		

1 Make the marinade by combining all the ingredients. Set aside for at least 1 hour, or up to 24 hours, so the flavors can blend.
2 Cut the papaya into slices 1 inch wide and about 4 inches long. Cut shallow slashes in the surface of the eggplants and pattypan squashes.
3 Put the papaya and all the vegetables into a nonreactive dish. Stir in the marinade, then let marinate in a cool place for 1 hour.
4 Lift the papaya and vegetables from the marinade (reserving the marinade) and thread alternately onto skewers. Brush liberally with the reserved marinade.
5 Grill on an oiled rack until lightly charred and sizzling all over, about 15 minutes, turning occasionally and brushing with marinade. Remove from the grill, sprinkle with cilantro, and serve with the flavored yogurt.

236 SPICED LENTIL BURGERS

PREPARATION TIME *15 minutes, plus 1 hour chilling* **COOKING TIME** *45–50 minutes* **SERVES 4**

1 heaped cup green or	2 garlic cloves, finely	1 tbsp lemon juice
brown lentils	chopped	salt and freshly ground
2 large onions, finely	1 tsp ground cumin	black pepper
chopped	1 tsp ground coriander	flour seasoned with salt
2 carrots, finely chopped	3 tbsp chopped fresh	and pepper for coating
1 celery stalk, finely	parsley	Avocado, Tomato, and Red
chopped	3 tbsp chopped fresh	Pepper Salsa *(see
olive oil for frying	cilantro	page 174)*

1 Cook the lentils in boiling unsalted water until tender, 20–30 minutes. Drain well and let cool.
2 Fry the onions, carrots, and celery in a little olive oil until soft and lightly browned, about 10 minutes. Remove from the heat and stir in the lentils, garlic, spices, herbs, lemon juice, and seasoning. Blend in a food processor until coarse-fine and the mixture will hold together. Alternatively, mash with a potato masher.
3 With floured hands, form into 12 flat patties ½–¾ inch thick. Coat them in seasoned flour and pat in gently. Cover and chill for at least 1 hour, to firm up, or, preferably, overnight, so that the flavors can blend.
4 Grill in an oiled hinged basket, or directly on an oiled rack, until crisp and browned, 6–8 minutes, turning once. Serve with the avocado, tomato, and red pepper salsa.

237 FALAFEL BURGERS WITH YOGURT AND MINT RELISH

PREPARATION TIME *10 minutes, plus 2 hours chilling* **COOKING TIME** *10 minutes* **SERVES 4–6**

28 oz canned chickpeas,
  drained and rinsed
1 garlic clove, chopped
2 tbsp tahini
1 tsp ground cumin
1 tsp ground coriander
1 cup fresh bread crumbs
3 tbsp chopped fresh
  cilantro

salt and freshly ground
  black pepper
flour seasoned with salt
  and pepper for coating
pita breads and lettuce
  leaves for serving

YOGURT AND MINT RELISH
1 small garlic clove
1 cup thick, plain yogurt
¼ cup chopped fresh mint
dash of hot pepper sauce
small sprig of fresh mint
  for garnish

1 Put all the burger ingredients, except the flour, into a food processor and blend until the chickpeas are finely chopped, but do not let the mixture turn to a purée.
2 Transfer to a bowl and stir in about 2 tablespoons of water, kneading until the mixture holds together. With well-floured hands, form the mixture into eight 1-inch-thick patties. Chill for at least 2 hours.
3 To make the relish, crush the garlic with a pinch of salt, then mix it with the yogurt. Add the chopped mint, and season with hot pepper sauce and black pepper to taste. Cover and chill. Garnish with the mint sprig before serving.
4 Grill the burgers in an oiled hinged basket, or directly on an oiled rack, until crisp and browned, about 5 minutes on each side.
5 Meanwhile, warm the pita breads at the side of the grill rack for 30 seconds on each side. Split the pita breads open, add the falafel, and top with lettuce and the yogurt and mint relish.

238 ASPARAGUS WITH CRISP CRUMBS, EGG, AND OLIVE GREMOLATA

PREPARATION TIME *10 minutes* **COOKING TIME** *6 minutes* **SERVES 4**

1 lb slim asparagus spears*
olive oil for brushing
4 tbsp unsalted butter,
  diced
½ cup fresh, coarse bread
  crumbs

grated zest of 1 lemon
2 tbsp chopped fresh
  parsley
⅓ cup chopped green
  olives

salt and freshly ground
  black pepper
1 large hard-cooked egg,
  peeled and finely
  chopped
lemon wedges for serving

1 Trim the tough ends from the asparagus spears. Brush the asparagus with oil, then grill on an oiled rack until tender and lightly charred, about 6 minutes, turning halfway through. Take care that the spears do not become too charred.
2 Meanwhile, make the gremolata: Heat the butter in a heavy-based frying pan, add the bread crumbs, and fry until crisp and golden, stirring frequently. Remove from the heat and stir in the lemon zest, parsley, olives, and seasoning.
3 Transfer the asparagus to a plate, or plates, and season. Scatter the crumb mixture and chopped egg evenly over the spears, leaving the tips uncovered. Serve with lemon wedges.
* If only fatter asparagus spears are available, pare off the tougher skin from the lower parts of the stalks using a potato peeler. Parboil the spears in boiling water, drain, and dry well before brushing with oil for grilling.

239 SPICED TOFU BURGERS WITH FRESH CILANTRO CHUTNEY

PREPARATION TIME *20 minutes, plus 2–24 hours marinating* **COOKING TIME** *15 minutes* **SERVES 4**

4 oz leeks, cut into 2-inch
   lengths
1 large celery stalk, about
   4 oz, cut into 2-inch
   lengths
olive oil for frying
2 garlic cloves, finely
   chopped
¾ tsp cumin seeds, crushed
2 tsp sun-dried tomato
   paste
1 tsp curry paste

8 oz firm tofu, drained
6 tbsp fresh bread crumbs
salt and freshly ground
   black pepper
beaten egg
flour seasoned with salt
   and pepper for coating

FRESH CILANTRO CHUTNEY
1 cup coarsely chopped
   fresh cilantro
2 tsp grated fresh
   gingerroot
1 garlic clove
2 tsp lime juice
1–2 peppadews (bottled
   mild sweet piquante
   peppers)*, finely
   chopped
pinch of sugar

1. Finely shred the leeks and celery lengthwise.
2. Heat the oil in a frying pan, add the leeks and celery, and fry, stirring, until softened and lightly colored. Add the garlic toward the end of cooking. Stir in the cumin, tomato paste, and curry paste. Cook, stirring, for a couple of minutes longer. Remove from the heat.
3. Mash the tofu. Using your hands or a fork, mix the tofu with the vegetable mixture, bread crumbs, seasoning, and enough egg to bind the mixture together (be careful not to use too much egg). With floured hands, press firmly into eight ½- to ¾-inch-thick patties. Chill, uncovered, for at least 2 hours, or overnight.
4. Make the cilantro chutney: Put half the cilantro, the ginger, garlic, lime juice, peppadews, and 2 tablespoons of water in a blender and blend until smooth. Add the remaining cilantro and blend again, leaving some texture in the leaves. Season to taste with sugar, salt, and pepper. Transfer to a small serving bowl, cover, and chill for up to 30 minutes.
5. Grill the burgers on an oiled rack until browned, about 4 minutes on each side, turning carefully once. Serve with the fresh cilantro chutney.
* Instead of peppadews you can use ½ fresh, hot red chile, seeded and finely chopped

240 LEEK AND GOAT CHEESE BURGERS

PREPARATION TIME *15 minutes, plus 4 hours chilling* **COOKING TIME** *20–25 minutes* **SERVES 4**

2 cups diced potatoes
3 oz soft goat cheese
4 oz leeks, finely chopped
   (about 1 cup)
1 tbsp butter
2 oz feta cheese, crumbled

½ cup fresh bread crumbs
salt and freshly ground
   black pepper
olive oil for brushing

FOR SERVING
Green Salad with Herbs
   (see page 167) and/or
   mayonnaise (see
   page 179)

1. Cook the potatoes in boiling salted water until tender, then drain well. Return to the pan over a low heat and shake the pan gently to dry the potatoes. Remove from the heat. Mash the potatoes and beat in the goat cheese.
2. Fry the leeks in the butter until very soft and dry. Beat them into the potato, along with the feta cheese, bread crumbs, and seasoning, adding plenty of black pepper. Transfer to a plate, cover, and chill for at least 4 hours.
3. With floured hands, shape into eight 2½-inch-diameter patties. Brush with oil. Grill on an oiled rack until browned and crisp, about 3 minutes, then turn over and grill on the other side. Serve with the green salad with herbs and/or mayonnaise.

241 GRILLED BABY EGGPLANTS WITH MOROCCAN TOPPING

PREPARATION TIME *10 minutes* **COOKING TIME** *4–6 minutes* **SERVES 4**

8 baby eggplants
olive oil for brushing
1 tbsp chopped fresh
   cilantro

MOROCCAN TOPPING
about 2 tbsp virgin olive oil
½ tbsp harissa sauce
1 plump garlic clove,
   finely chopped
1 tsp cumin seeds,
   toasted and ground
½ tbsp paprika

4 small, vine-ripened roma
   tomatoes, finely
   chopped
salt and freshly ground
   black pepper
pinch of sugar, or to taste

1   Make the topping: Combine the olive oil and harissa, then mix in the garlic, cumin, and paprika. Stir in the tomatoes and seasoning and sugar to taste. Cover and set aside until required.

2   Halve the eggplants lengthwise, leaving the stem on. Brush with olive oil and sprinkle with seasoning. Grill, cut-side down, on an oiled rack over medium-high heat until browned in patches. Turn over and grill until tender, 2–3 minutes longer.

3   Pile the topping onto the hot eggplant halves. Sprinkle with the chopped cilantro. Transfer to a serving dish and serve warm or cold.

242 TOFU BROCHETTES

PREPARATION TIME *15 minutes, plus 4 hours marinating* **COOKING TIME** *10–12 minutes* **SERVES 4**

	TOFU MARINADE	BROCHETTE MARINADE
8 oz firm tofu, drained and cut into 1-inch cubes	**1 tbsp dark soy sauce**	**1 tbsp sherry vinegar**
8 boiling onions, peeled	**1 tbsp dry sherry**	**½ tbsp Dijon vinegar**
8 cherry or baby roma tomatoes	**1 tbsp toasted sesame oil**	**1 small garlic clove, finely chopped**
1 large yellow bell pepper, grilled, peeled, and cut lengthwise into 8 strips	**1 tsp Dijon mustard**	**6 tbsp olive oil**
	1 plump garlic clove, finely chopped	**½ tbsp finely chopped mixed fresh herbs**
	2 tsp rice wine vinegar	

1 Make the tofu marinade by combining all the ingredients. Add the tofu and turn the cubes over to make sure they are evenly coated. Cover and let marinate in a cool place for at least 4 hours, preferably overnight.
2 Meanwhile, blanch the onions for 2–3 minutes, drain, and refresh under cold running water. Drain again and let dry on paper towels.
3 Make the brochette marinade by shaking the ingredients together in a lidded jar. Season.
4 Lift the tofu from the marinade and thread onto skewers alternately with the vegetables. Brush with the brochette marinade.
5 Grill on an oiled rack until browned, about 8 minutes, turning regularly.

243 SWEET POTATOES WITH FETA AND BLACK OLIVE RELISH

PREPARATION TIME *15 minutes* **COOKING TIME** *14–18 minutes* **SERVES 4**

7 oz feta cheese, crumbled	**2 tsp herbes de Provence**	**1 large, orange-fleshed sweet potato, about 1 lb**
1 plump garlic clove, crushed	**¼ cup virgin olive oil, plus extra for brushing**	**fresh cilantro for garnish**
⅓ cup chopped oil-cured black olives	**freshly ground black pepper**	

1 Mash the feta cheese with the garlic, olives, herbs, olive oil, and black pepper. Set aside.
2 Cut the sweet potato lengthwise into eight wedges. Add to a pan of boiling water, return quickly to a boil, and boil for 3 minutes. Drain, rinse under running cold water, and drain again.
3 Dry the sweet potato wedges to remove any remaining moisture, then brush with olive oil. Grind some black pepper over them. Grill on an oiled rack until well browned on all sides and tender, 10–15 minutes.
4 Garnish the relish with cilantro and serve with the sweet potatoes.

244 ZUCCHINI BURGERS WITH DILL TZATZIKI

PREPARATION TIME *15 minutes, plus 2 hours chilling* **COOKING TIME** *15–20 minutes* **SERVES 4**

1 lb small zucchini, grated (about 4 cups)	**1 heaped tbsp chopped fresh mint**	DILL TZATZIKI
salt and freshly ground black pepper	**2 heaped tbsp chopped fresh parsley**	**2 cups plain yogurt, preferably sheep-milk yogurt**
3 cups fresh bread crumbs	**4 ciabatta or other bread rolls, split in half**	**2 tbsp chopped fresh dill**
2 eggs, lightly beaten		
6 scallions, minced		

1 Layer the zucchini with a good sprinkling of salt in a colander. Let drain for 30–60 minutes.
2 Meanwhile, preheat the oven to 375°F. Reserve ¼ cup of the bread crumbs and spread the remainder on a baking sheet. Bake until brown and crisp, about 10 minutes, stirring occasionally. Spread out on a plate and set aside to cool.
3 Rinse the zucchini thoroughly and squeeze firmly to expel as much water as possible, then pat dry between two clean kitchen towels.
4 Mix the zucchini with the reserved bread crumbs, the eggs, scallions, herbs, and black pepper. With floured hands, form into 18 patties about ½–¾ inches thick. Coat evenly and thoroughly with the toasted bread crumbs, pressing the crumbs on firmly. Leave uncovered in the refrigerator for 1 hour or so to firm up.
5 Make the tzatziki by beating the yogurt until smooth, then stir in the dill and seasoning.
6 Grill the burgers in an oiled hinged basket, or directly on an oiled grill rack, until browned and crisp on the base, 3–4 minutes, then turn carefully and grill on the other side.
7 Meanwhile, lightly toast the rolls at the side of the grill rack. Serve the burgers in the rolls, with the tzatziki spooned on top.

245 ASH-BAKED ACORN SQUASH

PREPARATION TIME *10 minutes* **COOKING TIME** *20–30 minutes* **SERVES 4**

4 one-portion-sized acorn squash	FOR SERVING	**freshly grated Parmesan cheese**
salt and freshly ground black pepper	**Pesto (see pages 172–174), flavored mayonnaise (see pages 180–181), unsalted butter, or heavy cream**	**freshly ground black pepper**

1 Using a sharp knife, slice the cap off each squash and set aside. Scoop out and discard the central seeds and strings. With a small, sharp knife, cut slashes in the flesh. Season inside the squash, then replace the lid.
2 Wrap the squash individually in roomy but well-sealed, double-thickness, heavy-duty foil packets. Cook in the embers of the fire until tender, 20–30 minutes, turning occasionally.
3 Remove from the fire and serve with the chosen accompaniment(s).
   VARIATION Halved butternut squash can be cooked in the same way. Allow one half of a small to medium-sized squash per person.

246 CANNELLINI BEAN AND RED PESTO BURGERS WITH AIOLI

PREPARATION TIME *10 minutes, plus 2–24 hours chilling* **COOKING TIME** *6–8 minutes* **SERVES 2**

14-oz can cannellini
  beans, drained
2½ tbsp Red Pesto *(see
  page 173)*
2½ tbsp chopped fresh
  parsley

2 tbsp snipped fresh chives
1 cup fresh bread crumbs,
  preferably ciabatta or
  sourdough
1 egg yolk

salt and freshly ground
  black pepper
olive oil for brushing
aïoli *(see page 106)* for
  serving

1 Put the beans, pesto, herbs, bread crumbs, egg yolk, and seasoning into a food processor and blend until evenly combined. Make sure the beans are not reduced to a completely smooth purée (some should remain coarsely chopped).
2 With wet hands, shape the mixture into four 3-inch-diameter patties. Cover and chill for at least 1 hour to firm up, or, preferably, overnight so the flavors can develop.
3 Brush the burgers with olive oil and grill in an oiled hinged basket, or directly on an oiled grill rack, until marked lightly with charred lines, 3–4 minutes . Turn them over and brown on the other side. Serve with the aïoli.

247 ASH-BAKED SWEET POTATOES

PREPARATION TIME *5 minutes* **COOKING TIME** *45 minutes* **SERVES 4**

4 orange-fleshed sweet
  potatoes, pricked

FOR SERVING
freshly grated Parmesan
  cheese or ricotta cheese
salt and freshly ground
  black pepper

Pesto *(see pages 172–174)*,
  flavored mayonnaise
  (see pages 180–181),
  or flavored butter *(see
  pages 187–189)*

1 Wrap the sweet potatoes individually in roomy but well-sealed, double-thickness, heavy-duty foil packets. Cook in the embers of the fire until tender, about 45 minutes, turning occasionally.
2 Remove from the fire and serve with the chosen accompaniment(s).

248 GRILLED CORN WITH SOY BUTTER

PREPARATION TIME *10 minutes* **COOKING TIME** *30 minutes* **SERVES 6**

6 fresh ears of corn
olive oil for brushing
6 tbsp unsalted butter,
  chopped

1½ tbsp dark soy sauce
¾ tsp Sichuan peppercorns,
  toasted and finely
  ground

1 tsp finely chopped fresh,
  hot red chile

1 Shuck the corn, then brush with olive oil. Wrap the ears individually in heavy-duty foil packets.
2 Cook the foil packets on a grill rack over medium-high heat for 20 minutes, turning occasionally for even cooking.
3 Meanwhile, heat the butter with the soy sauce, Sichuan peppercorns, and chile in a small pan at the side of the grill rack until melted. Keep warm to allow the flavors to infuse.
4 Unwrap the corn and brush with some of the butter. Grill on the rack until flecked with brown and tender, about 10 minutes, turning frequently and brushing with the butter. Serve with any remaining butter.

249 ASPARAGUS WITH SESAME, GINGER, AND LIME MAYONNAISE

PREPARATION TIME *10 minutes* **COOKING TIME** *6 minutes* **SERVES 4–6**

1 lb slim asparagus spears*	2–3 tsp toasted sesame oil	salt and freshly ground
olive oil for brushing	1 heaped tsp sesame seeds,	black pepper
	lightly toasted and	
SESAME, GINGER, AND LIME	crushed	
MAYONNAISE	1–2 tsp ginger juice**	
grated zest and juice of	1¼ cups mayonnaise	
2 small limes	*(see page 179)*	

1   Make the mayonnaise by stirring the lime zest and juice, sesame oil, sesame seeds, and ginger juice to taste into the mayonnaise. Check the seasoning and set aside until required.

2   Trim the tough ends from the asparagus. Brush the spears with olive oil, then grill on an oiled rack until tender and lightly charred, about 6 minutes, turning halfway through the cooking. Take care that the spears do not become too charred.

3   Season the spears and serve warm with the mayonnaise.

*   If only fatter asparagus spears are available, pare off the tougher skin from the lower parts of the stalks using a potato peeler. Parboil the spears in boiling water, drain, and dry well before brushing with oil and grilling.

**   Ginger juice is made by squeezing grated fresh gingerroot in a garlic press.

VARIATION For a simpler version, omit the mayonnaise and instead mix together 3 tablespoons virgin olive oil, 1 tablespoon toasted sesame oil, 1 tablespoon lime juice, and seasoning. Pour this over the cooked asparagus spears.

250 MUSHROOM SKEWERS

PREPARATION TIME *10 minutes* **COOKING TIME** *5 minutes* **SERVES 2–4**

1 lb fresh oyster	Basil and Broiled Tomato
mushrooms	Pesto *(see page 172)*,
lemon juice	Tomato Tartar Sauce
freshly ground black	*(see page 179)*, or
pepper	Sun-Dried Tomato and
2 tbsp unsalted butter,	Garlic Mayonnaise *(see*
melted	*page 180) for serving*

1   Sprinkle the mushrooms with a little lemon juice and season them with black pepper.

2   Thread the mushrooms onto oiled skewers and brush with the melted butter.

3   Grill on an oiled rack for 5 minutes, turning frequently. Serve with your choice of the suggested accompaniments.

ACCOMPANIMENTS

This chapter covers accompaniments to serve with both vegetarian and non-vegetarian dishes. It includes recipes that are cooked on the grill as well as some that are prepared in advance. Potatoes baked in their skins, in the embers of the fire, are probably the first thing that springs to mind when thinking of a side dish to serve with grilled food. Whole small winter squash and sweet potatoes are also delicious cooked by this method.

Bread comes next on the accompaniments list, but you don't have to buy the loaf or make it beforehand in the kitchen. You can bake it on the grill rack and then serve while it is still warm and fragrant. Yeasted breads, such as naan breads, can be baked in this way (see the pizza recipe on page 20 to get an idea of how this is done). This chapter also includes two recipes made in minutes by simply stirring the ingredients together, kneading or shaping, and then baking on the grill rack. One is Herb Damper Bread and the other is Sun-Dried Tomato, Olive, and Goat Cheese Bread.

Strong flavors are needed—creamy dishes don't sit easily alongside grilled foods, and delicately-flavored dishes are lost against the robust tastes of food from the grill. Sophisticated side dishes are also out of place, not only with the food but also the setting and atmosphere. Instead, try a fresh Caesar Salad or Marinated Mushrooms, to complement your meal perfectly.

CHAPTER 6

251 MUSHROOM AND SPINACH SALAD

PREPARATION TIME *10 minutes* **COOKING TIME** *5 minutes* **SERVES 4**

4 handfuls of baby spinach
leaves
2½ cups thinly sliced button
mushrooms
2½ tbsp olive oil

½ tbsp hazelnut or walnut
oil
2 tsp balsamic vinegar
½ tbsp wholegrain mustard

salt and freshly ground
black pepper
1–2 tbsp pine nuts, lightly
toasted

1   Put the spinach into a bowl and add the sliced mushrooms.
2   Just before serving, whisk the oils, vinegar, mustard, and seasoning together until emulsified.
Pour over the salad and toss lightly. Sprinkle with the pine nuts and serve.

252 FRUITED COUSCOUS

PREPARATION TIME *10 minutes, plus cooling* **COOKING TIME** *None* **SERVES 4**

2½ cups hot vegetable
stock
1¼ cups couscous
½ cup chopped dried
apricots
⅓ cup raisins
⅓ cup chopped pitted
prunes*

⅓ cup pine nuts, lightly
toasted
⅓ cup pistachio nuts,
lightly toasted
¼ cup chopped fresh
flat-leaf parsley
2 tbsp chopped fresh
cilantro

1 tbsp chopped fresh mint
¼ cup olive oil
grated zest and juice of
1 orange
salt and freshly ground
black pepper

1   Pour the stock over the couscous, stir with a fork, and let cool.
2   Fluff up the couscous with a fork, then fork in the fruits, nuts, and herbs.
3   Combine the olive oil with the orange zest and juice, and some seasoning. Whisk until
emulsified, then stir into the couscous.
*   Pitted dates or dried figs can be used instead.

253 COOKED MEDITERRANEAN
FENNEL SALAD

PREPARATION TIME *10 minutes* **COOKING TIME** *5 minutes* **SERVES 4**

2 tbsp virgin olive oil
3 small fennel bulbs,
thinly sliced
½ cup sun-dried tomatoes
in oil, drained

12 oil-cured black olives,
halved and pitted
2 tbsp balsamic vinegar
pinch of sugar, or to
taste

salt and freshly ground
black pepper
fresh herb fennel for
garnish

1   Heat the oil in a saucepan and add the fennel and 1 tablespoon of water. Cover and cook until
the fennel has softened slightly and the water has evaporated, about 5 minutes .
2   Stir in the tomatoes, olives, vinegar, and sugar and black pepper to taste. Only add salt if
necessary. Heat through, then let cool.
3   Serve the salad at room temperature, garnished with herb fennel.

254 CAESAR SALAD

PREPARATION TIME *10 minutes* **COOKING TIME** *5 minutes* **SERVES 4-6**

**6 handfuls of romaine
leaves, torn into pieces**

CROUTONS
5 tbsp olive oil
**2-3 slices of sourdough
bread, crusts removed,
cut into ½-inch cubes**
**2 garlic cloves, lightly
crushed**

DRESSING
1 egg yolk
**2 tsp wholegrain
mustard**
6 tbsp olive oil
**3 garlic cloves, finely
chopped**
2 tbsp red wine vinegar
**4-6 tbsp freshly grated
Parmesan cheese**

**3 anchovy fillets, drained
and chopped**
**freshly ground black
pepper**

1   To make the croûtons, heat the oil in a frying pan, add the bread cubes and the garlic, and fry until crisp and lightly browned. Transfer to paper towels to drain.

2   Make the dressing: Mix the egg yolk with the mustard, then slowly pour in the oil, whisking. Add the garlic, vinegar, Parmesan cheese, anchovy fillets, and plenty of black pepper. Whisk until thoroughly mixed.

3   Just before serving, put the romaine into a salad bowl. Pour the dressing over and toss to combine, then add the croûtons and toss once more.

255 PARMESAN POLENTA

PREPARATION TIME *10 minutes, plus 1 hour chilling* **COOKING TIME** *20 minutes* **SERVES 4**

3 cups water
**salt and freshly ground
black pepper**
1⅛ cups instant polenta

**3 tbsp unsalted butter,
diced**
**1 cup freshly grated
Parmesan cheese**

**2 tbsp finely chopped
fresh parsley**

1   Bring the water and a large pinch of salt to a boil in a large saucepan. Add the polenta in a thin, steady stream, stirring constantly, and continue to stir until the polenta is thick and comes away from the sides of the pan.

2   Remove the pan from the heat and stir in the butter, Parmesan, parsley, and plenty of black pepper. Let cool for about 10 minutes.

3   Spread out a large sheet of plastic wrap. Spoon the polenta down the center and fold the wrap over it. Shape into a smooth cylinder 3½ inches wide and about 10 inches long, using the wrap to help you. Chill for 1 hour.

4   Remove the plastic wrap. With a large, sharp knife, cut the polenta roll into eight equal slices. Grill on an oiled rack until crisp and golden, about 3 minutes on each side, turning once.

256 MARINATED ZUCCHINI WITH LEMON AND MINT

PREPARATION TIME *10 minutes* **COOKING TIME** *3 minutes* **SERVES 4–6**

1 lb baby zucchini	DRESSING	salt and freshly ground
olive oil for brushing	5 tbsp extra virgin olive oil	black pepper
4 scallions, white parts	2 tbsp lemon juice	
only, finely chopped	1 garlic clove, chopped	
small fresh mint leaves	1 tbsp chopped fresh mint	
for garnish	pinch of sugar	

1. Using the point of a small, sharp knife, cut a shallow slash along the length of each zucchini. Brush with olive oil and grill the zucchini on an oiled rack until lightly charred and softened, about 3 minutes, turning once.
2. Meanwhile, make the dressing by whisking all the ingredients together.
3. Transfer the zucchini to a bowl and stir in the dressing, then cover and leave until cold.
4. To serve, add the scallions, adjust the seasoning, and scatter the mint leaves over.

257 ZUCCHINI SLICES WITH CHIVES AND TOMATOES

PREPARATION TIME *10 minutes* **COOKING TIME** *10 minutes* **SERVES 4**

⅓ cup finely snipped fresh	1 lb vine-ripened tomatoes,	4 small zucchini, about
chives	peeled, seeded, and	4 oz each
7 tbsp virgin olive oil, plus	finely chopped	
extra for brushing	salt and freshly ground	
finely grated zest and juice	black pepper	
of 1 lime		

1. Put the chives into a blender with the oil and lime juice. Blend to a purée, then pour into a bowl and stir in the lime zest, tomatoes, and seasoning.
2. Using a vegetable peeler, cut the zucchini lengthwise into long, thin strips. Arrange them in pairs and thread onto skewers. Brush the zucchini generously with olive oil and season them.
3. Grill on an oiled rack over high heat until tender and lightly charred, about 10 minutes, turning frequently and brushing with oil.
4. Remove from the grill and spoon some of the dressing over the zucchini. Serve with the remaining dressing.

258 SUN-DRIED TOMATO, OLIVE, AND GOAT CHEESE BREAD

PREPARATION TIME *15 minutes* **COOKING TIME** *20–25 minutes* **SERVES 4–6**

3¼ cups all-purpose flour
½ tbsp baking soda
salt and freshly ground
    black pepper
4–6 tbsp unsalted butter,
    diced

⅛ cup sun-dried tomatoes
    in oil, drained and
    chopped
12 oil-cured black olives,
    pitted and coarsely
    chopped

3 oz firm goat cheese,
    cut into small cubes
about 1 cup buttermilk or
    soured milk*

1. Sift the flour and soda into a bowl. Add seasoning. Toss in the butter and rub in with fingertips. Stir in the sun-dried tomatoes, olives, and cheese, followed by enough buttermilk or soured milk to form a medium-firm, soft but not sticky dough. If necessary, add a little more liquid.
2. Knead lightly on a floured surface until the dough just begins to come together and form a ball; do not over-handle or the bread will be heavy. Place on a lightly floured baking sheet and pat to a round no more than 1 inch thick.
3. Put the bread in the center of a large, oiled, double-thickness of heavy-duty foil. Fold the sides of the foil over the bread and pleat them firmly together to seal.
4. Cook on the grill rack over medium-hot heat until browned and cooked through (it should sound hollow when tapped), 10–12 minutes on each side. Serve warm, cut in thick wedges.
* To sour milk, add 1 tablespoon of lemon juice to 1 cup milk.

259 TOMATOES WITH TAPENADE AND PARSLEY TOPPING

PREPARATION TIME *10 minutes* **COOKING TIME** *6–8 minutes* **SERVES 4**

8 large, ripe but firm roma tomatoes, halved

olive oil for brushing

TOPPING

½ cup dry bread crumbs

2 tbsp extra virgin olive oil

2 tbsp tapenade

¼ cup chopped fresh flat-leaf parsley

salt and freshly ground black pepper

1 Brush the skin side of the tomatoes with oil.
2 Make the topping: Combine the bread crumbs with the oil, tapenade, and parsley. Season, taking care over the amount of salt you add. Divide the topping among the tomato halves, pressing it down lightly onto the cut sides.
3 Grill, skin-side down, on an oiled rack for 6–8 minutes.

260 PITA CHIPS WITH GARLIC AND HERBS

PREPARATION TIME *10 minutes* **COOKING TIME** *2–4 minutes* **SERVES 4**

4 pita breads

3 garlic cloves

salt and freshly ground black pepper

6 tbsp virgin olive oil

1 tsp dried oregano

1 tsp dried thyme

pinch of fennel seeds, finely crushed

1 Split each pita bread open into two halves.
2 Crush the garlic with a pinch of salt, then mix with the olive oil, herbs, seeds, and black pepper. Brush this over the inner surfaces of the pita bread halves.
3 Grill on an oiled rack until golden, 1–2 minutes on each side. Remove and let cool. Break the pita breads into pieces for serving.

261 GRILLED VEGETABLE PACKETS

PREPARATION TIME *10 minutes* **COOKING TIME** *8–10 minutes* **SERVES 4**

8 oz mixed mushrooms, such as shiitake, oyster, and cremini, thickly sliced

5 oz broccoli, broken into small florets

2 zucchini, cut lengthwise into slim batons

8 scallions, cut into 1-inch lengths

1½ tbsp peanut oil

2 tsp toasted sesame oil

2 tbsp rice wine

¼ cup soy sauce

2 garlic cloves, finely chopped

2-inch piece fresh gingerroot, finely chopped

1 tsp cardamom seeds, finely crushed

freshly ground black pepper

1 Pile the vegetables in the center of four 12-inch double-thickness squares of heavy-duty foil, making sure each portion has a good mix of vegetables. Fold up the sides.
2 Combine all the remaining ingredients. Divide among the vegetables, then twist the foil edges together to seal tightly.
2 Cook the packets at the side of the grill rack until the vegetables are tender, 8–10 minutes.

262 MASALA POTATO WEDGES

PREPARATION TIME *10 minutes* **COOKING TIME** *20–25 minutes* **SERVES 4**

2 large potatoes, unpeeled	**½ tbsp ground coriander**	**2 tbsp sun-dried tomato**
salt	**pinch of hot chile powder**	**paste**
1 tsp ground cumin	**2 tbsp olive oil**	**2 tbsp lemon juice**

1 Cook the whole potatoes in a pan of boiling, salted water until just tender, 15–20 minutes. Drain and leave until cool enough to handle, then remove the skins. Cut each potato lengthwise into eight wedges.
2 Mix together the spices, oil, sun-dried tomato paste, lemon juice, and 1 tablespoon of water.
3 Put the potatoes into a shallow dish, spoon the spice mixture evenly over them, and stir to ensure all the wedges are coated.
4 Grill the wedges on an oiled rack until tender and marked with charred lines, 5–6 minutes.

263 GARLICKY POTATO SLICES

PREPARATION TIME *10 minutes* **COOKING TIME** *20–25 minutes* **SERVES 4**

1¼ lb long white potatoes,	**2 garlic cloves**	FOR COOKING (OPTIONAL)
unpeeled	**¼ cup virgin olive oil**	**handful of fresh thyme or**
salt and freshly ground		**rosemary twigs**
black pepper		

1 Cook the potatoes in boiling water until just tender. Drain and, when cool enough to handle, cut into ½-inch-thick slices. Season the potatoes with plenty of black pepper.
2 Crush the garlic with a pinch of salt, then mix with the oil. Brush over the potato slices.
3 Put the optional herb twigs on the fire. Grill the potato slices on an oiled rack until crisp and lightly charred, about 5 minutes on each side.

264 HERB DAMPER BREADS

PREPARATION TIME *10 minutes* **COOKING TIME** *6–8 minutes* **SERVES 4-6**

3¼ cups all-purpose flour	**chopped fresh mixed herbs,**	**2-4 tbsp butter, melted**
4 tsp baking powder	**such as chives, parsley,**	**about 1½ cups milk**
salt and freshly ground	**thyme, tarragon,**	
black pepper	**oregano, and rosemary**	

1 Sift the flour, baking powder, and seasoning into a bowl. Stir in the herbs, then quickly stir in the butter and enough milk to make a soft but not sticky dough that comes together. Divide into eight equal pieces.
2 With floured hands, pat each piece into a round about ½ inch thick.
3 Grill the breads on an oiled rack until they are crisp, brown, and puffy, 3–4 minutes on each side. Serve warm.

265 ASH-BAKED POTATOES WITH SUN-DRIED TOMATO, BASIL, AND OLIVE BUTTER

PREPARATION TIME *5 minutes* **COOKING TIME** *1¼–1½ hours* **SERVES 4**

4 russet potatoes, about 10 oz each	SUN-DRIED TOMATO, BASIL, AND OLIVE BUTTER	**4 sun-dried tomatoes in oil, drained and minced**
2 tbsp olive oil	**½ cup unsalted butter, softened**	**1 tbsp chopped fresh basil**
salt and freshly ground black pepper	**3 tbsp finely chopped oil-cured black olives**	

1. Preheat the oven to 400°F. Prick the potatoes and bake in the oven until almost tender, 40–50 minutes.
2. Meanwhile, make the flavored butter. Beat the butter until softened, then add the remaining ingredients and beat together until evenly blended.
3. Spoon the flavored butter onto a sheet of plastic wrap or parchment paper. Using the wrap or paper to help, shape the butter into a roll about 1½ inches in diameter. Wrap tightly and chill until required. Cut into slices to serve. Alternatively, pack the butter into ramekin dishes.
4. Remove the potatoes from the oven and leave until cool enough to handle. Rub the skins liberally with olive oil and sprinkle with salt and pepper. Wrap individually in three layers of heavy-duty foil.
5. Push the packets into the embers of the grill fire and cook until tender and the skins are crisp, 30–40 minutes. Turn frequently so the potatoes cook evenly and do not burn. Serve the potatoes with the flavored butter (only about half will be needed). Warn people that the potatoes inside the packets will be very hot.
* Alternatively, serve with Arugula and Goat Cheese Pesto (see page 173).

266 POTATO SALAD

PREPARATION TIME *10 minutes* **COOKING TIME** *15 minutes* **SERVES 4**

1 lb round red or yellow flesh boiling potatoes	**⅓ cup virgin olive oil**
salt and freshly ground black pepper	**2½ tbsp tarragon vinegar**
2 shallots, finely chopped	**finely chopped fresh flat-leaf parsley or chives**

1. Put the potatoes in a saucepan of salted water and bring to a boil. Lower the heat and simmer until the potatoes are tender through to the center, but still firm.
2. Meanwhile, put the shallots, oil, vinegar, and seasoning in a lidded jar and shake vigorously until the dressing has emulsified.
3. Drain the potatoes and slice them thickly into a salad bowl. Pour the dressing over them, sprinkle with some parsley or chives, and toss everything together. Let cool before serving.

267 PEPPER AND ASPARAGUS NOODLE SALAD

PREPARATION TIME *15 minutes*   **COOKING TIME** *15 minutes*   **SERVES 4**

12 oz fettuccine

8 oz slim asparagus spears

½ cup virgin olive oil,
   plus extra for brushing

2 large, red bell peppers,
   grilled *(see page 20)*,
   peeled, and sliced

4 sun-dried tomatoes
   in oil, drained and sliced

2 tbsp salted capers, well
   rinsed and dried

10 Kalamata olives, pitted
   and sliced

1½ tbsp balsamic vinegar

salt and freshly ground
   black pepper

3 tbsp chopped fresh basil

1. Cook the pasta in a large saucepan of boiling salted water according to the package directions, until al dente. Drain well.
2. Meanwhile, blanch the asparagus in boiling water for 3 minutes; drain well and pat dry.
3. Heat a heavy, ridged, cast-iron grill pan. Brush the asparagus with olive oil and pan-grill until charred and tender, 3–4 minutes. Remove and chop into short lengths.
4. Toss the pasta with the asparagus, red peppers, sun-dried tomatoes, capers, and olives.
5. Whisk together the oil, vinegar, and seasoning. Trickle this dressing over the salad, add the basil, and gently toss everything together.

268 NEW POTATO SKEWERS WITH BASIL AÏOLI

PREPARATION TIME *10 minutes* **COOKING TIME** *15-20 minutes* **SERVES 4**

1 lb boiling potatoes, halved if large	BASIL AÏOLI	**1 tbsp lemon juice**
3 tbsp olive oil	**2 heaped cups fresh basil leaves**	**¾ cup olive oil**
salt and freshly ground black pepper	**1 garlic clove**	
	1 egg yolk	

1 Make the aïoli: Put the basil, garlic, egg yolk, and lemon juice into a blender or food processor. Add a little of the oil and blend together. With the machine running, slowly add the remaining oil. Season and transfer to a bowl.

2 Put the potatoes in a saucepan of salted water and bring to a boil. Lower the heat and simmer until the potatoes are almost tender. Drain well, then return to the pan and add the oil and seasoning. Toss and shake the potatoes around to coat with oil.

3 Thread the potatoes onto skewers and grill on an oiled rack until tender, 7-8 minutes, turning regularly. Serve the potatoes with the basil aïoli.

269 MARINATED MUSHROOMS

PREPARATION TIME *5 minutes, plus 12 hours marinating* **COOKING TIME** *15-20 minutes* **SERVES 4**

1 lb small mushrooms	**2 fresh thyme sprigs**	**shredded fresh basil or**
2 tbsp olive oil	**2 tbsp tomato paste**	**flat-leaf parsley for**
6 tbsp white wine	**1 tbsp lemon juice, or**	**garnish**
1 cup fresh vegetable stock or water	**to taste**	
2 tsp black peppercorns	**salt and freshly ground black pepper**	
1 bay leaf, torn across	**4 tomatoes, chopped**	

1 Put the mushrooms, oil, wine, stock, peppercorns, herbs, and tomato paste into a saucepan. Bring to a boil, then cover and simmer until the mushrooms are tender, 10-15 minutes.

2 Using a slotted spoon, transfer the mushrooms from the liquid to a bowl. Boil the liquid hard until reduced to a light sauce. Add the lemon juice and seasoning. Pour this over the mushrooms, add the tomatoes, and let cool. Cover and keep in a cool place for 12 hours.

3 To serve, stir the mushrooms and scatter the shredded herbs over the top.

270 GRILLED ONION SLICES

PREPARATION TIME *10 minutes* **COOKING TIME** *8 minutes* **SERVES 4**

2 large red onions, cut into ½-inch-thick rounds	**salt and freshly ground black pepper**	**freshly grated pecorino or Parmesan cheese**
olive oil for brushing		**for sprinkling**

1 Thread the onion rounds onto skewers, pushing the skewers in from side to side so the onion rounds lie flat. Brush with olive oil.

2 Grill on an oiled rack for 2 minutes. Lift the skewers and give them a quarter turn, to create a crisscross pattern of charred lines. Grill for 2 minutes longer, then turn the onions over and repeat on the other side.

3 Transfer to a dish, season, and sprinkle with pecorino or Parmesan cheese. Serve straightaway.

271 CARAMELIZED SHALLOTS

PREPARATION TIME *5 minutes* **COOKING TIME** *40 minutes* **SERVES 4**

1 lb shallots, peeled
3 fresh thyme sprigs
1 bay leaf, torn across
2 tbsp brown sugar

few dashes of balsamic
   vinegar, to taste
2 tbsp unsalted butter,
   diced

salt and freshly ground
   black pepper

1 Put the shallots in the center of a large sheet of double-thickness, heavy-duty foil, nestling the thyme sprigs and bay leaf among them. Fold the foil loosely over the shallots and twist the edges together to seal them firmly.
2 Put the packet on the side of the grill rack and cook for 30 minutes.
3 Open the foil (the shallots should be soft). Carefully stir in the sugar, sprinkle with a little balsamic vinegar, and dot with the butter. Season, and re-seal the foil. Return to the grill rack and cook for 10 minutes longer, by which time the shallots should be a rich golden brown.

272 MIXED TOMATO SALAD

PREPARATION TIME *10 minutes* **COOKING TIME** *None* **SERVES 4**

2 oz watercress
2 tbsp pine nuts
1 small garlic clove
⅓ cup sun-dried tomatoes
   in oil, drained and
   shredded, plus ¼ cup oil
   from the jar

2 tbsp freshly grated
   Parmesan cheese
salt and freshly ground
   black pepper
6 oz vine-ripened roma
   tomatoes, quartered

6 oz cherry tomatoes,
   halved
3 ripe, beefsteak tomatoes,
   chopped

1 Put the watercress, pine nuts, garlic, and 2 tablespoons of the oil in a food processor or small blender and blend until almost smooth.
2 With the motor still running, slowly trickle in the remaining oil. Add the cheese and blend briefly, then add seasoning.
3 Toss all the tomatoes with the dressing and serve as soon as possible.

273 ASIAN BREAD SALAD

PREPARATION TIME *10 minutes* **COOKING TIME** *None* **SERVES 3-4**

1 naan bread, cut into
   ½-inch pieces
flesh from 1 ripe mango,
   cut into ½-inch pieces
5-6 scallions, including
   a little green, finely
   chopped

1 red bell pepper, seeded
   and diced
1 fresh, hot red chile,
   seeded and finely
   chopped (optional)
3 tbsp chopped fresh
   cilantro leaves

1 small garlic clove,
   chopped
salt and freshly ground
   black pepper
2 tbsp lime juice
6 tbsp plain yogurt
1 tbsp mint jelly

1 Toss the naan, mango, scallions, red pepper, optional chile, and cilantro together.
2 Crush the garlic to a paste with a pinch of salt and mix with the lime juice, yogurt, mint jelly, and black pepper. Stir into the salad. Serve as soon as possible.

274 RATATOUILLE SALAD

PREPARATION TIME *10 minutes, plus 1 hour draining* **COOKING TIME** *50 minutes* **SERVES 4-6**

2 eggplants, sliced
salt and freshly ground
 black pepper
olive oil for cooking
2 red bell peppers, sliced

6 small zucchini, thickly
 sliced
1 large onion, thinly sliced
3 garlic cloves, crushed
 and chopped

2 large, ripe tomatoes,
 chopped
a few sprigs of fresh thyme,
 marjoram, and parsley
leaves from a few sprigs
 of fresh basil, shredded

1   Sprinkle the eggplants with salt and let drain in a colander for 1 hour. Rinse them thoroughly, then dry well.

2   Heat a little oil in a large frying pan, add the eggplant slices, in batches if necessary, and fry until lightly browned. Remove and drain on paper towels.

3   Add the red peppers to the pan and fry for a few minutes until softened, but take care not to overcook them. Remove to paper towels.

4   Fry the zucchini (add a little more oil if necessary) until just beginning to soften, stirring occasionally. Remove to paper towels.

5   Fry the onion (add a little more oil if necessary) until softened, stirring frequently. Stir in the garlic and tomatoes for few minutes, then return the other vegetables to the pan and add the thyme, marjoram, and parsley. Season lightly, and add 2 tablespoons of oil, if desired. Cover and cook gently for 30–35 minutes, stirring occasionally.

6   Stir in the basil, remove from the heat, and let cool, uncovered. Serve at room temperature.

275 CILANTRO NOODLE SALAD

PREPARATION TIME *10 minutes* **COOKING TIME** *5 minutes* **SERVES 4**

8 oz dried Chinese egg noodles	2 tbsp Thai fish sauce	3 tbsp chopped fresh cilantro
1 garlic clove, finely crushed	1½ tbsp toasted sesame oil grated zest and juice of 1 lime	2 tbsp Japanese pickled ginger*, shredded
6 scallions, thinly sliced on the diagonal	2 tbsp peanut oil	few drops of chile oil
1 tbsp soy sauce	2 tbsp sesame seeds, lightly toasted	freshly ground black pepper

1 Cook the noodles in a saucepan of boiling water, according to the package directions.
2 Meanwhile, combine all the remaining ingredients.
3 Drain the noodles in a colander, then tip into a serving bowl. Toss with the dressing.
* Japanese pickled ginger can be bought from Asian markets and some supermarkets, but it is very easy to make. Combine 6 tablespoons rice vinegar, 1 tablespoon sugar, 1 teaspoon salt, and a 2-oz piece fresh gingerroot, very thinly sliced, in a small saucepan. Bring to a boil and simmer for 1–2 minutes, then let cool. The pickled ginger can be stored in a lidded jar in the refrigerator for up to 1 month.

276 GREEN SALAD WITH HERBS

PREPARATION TIME *10 minutes* **COOKING TIME** *None* **SERVES 4-6**

4 handfuls of mixed salad leaves, such as mâche, frisée, arugula, and radicchio, torn into bite-sized pieces	4 tbsp chopped mixed fresh herbs, such as chervil, marjoram, flat-leaf parsley, dill, tarragon, and mint	¼ cup extra virgin olive oil 1½ tbsp balsamic vinegar salt and freshly ground black pepper

1 Toss the salad leaves and herbs together in a salad bowl.
2 Whisk the oil with the vinegar and seasoning until emulsified. Pour over the salad and toss so the leaves are evenly coated. Serve within 30 minutes.

277 ASIAN COLESLAW

PREPARATION TIME *10 minutes* **COOKING TIME** *None* **SERVES 4-6**

½ small head white cabbage, about 5 oz	1 carrot, finely shredded	DRESSING
½ head napa cabbage, about 7 oz, finely shredded	¼ cup chopped canned water chestnuts	1 tbsp soy sauce
		½ tbsp toasted sesame oil
		3 tbsp orange juice
2 small fennel bulbs, thinly sliced		1½ tbsp rice wine vinegar
		2 tsp grated fresh gingerroot

1 Discard the outer leaves of the white cabbage. Cut the piece in half and cut away the core and any large ribs. Finely shred the cabbage. Put into a large bowl with the napa cabbage, fennel, carrot, and water chestnuts.
2 Make the dressing by whisking all the ingredients together until emulsified. Pour over the salad and toss so the leaves are evenly coated. Serve within 30 minutes.

278 WILTED TOMATOES

PREPARATION TIME *10 minutes* **COOKING TIME** *15 minutes* **SERVES 4**

7 tbsp virgin olive oil
2 shallots, finely chopped
2 garlic cloves, finely
    chopped
2 anchovy fillets, chopped

1 tsp chile oil
1 lb roma tomatoes,
    peeled, seeded, and
    finely diced

1 tbsp sun-dried tomato
    paste
salt and freshly ground
    black pepper

1   Warm the olive oil in a saucepan. Add the shallots, garlic, and anchovy, and sweat very gently until the shallots have softened and the flavors have mellowed.
2   Add the chile oil, tomatoes, and tomato paste to the pan. Continue to cook gently until the tomatoes wilt and soften, 3–4 minutes. Taste for seasoning and add salt and pepper if necessary. Serve while still warm.

279 SUMMER TABOULEH

PREPARATION TIME *10 minutes* **COOKING TIME** *None* **SERVES 4**

1¼ cups bulghur wheat
2–3 garlic cloves, crushed
1 cup oil-cured black olives,
    pitted
3 vine-ripened tomatoes,
    chopped
6 scallions, finely chopped

2 tbsp chopped fresh
    cilantro
1 tbsp chopped fresh mint
1 tbsp chopped fresh
    flat-leaf parsley
6 sun-dried tomatoes in oil,
    drained and sliced

3 tbsp virgin olive oil
juice of 1 lemon
salt and freshly ground
    black pepper

1   Put the bulghur wheat into a bowl and pour over boiling water to cover. Let soak for 30 minutes.
2   Drain off any remaining water.
3   Fold all the remaining ingredients into the bulghur, using plenty of seasoning.

280 BEET SALAD

PREPARATION TIME *10 minutes, plus 30 minutes chilling* **COOKING TIME** *None* **SERVES 4**

1 cup plain yogurt
freshly ground black
    pepper
1 lb cooked beets, peeled
    and cut into ½-inch cubes

leaves from a small bunch
    of fresh cilantro,
    chopped
2 oz small arugula leaves
5–6 oz feta cheese, cubed

chopped walnuts for
    garnish (optional)

1   Season the yogurt with black pepper, then stir in the beet cubes and chopped cilantro. Chill for 30 minutes.
2   Make a ring of arugula on a deep serving plate. Pile the beet mixture in the center and scatter the feta cheese over the top. Sprinkle with the optional walnuts and serve.

281 WATERCRESS, ENDIVE, AND ORANGE SALAD

PREPARATION TIME *15 minutes* **COOKING TIME** *None* **SERVES 4**

1 large bunch of
   watercress, coarse
   stems removed
1 fennel bulb, cored and
   thinly sliced across

1 red onion, very thinly
   sliced
2 heads Belgian endive,
   leaves separated, torn
   into pieces, if desired

2–3 juicy oranges
3 tbsp virgin olive oil
salt and freshly ground
   black pepper

1   Combine the watercress, fennel, red onion, and endive in a salad bowl.
2   Working over a bowl to catch the juice and using a small, sharp knife, carefully cut off the orange peel and pith. Put the oranges on a plate (again to catch the juice) and cut across into slices. Add the slices to the salad and the orange juice from the plate into the bowl of orange juice.
3   Whisk the oil with the orange juice and season to taste. Pour over the salad and toss to mix. Serve within 30 minutes.

SALSAS, MARINADES, SAUCES, AND BUTTERS

The recipes in this chapter can all be used to turn plain grilled food into a real treat. Most marinades are mixtures of oil (which moistens the food), an acid ingredient (which tenderizes), and flavorings. Marinades are best made in advance (especially if the food will not be marinated for long) to allow the flavors time to develop. Don't overdo the oil, as this can cause a flareup.

Let foods marinate or absorb a rub or paste in a cool place rather than the refrigerator, to avoid dulling the flavor. If foods are refrigerated, return them to room temperature 30–60 minutes before grilling. The more tender a food, the shorter the time it should be marinated, otherwise the acid in a marinade will make it soft. Use nonreactive dishes for marinating, because acids do not react with them. Allow about ½ cup of marinade per pound of food. Cutting slashes in food will allow the marinade or rub to penetrate. Drain marinated food and pat dry before cooking (moisture prevents it from browning), and scrape off any particles such as herbs.

Honey, sugar, or maple syrup-based mixtures give a sweet, rich coating to grilled food. However, they can burn, so are best brushed on halfway through cooking, or just before the end. Herb and spice rubs, which give a deliciously crisp finish, can be either rubbed into the food or combined with a little oil first.

282 PESTO

PREPARATION TIME *10 minutes* **COOKING TIME** *None* **SERVES 4**

2 garlic cloves, chopped
2 handfuls of fresh basil
  leaves
⅛ cup pine nuts

⅔ cup olive oil
½ cup freshly grated
  Parmesan cheese

salt and freshly ground
  black pepper

1 Put the garlic, basil, and pine nuts into a small blender or food processor. Blend to a paste. With the motor running, slowly pour in the oil to make a creamy paste.
2 Add the cheese, season to taste, and blend briefly.

283 FRESH COCONUT, LEMON GRASS, AND CHILE PESTO

PREPARATION TIME *10 minutes* **COOKING TIME** *None* **SERVES 4**

½ cup freshly grated
  coconut
3–4 lemon grass stems,
  outer layers discarded,
  chopped

1 plump garlic clove,
  chopped
1 fresh, mild red chile,
  seeded and chopped

juice of 1 lime or small
  lemon
4–6 tbsp peanut oil
salt

1 Put the coconut, lemon grass, garlic, chile, and juice into a small blender or food processor.
2 With the motor running, slowly pour in the oil to make a thick sauce. Season with salt.

284 BASIL AND BROILED TOMATO PESTO

PREPARATION TIME *10 minutes* **COOKING TIME** *5–10 minutes* **SERVES 4-6**

12 oz vine-ripened roma
  tomatoes
1 cup fresh basil leaves
2 garlic cloves, chopped
⅔ cup chopped blanched
  almonds

½ cup chopped walnuts
½ cup fruity olive oil
½ cup freshly grated
  pecorino cheese
salt and freshly ground
  black pepper

sun-dried tomato paste
  or a pinch of sugar
  (optional)

1 Preheat the broiler and line the broiler pan with foil. Broil the tomatoes, turning them frequently, until they are blistered and lightly charred. Leave until cool enough to handle, then remove the blackened patches.
2 Put the broiled tomatoes, basil leaves, garlic, nuts, and a little of the oil into a small blender or food processor. Pulse until chopped together.
3 With the motor running, slowly pour in the rest of the oil to make a paste. Add the cheese. Season and add a little tomato paste or sugar, if necessary.

285 ARUGULA AND GOAT CHEESE PESTO

PREPARATION TIME *10 minutes* **COOKING TIME** *None* **SERVES 6**

1 garlic clove, peeled	2 tbsp freshly grated
3 tbsp shelled pistachio	Parmesan cheese
nuts	scant 1 cup olive oil
4 oz soft goat cheese	salt and freshly ground
3 oz arugula	black pepper

1 Put the garlic, nuts, goat cheese, arugula, and Parmesan into a small blender or food processor with a little of the oil. Blend together briefly.

2 With the motor running, pour in the remaining oil. Season.

286 RED PESTO

PREPARATION TIME *5 minutes* **COOKING TIME** *20 minutes* **SERVES 4**

1 large, red bell pepper	1 plump garlic clove,	½ cup freshly grated
3 sun-dried tomatoes	chopped	pecorino or Parmesan
in oil, drained and	⅓ cup pine nuts	cheese
chopped	about 5 tbsp virgin olive oil	salt

1 Preheat the oven to 400°F. Roast the pepper until it starts to soften and the skin begins to blister, about 20 minutes. Remove from the oven and leave until cool enough to handle.

2 Peel off the skin and discard, along with the seeds. Chop the flesh and put into a small blender or food processor with the sun-dried tomatoes, garlic, and pine nuts.

3 With the motor running, slowly pour in the oil to make a paste. Add the cheese. Season with salt.

287 CILANTRO, GINGER, AND CASHEW NUT PESTO

PREPARATION TIME *10 minutes* **COOKING TIME** *None* **SERVES 4**

1 cup fresh cilantro leaves
2 tbsp grated fresh
  gingerroot
½ cup chopped cashew nuts
2 garlic cloves, chopped

juice of 1 lime or small
  lemon
½–¾ cup olive oil
salt and freshly ground
  black pepper

1 Put the cilantro, ginger, cashew nuts, garlic, and lime or lemon juice into a small blender or food processor. Blend to a paste.
2 With the motor running, slowly pour in the oil to make a creamy paste. Season to taste.

288 DILL PESTO

PREPARATION TIME *10 minutes* **COOKING TIME** *None* **SERVES 4**

2 garlic cloves, chopped
large handful of fresh dill
⅓ cup blanched almonds
⅔ cup olive oil

¼ cup freshly grated
  Parmesan cheese
salt and freshly ground
  black pepper

1 Put the garlic, dill, and almonds in a small blender or food processor. Blend to a paste. With the motor running, slowly pour in the oil to make a creamy paste.
2 Add the cheese, season to taste, and blend briefly.

289 AVOCADO, TOMATO, AND RED PEPPER SALSA

PREPARATION TIME *10 minutes, plus 30 minutes chilling* **COOKING TIME** *20 minutes* **SERVES 4**

1 red bell pepper
2 large, ripe avocados
1 garlic clove, finely
  chopped
1 roma tomato, finely
  chopped

1 small red onion, minced
1 fresh, hot red chile,
  seeded and finely
  chopped
juice of 1 small lime

¼ cup chopped fresh
  cilantro
salt and freshly ground
  black pepper

1 Grill the red pepper on an oiled rack, or under a preheated broiler, turning occasionally, until well charred and soft. Leave until cool enough to handle, then remove the skin and discard the seeds. Mince the flesh. Put into a bowl.
2 Peel the avocados, remove the pits, and chop the flesh finely. Add to the bowl with the remaining ingredients. Toss gently to combine. Cover and chill for 30 minutes.

290 GRILLED TOMATO SALSA

PREPARATION TIME *10 minutes* **COOKING TIME** *6–7 minutes* **SERVES 4-6**

6 ripe tomatoes, halved	5 scallions, finely chopped	1 tsp ground cumin
2-3 tbsp lime juice	2 garlic cloves, finely	salt
2 tbsp olive oil	chopped	
3 tbsp chopped fresh	1 fresh, hot chile, seeded	
cilantro	and chopped	

1 Grill the tomatoes, skin-side down, on an oiled rack until slightly softened and the skin is charred in patches, 6–7 minutes.
2 Remove from the grill and leave until cool enough to handle, then peel off the skins. Coarsely chop the flesh and mix with the remaining ingredients. Serve warm.

291 NUTTY BANANA SALSA

PREPARATION TIME *10 minutes* **COOKING TIME** *None* **SERVES 4**

½ small red onion, finely	grated zest and juice of	salt and freshly ground
chopped, rinsed, and	1 lime	black pepper
dried	dash of sweet chile sauce	3 bananas
1 small garlic clove, finely	¼ cup unsweetened	
chopped	flaked coconut	

1 Put the red onion, garlic, lime zest and juice, chile sauce, and coconut into a bowl. Stir together and season to taste.
2 Just before serving, dice the bananas and add to the bowl. After mixing, check the seasoning. Serve within 30 minutes.

292 FRESH PINEAPPLE AND MANGO SALSA

PREPARATION TIME *15 minutes, plus 1 hour chilling* **COOKING TIME** *None* **SERVES 6-8**

½ large, ripe pineapple	5 scallions, finely chopped
1 small, ripe but firm	1 tbsp chopped fresh mint
mango, peeled, pitted,	2½ tbsp lime juice
and finely chopped	salt and freshly ground
1 fresh, hot red chile,	black pepper
seeded and minced	
1-inch piece fresh	
gingerroot, finely grated	

1 Using a large, sharp knife, trim and peel the pineapple. Make sure all the "eyes" are removed. Cut the pineapple into wedges from top to bottom, then cut out the core. Chop the flesh finely and put into a bowl.
2 Add the remaining ingredients to the bowl and stir to combine. Chill for 1 hour before serving.

293 SPICED PEAR SALSA

PREPARATION TIME *15 minutes, plus 1 hour chilling* **COOKING TIME** *None* **SERVES 8**

grated zest and juice
   of 1 lime
1 piece stem ginger in
   syrup, drained and finely
   chopped, plus 1 tbsp
   syrup from the jar
3 scallions, chopped

2 large, ripe pears, about
   8 oz each, cored and
   cut into ½-inch cubes
2 dried pear halves,
   chopped
1-inch piece fresh
   gingerroot, grated

1 fresh, hot red chile,
   seeded and finely
   chopped
½ English cucumber, peeled,
   seeded, and chopped
2 tbsp chopped fresh mint

1 Stir together the lime zest and juice and the ginger syrup.
2 Put the remaining ingredients into a bowl. Pour the lime mixture over and stir all the ingredients together. Cover and chill for up to 1 hour.

294 SALSA VERDE

PREPARATION TIME *10 minutes* **COOKING TIME** *None* **SERVES 4-6**

2 garlic cloves, chopped
3 anchovy fillets, drained
   and chopped
leaves from a bunch of
   fresh flat-leaf parsley

15 fresh basil leaves
10 fresh mint leaves
1 tbsp capers, drained
2 tsp Dijon mustard

⅔ cup fruity olive oil
freshly ground black
   pepper

1 Put the garlic, anchovies, herbs, capers, mustard, and a few tablespoons of the oil into a small blender or food processor.
2 Blend briefly to a smooth paste, then, with the motor running, slowly pour in the remaining oil to produce a consistency like a coarse, green mayonnaise. Season with black pepper.

295 MEXICAN TOMATO SALSA FRESCA

PREPARATION TIME *10 minutes* **COOKING TIME** *None* **SERVES 6-8**

6 vine-ripened tomatoes,
   seeded and finely
   chopped
1 fresh, hot green chile,
   seeded and minced

2 garlic cloves, finely
   chopped
1 small red onion, finely
   chopped
1 tbsp lime juice

leaves from a small bunch
   of fresh cilantro
2 tbsp olive oil
salt and freshly ground
   black pepper

1 Put the tomatoes, chile, garlic, red onion, lime juice, and cilantro into a bowl. Stir together and season to taste.
2 Cover and leave at room temperature for 30 minutes. Chill, if desired, before serving. Serve within 30–60 minutes.

296 MANGO AND MINT SALSA

PREPARATION TIME *10 minutes* **COOKING TIME** *None* **SERVES 4**

¾ cup plain yogurt
1 tsp curry paste
flesh from 1 mango, cubed

2 tbsp chopped fresh mint
    leaves

1 fresh, hot red chile,
    seeded and minced
salt

1 Beat the yogurt and curry paste together until the paste is evenly mixed, then stir in the remaining ingredients.

297 LYCHEE, GRAPE, AND FRESH COCONUT SALSA

PREPARATION TIME *20 minutes, plus 1 hour chilling* **COOKING TIME** *None* **SERVES 4**

1 small coconut
4 oz fresh lychees, peeled
    and pitted
6 oz seedless green
    grapes, halved

1 tbsp shredded fresh basil
1-inch piece fresh
    gingerroot, grated
grated zest and juice of
    1 lime

½ tsp Thai fish sauce
1 tsp clear honey
dash of chile sauce, to taste

1 Using a skewer or screwdriver, pierce the three coconut "eyes." Drain off the water and reserve for use in another recipe.
2 Put the coconut into a plastic bag, seal the end, and place on the floor or a firm worktop. Using a hammer, hit the coconut firmly and hard to crack it open. Use a small, sturdy, sharp knife to prize the flesh from the shell. If necessary, break the flesh into smaller pieces. Shred the flesh into a bowl. Use half the flesh in this recipe and save the rest for another use.
3 Add the lychees, grapes, and basil to the shredded coconut and toss together.
4 Stir the ginger, lime zest and juice, fish sauce, honey, and chile sauce together. Pour this over the coconut mixture and toss to combine evenly. Cover and chill for 1 hour.

298 PROVENCAL SAUCE

PREPARATION TIME *10 minutes* **COOKING TIME** *None* **SERVES 4**

3 tbsp coarsely chopped oil-cured black olives
3 garlic cloves, minced
⅛ cup sun-dried tomatoes in oil, sliced

2-oz can anchovy fillets, drained and chopped
juice of 2 lemons
6 tbsp virgin olive oil
¼ cup chopped fresh basil

salt and freshly ground black pepper

1 Put all the ingredients into a bowl, being careful when adding salt, and stir together.

299 PINEAPPLE AND MACADAMIA NUT SALSA

PREPARATION TIME *15 minutes* **COOKING TIME** *None* **SERVES 4**

1 small pineapple
¼ cup chopped macadamia nuts

1 red onion, finely chopped
1 garlic clove, finely chopped
1 tbsp light soy sauce

3 tbsp lime juice
freshly ground black pepper

1 Using a large, sharp knife, trim and peel the pineapple. Make sure all the "eyes" are removed. Cut the pineapple into quarters from top to bottom, then cut out the core. Chop the flesh finely and put into a bowl.
2 Add all the remaining ingredients to the bowl and toss together.

300 CILANTRO, LEMON GRASS, AND COCONUT SAUCE

PREPARATION TIME *10 minutes* **COOKING TIME** *1 minute* **SERVES 4**

5 oz creamed coconut, crumbled
1¼ cups boiling water
2 tsp cumin seeds
1 fresh, hot red chile, seeded and chopped

3 garlic cloves, coarsely chopped
½ tsp salt
1 lemon grass stem, outer layer removed, thinly sliced

2 tbsp lime juice
3 tbsp chopped fresh cilantro
3 tbsp chopped fresh flat-leaf parsley

1 Put the creamed coconut in a bowl, pour on the boiling water, and stir until smooth.
2 Heat a small, heavy-based frying pan, add the cumin seeds, and toast until fragrant, about 10 seconds. Tip into a small blender or food processor. Add the chile, garlic, salt, and lemon grass. Mix together, then add the creamed coconut liquid, lime juice, cilantro, and parsley. Process to a smooth paste.
3 Pour the sauce into a small saucepan and put on the side of the grill rack to warm through while the food is grilling.

301 TOMATO TARTAR SAUCE

PREPARATION TIME *15 minutes* **COOKING TIME** *5 minutes* **SERVES 4**

3 tbsp white wine vinegar
½ shallot, finely chopped
4 black peppercorns, lightly
    crushed
a few tarragon stems,
    coarsely chopped

½ cup mayonnaise
    (see below)
1 tsp Dijon mustard
2 roma tomatoes, seeded
    and finely chopped

2 tbsp finely chopped
    green olives
2 tbsp finely chopped
    sweet-sour gherkins

1   Put the vinegar in a small saucepan with the shallot, peppercorns, and tarragon stems, and boil until reduced to 1 teaspoon. Let cool.
2   Mix the mayonnaise and mustard together. Strain the vinegar into the mustard mayonnaise. Stir in the remaining ingredients. Taste for seasoning.

302 BARBECUE SAUCE

PREPARATION TIME *10 minutes* **COOKING TIME** *5 minutes* **SERVES 4**

1¼ cups ketchup *(see
    page 184)*
¾ cup cider vinegar or
    red wine vinegar
3 tbsp soy sauce
3 tbsp Worcestershire
    sauce

1 garlic clove, finely
    chopped
½ cup light brown sugar
1½ tbsp English mustard
    powder
2 tsp grated fresh
    gingerroot

1 tbsp hot chile powder
squeeze of lemon juice
salt and freshly ground
    black pepper

1   Put all the ingredients into a saucepan and bring to a boil, stirring.
2   Simmer for 5 minutes, stirring frequently. Let cool.

303 MAYONNAISE

PREPARATION TIME *10 minutes* **COOKING TIME** *None* **SERVES 4-6**

2 egg yolks, at room
    temperature
1 tsp Dijon mustard, or
    to taste

2-3 tsp white wine vinegar
    or lemon juice
salt and freshly ground
    black pepper

1¼ cups mild olive oil, at
    room temperature

1   Put the egg yolks, mustard, vinegar or lemon juice, and a pinch of salt into a blender. Blend for about 10 seconds, then, with the motor running, pour in the oil in a slow, steady stream until the mixture is thick and creamy.
2   Adjust the seasoning levels of mustard and vinegar or lemon juice, if necessary. Store in a lidded jar in the refrigerator for up to 3 days.
*   **NOTE** Pregnant women, young children, the elderly, and those with impaired immune systems should avoid eating raw eggs, because of the potential risk of salmonella food poisoning.

304 SUN-DRIED TOMATO AND GARLIC MAYONNAISE

PREPARATION TIME *10 minutes* **COOKING TIME** *None* **SERVES 4**

2 egg yolks
4 garlic cloves, crushed
juice of ½ lemon, or to taste
1 cup olive oil

8 sun-dried tomatoes
in oil, drained and finely
chopped, plus ¼ cup oil
from the jar

salt and freshly ground
black pepper

1 Put the egg yolks, garlic, and lemon juice into a blender or food processor. Blend briefly. With the motor running, slowly pour in the oils until the mixture forms a thick cream.
2 Transfer to a bowl, stir in the chopped sun-dried tomatoes, and season to taste, adding a little more lemon juice, if necessary.

305 SALSA VERDE MAYONNAISE

PREPARATION TIME *10 minutes* **COOKING TIME** *None* **SERVES 4**

3 heaped tbsp fresh
flat-leaf parsley leaves
1 heaped tbsp fresh mint
leaves
3 tbsp capers, rinsed

6 anchovy fillets in oil,
drained
1 garlic clove
6 tbsp mayonnaise
(see page 179)

1 tsp Dijon mustard
1 tbsp lemon juice
salt

1 Coarsely chop the parsley, mint, capers, anchovies, and garlic together.
2 Stir into the mayonnaise, along with the mustard, lemon juice, and salt.

306 CILANTRO AND GINGER MAYONNAISE

PREPARATION TIME *10 minutes* **COOKING TIME** *None* **SERVES 4**

2 egg yolks	1¼ cups mixed peanut oil	salt and freshly ground
1 garlic clove, crushed	and sunflower oil	black pepper
½ tsp Dijon mustard	2–3 tbsp rice wine vinegar	
1 tsp grated fresh	3 tbsp chopped fresh	
gingerroot	cilantro	

1   Put the egg yolks, garlic, mustard, and ginger into a blender or food processor. Blend briefly. With the motor running, slowly pour in the oils until the mixture forms a thick cream; slowly pour in the vinegar toward the end.

2   Transfer to a bowl, stir in the cilantro, and season, adding more rice vinegar if necessary.

307 CAJUN REMOULADE

PREPARATION TIME *5 minutes* **COOKING TIME** *None* **SERVES 6–8**

6 scallions, chopped	1 fresh, hot red chile,	1 tbsp Worcestershire
2 anchovy fillets in oil,	seeded and finely	sauce
chopped	chopped	1 tbsp Dijon mustard
2 tbsp chopped fresh	1 tbsp capers, chopped	juice of 1 lemon
flat-leaf parsley	3 tbsp ketchup	2½ cups mayonnaise
2 tbsp snipped fresh chives	*(see page 184)*	*(see page 179)*

1   Beat all the ingredients into the mayonnaise.

308 MEXICAN MARINADE

PREPARATION TIME *10 minutes* **COOKING TIME** *None* **SERVES 4**

2 garlic cloves, crushed	2 tbsp olive oil	¾ tsp dried oregano
salt and freshly ground	2 tsp paprika	juice of 1½ limes
black pepper	1–2 tsp hot chile powder	
2 tbsp tequila	¾ tsp ground cumin	

1   Mash the garlic to a paste with a pinch of salt. Combine with the remaining ingredients.

309 THAI-STYLE MARINADE

PREPARATION TIME *5 minutes* **COOKING TIME** *None* **SERVES 4**

2 garlic cloves, chopped	juice of 2 small limes	2 tbsp chopped fresh
1-inch piece fresh	1 fresh, hot red chile,	cilantro
gingerroot, chopped	seeded and chopped	
2 lemon grass stems, outer	⅔ cup canned coconut milk	
leaves removed,	1–2 tbsp brown sugar	
chopped		

1   Put all the ingredients into a blender or food processor and blend to a purée.

310 NORTH AFRICAN MARINADE

PREPARATION TIME *5 minutes* **COOKING TIME** *None* **SERVES 4**

1 tsp ground cumin	1 tsp ground ginger	pinch of hot chile powder
1 tsp ground coriander	1 tsp paprika	sunflower oil

1   Combine the spices, then mix with enough oil to make a paste.

311 HARISSA MARINADE

PREPARATION TIME *5 minutes* **COOKING TIME** *None* **SERVES 4**

3 tbsp olive oil	1 garlic clove, finely	1 tsp ground cardamom
2 tbsp lemon juice	chopped	1 tsp ground cumin
1 tsp harissa sauce	½ tbsp pimenton (smoked paprika)	

1   Put all the ingredients into a bowl and stir together until evenly blended.

312 TANDOORI MARINADE

PREPARATION TIME *5 minutes* **COOKING TIME** *None* **SERVES 6**

1 onion, coarsely chopped	¼ cup lemon juice	½ tsp grated nutmeg
4 large garlic cloves, chopped	1 cup plain yogurt	½ tsp freshly ground black pepper
1oz fresh gingerroot, chopped	1 tbsp turmeric	¼ tsp ground cloves
	1 tbsp ground coriander	¼ tsp ground chile
¼ cup peanut oil	1 tsp ground cumin	
	½ tsp ground cinnamon	

1   Put the onion, garlic, and ginger into a blender and process until reduced to a paste.
2   Add the remaining ingredients and blend until smooth.

313 COCONUT, LIME, AND PINEAPPLE MARINADE

PREPARATION TIME *10 minutes* **COOKING TIME** *None* **SERVES 4**

1 cup canned coconut milk	¼ pineapple, peeled and	1 tbsp hot pepper sauce
flesh from ½ lime, chopped	chopped	salt

1   Pour the coconut milk into a small blender. Add the remaining ingredients and blend together until evenly mixed.

314 LEMON AND DILL MARINADE

PREPARATION TIME *10 minutes* **COOKING TIME** *None* **SERVES 4**

¾ cup grapeseed oil
grated zest and juice of
   1 small lemon

2 tbsp chopped fresh dill
salt and freshly ground
   black pepper

1 Put all the ingredients into a bowl and whisk together.

315 GINGER AND CILANTRO MARINADE

PREPARATION TIME *5 minutes* **COOKING TIME** *None* **SERVES 4**

½-inch piece fresh
   gingerroot, grated
2 tbsp chopped fresh
   cilantro

1 garlic clove, crushed
1 tbsp peanut oil
1 tbsp rice wine vinegar
½ tsp turmeric

½ tsp sweet chile sauce

1 Put all the ingredients into bowl. Add 1 tablespoon of water and stir everything together.

316 TAMARIND MARINADE

PREPARATION TIME *10 minutes* **COOKING TIME** *10 minutes* **SERVES 4**

2 walnut-sized lumps of
   tamarind, soaked and
   squeezed
3 garlic cloves, crushed
1-inch piece fresh
   gingerroot, chopped

2 lemon grass stems, outer
   leaves removed,
   chopped
4 lime leaves, sliced
2 shallots, chopped

2 fresh, hot chiles, seeded
   and chopped
2 tbsp peanut oil
salt and freshly ground
   black pepper

1 Put all the ingredients into a blender or food processor and blend to a purée.
2 Transfer to a small frying pan and cook, stirring frequently, for about 10 minutes. Spoon into a bowl and let cool.

317 ROUILLE

PREPARATION TIME *10 minutes* **COOKING TIME** *None* **MAKES** *about 2½ cups*

2 extra large egg yolks
5 garlic cloves, crushed
2 tbsp chopped red bell
   pepper
1 tbsp lemon juice

1 tsp Dijon mustard
1 tsp tomato paste
1 tsp paprika
pinch of cayenne pepper
1½ cups virgin olive oil

½ cup extra virgin olive oil
salt

1 Put the egg yolks, garlic, red pepper, lemon juice, mustard, tomato paste, paprika, and cayenne into a blender. Blend together, then, with the motor running, add 1 tablespoon of oil. When this is incorporated, slowly pour in the remaining oils.
2 Add salt to taste, and any other flavorings you feel need boosting. Store, covered, in the refrigerator for up to 1 week.

318 HOMEMADE KETCHUP

PREPARATION TIME *10 minutes* **COOKING TIME** *20–30 minutes* **MAKES** *about 3 cups*

3 lb tomatoes, chopped
1 fleshy red bell pepper,
   seeded and sliced
2 red onions, chopped

½ tsp paprika
¾ cup spiced red wine
   vinegar*

1. Put the tomatoes, red pepper, red onion, and paprika into a nonreactive saucepan with the vinegar. Simmer until pulped, stirring occasionally.
2. Press through a nylon or plastic strainer. Return the juice to the rinsed pan and boil vigorously until thick. Pour into warmed, sterilized jars, cover, and let cool. Store in the refrigerator for up to 3 months.
* To make the spiced red wine vinegar, combine the vinegar with 1 teaspoon celery seeds, 1 small mace blade, and 1 teaspoon black peppercorns and bring to a boil. Remove from the heat, cover, and let infuse for a day before straining and using.

319 MANGO DRESSING

PREPARATION TIME *10 minutes* **COOKING TIME** *None* **SERVES 4**

1 very ripe mango
1 tbsp white wine vinegar
1 tbsp Dijon mustard

1 tbsp clear honey
½ cup virgin olive oil
hot pepper sauce

salt and freshly ground
   black pepper

1. Put the mango flesh into a blender or food processor. Add the vinegar, mustard, and honey. Blend briefly, then, with the motor running, slowly pour in the olive oil until evenly mixed.
2. Add a few drops of hot pepper sauce and season to taste. Cover and chill until required.

320 SMOKY BARBECUE RELISH

PREPARATION TIME *10 minutes* **COOKING TIME** *35 minutes* **SERVES 4**

3 tbsp olive oil
2 large onions, finely
   chopped
1 fresh, hot red chile,
   seeded and finely
   chopped

1½ lb ripe tomatoes,
   coarsely chopped
¼ cup maple syrup
3 tbsp smoky barbecue
   sauce, or to taste
2 tbsp sherry vinegar

2 ears of corn, shucked
salt and freshly ground
   black pepper

1. Heat the oil in a heavy-based pan and fry the onions and chile gently until soft and pale brown, stirring occasionally.
2. Increase the heat and add the tomatoes, maple syrup, barbecue sauce, and vinegar. Heat until bubbling, then adjust the heat so the sauce is simmering. Cook until thick, about 25 minutes, stirring occasionally.
3. Meanwhile, cut the kernels from the corn and toast in a large, heavy-based frying pan until tender and speckled with brown, about 25 minutes . Stir into the relish and season to taste.

321 TOASTED CORN AND ROASTED RED PEPPER RELISH

PREPARATION TIME *10 minutes* **COOKING TIME** *10 minutes* **SERVES 4**

1 ear of corn, shucked
1 red bell pepper, roasted, peeled, and diced *(see page 173)*

1 small red onion, finely diced
2 tbsp lime juice
2 tbsp olive oil

3-4 tsp finely chopped fresh sage
salt and freshly ground black pepper

1 Heat a heavy, ridged, cast-iron grill pan and toast the ear of corn until tender and nicely charred, about 10 minutes, turning frequently. Let cool.
2 Using a large, heavy knife, slice the corn kernels off the cob and put into a bowl. Stir in the red pepper, red onion, lime juice, olive oil, and sage, and season to taste. Cover and chill until required.

322 RED PEPPER, BLACK OLIVE, AND CAPER RELISH

PREPARATION TIME *10 minutes* **COOKING TIME** *10 minutes* **SERVES 4**

3 red bell peppers
1 cup chopped oil-cured Kalamata olives
⅓ cup capers, rinsed and coarsely chopped

2 heaped tbsp coarsely chopped fresh basil
2 heaped tbsp coarsely chopped fresh flat-leaf parsley

2 tbsp olive oil
salt and freshly ground black pepper

1 Preheat the broiler. Broil the peppers, turning frequently, until the skins char and blister. Leave until cool enough to handle, then peel off and discard the skins, seeds, and core. Chop the flesh.
2 Mix the pepper flesh with the olives, capers, herbs, and oil. Season to taste, then cover and chill until required.

323 SPICED SWEET MUSTARD RUB

PREPARATION TIME *10 minutes* **COOKING TIME** *None* **SERVES 4**

2 tbsp wholegrain mustard
2 garlic cloves, finely chopped
grated zest and juice of ½ lemon

1 tsp Sichuan peppercorns, toasted and finely crushed
1 tsp dried oregano

2 tbsp chopped fresh cilantro
2 tbsp pomegranate molasses

1 Put all the ingredients into a bowl. Stir everything together to make a light paste.

324 PAPRIKA SPICE RUB

PREPARATION TIME *5 minutes* **COOKING TIME** *2 minutes* **SERVES 5-6**

3 tbsp paprika

1 tbsp ground cumin

2 tsp hot chile powder

¼ tsp cayenne pepper

¼ tsp ground cinnamon

salt

1 Set a heavy, nonstick frying pan over medium heat.
2 Add all the ingredients and stir together for 2 minutes.

325 TEXAN SPICE RUB

PREPARATION TIME *5 minutes* **COOKING TIME** *None* **SERVES 6**

1 tsp black mustard seeds

1 garlic clove

2 tsp salt

1 tsp paprika

2 tsp hot chile powder

½ tsp ground coriander

½ tsp ground cumin

1 Crush the mustard seeds, garlic, and salt to a paste with a mortar and pestle, or put into a small bowl and crush with the end of a rolling pin.
2 Add the remaining ingredients and combine thoroughly.

326 LEMON AND HERB RUB

PREPARATION TIME *5 minutes* **COOKING TIME** *None* **SERVES 6**

grated zest of 1 lemon

3 garlic cloves

salt

1 tsp dried basil

½ tsp dried thyme

2 tsp dried rosemary

freshly ground black
pepper

1 Crush the lemon zest, garlic, and salt together with a mortar and pestle, or put into a small bowl and crush with the end of a rolling pin.
2 Finely chop the basil, thyme, and rosemary together. Combine with the lemon zest mixture and season with pepper.

327 SWEET SPICED RUB

PREPARATION TIME *5 minutes* **COOKING TIME** *None* **SERVES 6**

1 tbsp brown sugar

2 tsp hot chile powder

2 tsp freshly ground black
pepper

1 tsp cayenne pepper

1 tsp mustard powder

1 tsp ground cumin

1 tsp garlic salt

1 Put all the ingredients into a bowl and stir them together thoroughly.

328 GINGER AND ORANGE BUTTER

PREPARATION TIME *10 minutes* **COOKING TIME** *None* **SERVES 8**

½ cup unsalted butter,
   softened
1 tbsp grated fresh
   gingerroot

1 tbsp orange juice
1 tbsp grated orange zest
salt and freshly ground
   black pepper

1 Beat the butter until softened, then add the remaining ingredients and mix everything together until evenly blended.
2 Spoon the flavored butter onto a sheet of plastic wrap or parchment paper. Using the wrap or paper to help, shape the butter into a roll about 1½ inches in diameter. Wrap tightly and chill until required. Cut into slices to serve. Alternatively, pack the butter into ramekin dishes.

329 BLACK OLIVE, CAPER, AND ANCHOVY BUTTER

PREPARATION TIME *10 minutes* **COOKING TIME** *None* **SERVES 8**

7 tbsp unsalted butter
10 oil-cured black olives,
   pitted and finely
   chopped

6 capers, drained and
   finely chopped
3 anchovy fillets in oil,
   finely chopped

freshly ground black
   pepper

1 Beat the butter until softened, then add the remaining ingredients and mix everything together until evenly blended.
2 Spoon the flavored butter onto a sheet of plastic wrap or parchment paper. Using the wrap or paper to help, shape the butter into a roll about 1½ inches in diameter. Wrap tightly and chill until required. Cut into slices to serve. Alternatively, pack the butter into ramekin dishes.

330 ROASTED CHILE BUTTER

PREPARATION TIME *10 minutes* **COOKING TIME** *10–15 minutes* **SERVES 8**

2 large, fresh, medium-hot
   red chiles
1 tbsp olive oil

½ cup unsalted butter
½ tbsp chopped fresh
   parsley

salt

1 Preheat the oven to 450°F. Brush the chiles with the oil and lay them in a single layer in a small roasting pan. Roast until the skin is charred and blistered, 10–15 minutes, turning halfway through the roasting. Let cool, then scrape out and discard the seeds and finely chop the flesh.
2 Beat the butter until softened, then add the remaining ingredients and mix everything together until evenly blended.
3 Spoon the flavored butter onto a sheet of plastic wrap or parchment paper. Using the wrap or paper to help, shape the butter into a roll about 1½ inches in diameter. Wrap tightly and chill until required. Cut into slices to serve. Alternatively, pack the butter into ramekin dishes.

331 PARSLEY AND CHIVE BUTTER

PREPARATION TIME *10 minutes* **COOKING TIME** *None* **SERVES 8**

½ cup unsalted butter
2 tbsp chopped fresh
    parsley

2 tbsp snipped fresh chives
2 tbsp lemon juice
grated zest of 1 lemon

salt and freshly ground
    black pepper

1   Beat the butter until softened, then add the remaining ingredients and mix everything together until evenly blended.
2   Spoon the flavored butter onto a sheet of plastic wrap or parchment paper. Using the wrap or paper to help, shape the butter into a roll about 1½ inches in diameter. Wrap tightly and chill until required. Cut into slices to serve. Alternatively, pack the butter into ramekin dishes.

332 BASIL AND SUN-DRIED TOMATO BUTTER

PREPARATION TIME *10 minutes* **COOKING TIME** *None* **SERVES 8**

½ cup unsalted butter
3 tbsp coarsely chopped
    fresh basil

3 sun-dried tomatoes in oil,
    drained and chopped

salt and freshly ground
    black pepper

1   Beat the butter until softened, then add the remaining ingredients and mix everything together until evenly blended.
2   Spoon the flavored butter onto a sheet of plastic wrap or parchment paper. Using the wrap or paper to help, shape the butter into a roll about 1½ inches in diameter. Wrap tightly and chill until required. Cut into slices to serve. Alternatively, pack the butter into ramekin dishes.

333 GINGER AND MINT BUTTER

PREPARATION TIME *10 minutes* **COOKING TIME** *None* **SERVES 8**

½ cup unsalted butter	1 tbsp grated fresh	salt and freshly ground
2 tbsp chopped fresh mint	gingerroot	black pepper

1   Beat the butter until softened, then add the remaining ingredients and mix everything together until evenly blended.

2   Spoon the flavored butter onto a sheet of plastic wrap or parchment paper. Using the wrap or paper to help, shape the butter into a roll about 1½ inches in diameter. Wrap tightly and chill until required. Cut into slices to serve. Alternatively, pack the butter into ramekin dishes.

334 JAMAICAN SPICED BASTE

PREPARATION TIME *10 minutes* **COOKING TIME** *none* **SERVES 4**

2 garlic cloves, chopped	1 tsp ground allspice	2 tbsp dark rum
salt and freshly ground	2 fresh, hot red chiles,	2 tbsp ketchup *(see*
black pepper	seeded and minced	*page 184)*

1   Mix the ingredients together thoroughly.

335 JAMAICAN JERK SEASONING

PREPARATION TIME *5 minutes* **COOKING TIME** *None* **SERVES 4**

5 fresh, hot red chiles,	2 tbsp orange juice	1 tsp ground cloves
seeded and chopped	2 tbsp white wine vinegar	salt and freshly ground
2 scallions, chopped	1 tbsp yellow mustard	black pepper
1 tbsp dried thyme	seeds	
1 tbsp dried basil	1 tsp ground allspice	

1   Put all the ingredients into a blender and blend to a thick sauce. If necessary, add a little more orange juice or vinegar to obtain the right consistency.

336 CHIMICHURRI

PREPARATION TIME *10 minutes, plus 3 hours marinating* **COOKING TIME** *None* **SERVES 4**

½ cup olive oil	1 tsp dried oregano	salt and freshly ground
¼ cup red wine vinegar	¼ cup chopped mixed	black pepper
1 small red onion, finely	fresh parsley and	
chopped	cilantro	
3 garlic cloves, finely	dash of hot pepper sauce,	
chopped	or to taste	

1   Whisk the oil with the vinegar until emulsified. Stir in the remaining ingredients. Cover and leave the marinade for at least 3 hours before serving, or refrigerate for up to 2 days.

DESSERTS

Grilled desserts are the most appropriate and delicious way to end your meal. Some people might be surprised at the variety of desserts that can be cooked on a grill; if the grill is covered, the possibilities are even greater.

Choose fruits that are ripe but not too soft, and remove them from the grill before they overcook. Tropical fruits, such as pineapple and mango, are always popular, but there are many others that work equally well. For example, pears, peaches, and bananas cooked in their skins all become wonderful treats when grilled until sizzling and lightly caramelized. Add some spices, either simply sprinkled on or in a marinade, baste, or butter, and these familiar fruits become exotic.

Individual fruits or combinations can be enclosed in foil packets for grilling. This is a particularly good method for fragile fruit, such as strawberries and raspberries, and for fruits that are too ripe and soft to be cooked directly on the grill rack. Slices of sweet breads and cakes also grill well, and provide bases for the fruit, making more substantial desserts.

Clean any particles of savory food off the grill rack before cooking desserts on it. If possible, grill the fruit on an oiled fine mesh, or in an oiled hinged basket, to make turning and lifting easy.

337 GRILL-BAKED APPLES

PREPARATION TIME *10 minutes* **COOKING TIME** *30–40 minutes* **SERVES 4**

4 large baking apples,
   such as Braeburn or
   Rome Beauty
¼ cup sugar
1 tsp ground cinnamon
2 oz marzipan, chopped

¼ cup chopped blanched
   almonds
¼ cup chopped dried
   mango
1 tbsp unsalted butter,
   cut into 4 pieces

sour cream or vanilla
   ice cream for serving

1 Keeping the apples intact, remove the cores, cutting from top to bottom.
2 Using the point of a small, sharp knife, score the skin around the circumference of each apple. Place each apple on a double-thickness piece of heavy-duty foil large enough to enclose it.
3 Mix the sugar with the cinnamon, then add the marzipan, almonds, and mango. Use to fill the core-hollows in the apples. Put a piece of butter on top of each. Fold the foil loosely around the apples and twist the edges together firmly to seal tightly.
4 Place the packets at the side of the grill rack and cook for 30–40 minutes. Serve with sour cream or vanilla ice cream.

338 STUFFED PEACHES

PREPARATION TIME *10 minutes* **COOKING TIME** *8–10 minutes* **SERVES 4**

8 amaretti cookies,
   coarsely crushed
1 cup crumbled pound cake
¼ cup amaretto liqueur

4 ripe but firm, large
   peaches, halved and
   pitted
½ cup orange juice

¼ cup sliced almonds,
   toasted

1 Mix together the amaretti cookies, cake crumbs, and 2 tablespoons of amaretto. Divide among the hollows in the peaches.
2 Combine the remaining amaretto with the orange juice.
3 Put two peach halves on a piece of heavy-duty foil that is large enough to enclose them. Fold up the sides of the foil. Sprinkle one-quarter of the nuts over the filling. Drizzle one-quarter of the orange juice mixture over. Fold the foil loosely over the peaches and pleat the sides together to make a secure packet. Repeat with the remaining peach halves.
4 Cook on a grill rack until the peaches have softened and are warmed through, 8–10 minutes.

339 HONEYED APRICOT SKEWERS WITH LEMON TZATZIKI

PREPARATION TIME *10 minutes* **COOKING TIME** *5–7 minutes* **SERVES 4**

2 lemons	12 small bay leaves
8 ripe but not too soft apricots, quartered and chilled	1 cup thick, plain yogurt, chilled
	¼ cup clear honey

1 Grate the zest and squeeze the juice from one lemon. Cut the other lemon into about 12 pieces. Thread the pieces alternately with the apricot quarters and bay leaves onto skewers, beginning and ending with an apricot quarter.

2 To make the tzatziki, combine the lemon zest with the yogurt and chill until required.

3 Melt the honey with the lemon juice in a small pan and bubble until reduced by about half, 3–4 minutes. Brush the skewers with some of the hot honey mixture and grill on an oiled rack until the edges of the apricots begin to caramelize, 2–3 minutes, turning once.

4 Serve with the remaining honey mixture trickled over and accompanied by the lemon tzatziki.

340 CARAMELIZED APPLES WITH BRIOCHE TOASTS

PREPARATION TIME *10 minutes* **COOKING TIME** *4–5 minutes* **SERVES 4**

4 apples, cored and thickly sliced	1 tsp ground cinnamon	sour cream for serving
juice of 1 lime	4 tbsp unsalted butter, melted	
2 tbsp sugar	4 thick slices brioche	

1 Sprinkle the cut surfaces of the apples with lime juice.

2 Stir the sugar and cinnamon together. Stir half of the mixture into the warm butter until the sugar has dissolved. Brush over the brioche and apple slices.

3 Grill the apples on an oiled rack until browned, 4–5 minutes, turning once. Add the brioche slices to the side of the grill rack and toast them lightly on both sides; keep an eye on them as they can burn easily.

4 Remove the brioche slices to plates. Cut the apple slices into halves or quarters and put onto the brioche slices. Sprinkle with the remaining sugar and cinnamon. Serve with sour cream.

341 FRUIT BROCHETTES WITH HONEY, ORANGE, AND PECAN SAUCE

PREPARATION TIME *10 minutes* **COOKING TIME** *6–8 minutes* **SERVES 4**

2 apples, cored and cut into wedges	HONEY, ORANGE, AND PECAN SAUCE	2-inch fresh rosemary sprig
2 pears, cored and cut into wedges	1 orange	½ cup pecan halves
6 plums, pitted and cut into wedges	2 tbsp clear honey	
	4 tbsp unsalted butter	
	1 tbsp confectioners' sugar	

1 Make the sauce: Pare the zest from the orange and cut it into fine shreds. Blanch the shreds in boiling water for 1 minute. Drain and blanch once more. Set aside.
2 Squeeze the juice from the orange and pour into a small saucepan. Add the honey, butter, and sugar. Add the rosemary and heat gently for 5 minutes, stirring occasionally.
3 Thread the fruits alternately onto skewers. Brush the fruit with the honey mixture and grill on an oiled rack until sizzling and lightly browned.
4 Meanwhile, discard the rosemary from the sauce; add the pecans and reheat.
5 Transfer the brochettes to plates, pour some of the sauce around them, and sprinkle with the blanched orange zest shreds.

342 PAPAYA, PEAR, ORANGE, AND GINGER BROCHETTES

PREPARATION TIME *15 minutes* **COOKING TIME** *15 minutes* **SERVES 4**

3 small oranges	flesh from 1 ripe but firm (unpeeled) pear, cut into 1-inch cubes	2 tbsp unsalted butter, chopped
flesh from 1 ripe but firm papaya, cut into 1-inch cubes	18 slices of crystallized ginger, plus ¼ cup syrup from the jar	1 tbsp brown sugar

1 Cut a slice from each end of the oranges. Stand each orange in turn upright on a plate (to catch any juice) and slice off all the skin and pith. Cut across each orange to make six slices, then cut each slice in half.
2 Thread the papaya, pear, orange, and ginger alternately onto eight parallel pairs of soaked bamboo skewers (see page 10).
3 Heat the butter, sugar, ginger syrup, and orange juice in a small saucepan over low heat until smooth, stirring occasionally. Remove from the heat. Let cool slightly, then brush over the fruit.
4 Grill the brochettes on an oiled rack for about 10 minutes, turning once and brushing with any remaining butter mixture.

343 PAPAYA WITH CHILE-LIME SYRUP

PREPARATION TIME *5 minutes* **COOKING TIME** *10 minutes* **SERVES 4**

½ cup light brown sugar
1 fresh, hot red chile,
   seeded and cut into
   thin strips

pared zest of 2 limes,
   cut into fine strips
juice of 2 limes
2 papayas

1   First make the syrup: Put the sugar, chile, and 1 cup water in a saucepan and bring to a boil.
   Reduce the heat and simmer for 5 minutes to make a syrup. Add the lime zest and juice and
   pour into a bowl.
2   Cut the papayas into thin wedges. Brush with some of the syrup and grill on an oiled rack until
   lightly caramelized, about 4 minutes. Serve with the remaining syrup.

344 SEARED CINNAMON-GLAZED PEACHES

PREPARATION TIME *5 minutes* **COOKING TIME** *8 minutes* **SERVES 4**

2 tbsp light brown sugar
2 tsp ground cinnamon

4 large, ripe but firm
   peaches, halved and
   pitted

vanilla ice cream for
   serving

1 Combine the brown sugar and cinnamon, and sprinkle over the peaches.
2 Grill, cut-side down, on an oiled rack until very lightly charred but still firm, about 8 minutes.
   Serve with vanilla ice cream

345 KIWI, PINEAPPLE, AND BANANA WITH VANILLA MASCARPONE DIP

PREPARATION TIME *10 minutes* **COOKING TIME** *10 minutes* **SERVES 6**

1 small pineapple,
   unpeeled and leafy top
   left on, cut lengthwise
   into equal wedges
3 bananas, unpeeled,
   halved

6 kiwi fruit, unpeeled,
   quartered lengthwise
confectioners' sugar for
   sprinkling

VANILLA MASCARPONE DIP
1 vanilla bean, split open
1 cup mascarpone cheese,
   chilled
confectioners' sugar to
   taste

1 Make the dip by scraping the seeds from the vanilla bean into the mascarpone. Stir well, then
   add sugar to taste. Chill until required.
2 Remove the fibrous core from the pineapple wedges. Sprinkle all the fruit lightly with sugar.
3 Grill the fruit on an oiled rack until lightly caramelized, about 10 minutes, turning a couple of
   times. Serve the warm fruit with the dip.

346 GRILLED FIGS WITH BITTERSWEET CHOCOLATE AND PISTACHIOS

PREPARATION TIME *10 minutes* **COOKING TIME** *5–8 minutes* **SERVES 3–6**

6 large, ripe but not too soft
   black figs
4 oz bittersweet chocolate
   with at least 70% cocoa
   solids, chopped

1 tsp unsalted butter
Vanilla Cream *(see page
   200)*
1 tbsp coarsely chopped
   pistachio nuts

1 Cut the figs from top to bottom into quarters, without cutting all the way through.
2 Grill the figs on an oiled rack until heated through but not too soft, 5–8 minutes.
3 Meanwhile, melt the chocolate and butter with 2 tablespoons of hot water in a small pan at the
   side of the grill rack, stirring to make a smooth sauce.
4 Remove the figs from the grill. Put a spoonful of vanilla cream into the center of each one. Trickle
   the sauce over, sprinkle with the pistachio nuts, and serve.

347 PEARS WITH CHOCOLATE SAUCE

PREPARATION TIME *5 minutes* **COOKING TIME** *12-15 minutes* **SERVES 4**

4 ripe but firm pears

CHOCOLATE SAUCE
**3 oz bittersweet chocolate
with at least 70% cocoa
solids, chopped
⅔ cup boiling water**

**½ cup unsweetened cocoa
powder
2 tbsp sugar, or to taste**

1   First make the sauce: Melt the chocolate with ½ cup of the boiling water in a double boiler,
    or a small bowl set over a saucepan of hot water. Stir regularly until smooth.
2   Dissolve the cocoa powder and sugar in the remaining boiling water, then pour into the melted
    chocolate, stirring. Set aside, off the heat.
3   Cut the pears lengthwise into quarters and remove the cores. Grill on an oiled rack (in an oiled
    hinged basket for ease of turning) until warmed, slightly softened, and lightly charred, about
    4 minutes on each side.
4   Meanwhile, warm the bowl of sauce over the saucepan of hot water at the side of the grill rack.
    Serve the pears with the warm sauce poured over.

348 NECTARINES WITH CARAMEL ORANGE SAUCE

PREPARATION TIME *10 minutes* **COOKING TIME** *15 minutes* **SERVES 4**

**4 ripe but firm nectarines,
halved and pitted
confectioners' sugar for
sprinkling**

CARAMEL ORANGE SAUCE
**½ cup granulated sugar
grated zest and juice of
1 orange**

¼ cup light cream

1   First make the sauce: Put the sugar and orange zest into a heavy-based saucepan. Add
    2 tablespoons of water and heat gently, stirring, until the sugar has dissolved. Increase the heat
    and boil until the sauce turns to a golden caramel color, 4–5 minutes. Immediately remove from
    the heat and whisk in the cream and orange juice; take care because it might splutter. Return the
    pan to low heat and cook, stirring, until the sauce is smooth.
2   Sprinkle confectioners' sugar over the cut side of the nectarine halves, then place them, cut-side
    down, on the grill rack. Grill over medium heat until warm and lightly charred but still firm,
    about 5 minutes .
3   Meanwhile, warm the sauce at the side of the grill rack. Serve the nectarines with the sauce.

349 CARAMEL ORANGES

PREPARATION TIME *15 minutes* **COOKING TIME:** *12–14 minutes* **SERVES 4**

4 large oranges
melted unsalted butter
　for brushing
1–2 tbsp brown sugar

2 tbsp Orange Nassau,
　Cointreau, Grand
　Marnier, or other
　orange liqueur

vanilla ice cream for
　serving

1   Working over a bowl to catch any juice, carefully cut away all the orange peel and white pith. Reserve some of the peel. Cut across each orange to make six slices.
2   Remove the pith from the reserved peel, then cut the peel into very fine shreds. Blanch these in boiling water for 2–3 minutes. Drain and dry.
3   Cut four double-thickness squares of heavy-duty foil that are large enough to wrap loosely around an orange. Butter the center of each square thoroughly with unsalted butter.
4   Divide the orange slices among the foil squares. Fold up the sides of the foil. Divide the orange juice from the bowl, the sugar, and liqueur among the oranges, then twist the edges of the foil firmly together to make roomy but tightly sealed packets.
5   Cook the packets of oranges at the side of the grill rack for about 10 minutes.
6   Carefully transfer the cooked packets to serving plates and open up the foil. Add a scoop of vanilla ice cream to each.

350 GRILLED MANGO WITH LIME SYRUP

PREPARATION TIME *10 minutes* **COOKING TIME** *5 minutes* **SERVES 4**

2 mangoes, peeled, pitted, and thickly sliced	**2 tbsp bottled sweetened lime juice**	**pinch of ground ginger**
	2 tbsp sugar	**chilled crème fraîche for serving**

1 Grill the mango slices on an oiled rack for 3–4 minutes on each side.
2 Meanwhile, put the lime juice, sugar, and ginger into a small pan and heat gently at the side of the grill rack, stirring until the sugar has dissolved.
3 Remove the mango from the grill, trickle the syrup over, and serve with chilled crème frâiche.

351 SEARED PEARS WITH CARDAMOM BUTTER

PREPARATION TIME *15 minutes* **COOKING TIME** *8–12 minutes* **SERVES 4**

4 ripe but firm pears, cored and thickly sliced	CARDAMOM BUTTER:	**seeds from 3 cardamom pods, crushed**
granulated sugar or brown sugar for sprinkling	**6 tbsp unsalted butter, diced**	
	½ tbsp lemon juice	

1 Make the cardamom butter: Melt the butter with the lemon juice and cardamom seeds in a small saucepan set at the side of the grill rack.
2 Brush the pears with some of the butter and sprinkle with sugar.
3 Grill the slices on an oiled fine mesh, in an oiled hinged basket, or directly on an oiled rack, until softening and beginning to caramelize, 4–6 minutes on each side, turning occasionally and brushing with the butter. Serve the pears with any remaining butter spooned over.

352 PLUMS WITH CINNAMON CREAM

PREPARATION TIME *10 minutes* **COOKING TIME** *5 minutes* **SERVES 4**

8 large, ripe but not too soft plums, halved and pitted	CINNAMON CREAM
	1 cup heavy cream
1 tbsp clear honey, warmed slightly	**½ tsp ground cinnamon**
	1 tbsp confectioners' sugar

1 Make the cinnamon cream: Whip the cream until it will hold soft peaks. Combine the cinnamon with the sugar and fold into the cream. Cover and chill until required.
2 Thread the plum halves onto bamboo skewers that have been soaked in water for 30 minutes. Brush the plums with the honey and grill on an oiled rack until warmed and just softened, about 5 minutes, turning once.
3 Remove from the grill and serve with the cinnamon cream.

353 STRAWBERRY AND BROWNIE SKEWERS WITH VANILLA CREAM

PREPARATION TIME *10 minutes* **COOKING TIME** *3 minutes* **SERVES 4**

8 large, ripe but firm
   strawberries, hulled
8 1¼-inch-square pieces of
chocolate brownie

VANILLA CREAM
1-2 tbsp vanilla sugar,
   or to taste*
¾ cup heavy cream

1 Make the vanilla cream: Whip the vanilla sugar into the cream until soft peaks form. Chill.
2 Thread the strawberries and brownie squares alternately onto skewers. Grill on an oiled rack for about 3 minutes, turning once or twice. Serve with the vanilla cream.
* To make vanilla sugar, simply insert a vanilla bean into a jar of granulated sugar and leave for 2 weeks before using. The jar can be replenished with more sugar as it empties.

354 FIGS WITH GOAT CHEESE, HONEY, AND THYME

PREPARATION TIME *10 minutes* **COOKING TIME** *5-6 minutes* **SERVES 4**

12 ripe but not too soft figs,
   halved lengthwise

½ cup soft, mild goat cheese
fresh thyme for sprinkling

¼ cup clear honey

1 Spread the cut side of each fig half with goat cheese. Sprinkle lightly with thyme and trickle the honey over.
2 Grill the figs, cut-side up, on an oiled rack over low heat until soft, 5-6 minutes.

355 GRILLED PLUM BRUSCHETTAS

PREPARATION TIME *10 minutes* **COOKING TIME** *10 minutes* **SERVES 4**

8-10 ripe but firm plums,
   quartered and pitted
1 vanilla bean, split open

2 tbsp kirsch
2 tbsp sugar
4 slices brioche

chilled mascarpone cheese
for serving

1 Put the plums on a large square of buttered heavy-duty foil. Add the vanilla bean, kirsch, and sugar. Fold up the foil to make a packet and twist the edges together to seal. Put the packet on the grill rack and cook for 10 minutes.
2 Meanwhile, grill the brioche slices on the rack until nicely browned on both sides.
3 Spread the mascarpone thickly over the toasted brioche. Pile the fruit on top and trickle the juices from the foil parcel over. Serve straightaway.

356 FRUIT BROCHETTES WITH PEAR SAUCE

PREPARATION TIME *15 minutes, plus 30 minutes soaking* **COOKING TIME** *5 minutes* **SERVES 6**

6 large, ripe lychees, peeled, pitted, and halved	**1 tbsp dark clear honey, warmed slightly**	**½ tsp ground cinnamon, plus extra for dusting**
flesh from 1 baby pineapple, or 2 thick slices, cubed	PEAR SAUCE **1 heaped cup dried pears**	**juice of 1 orange** **½ tsp vanilla extract** **¼ cup plain yogurt**
3 large figs, quartered lengthwise	**1 tsp grated fresh gingerroot**	**1 tsp dark clear honey**

1   Make the sauce: Just cover the pears with hot water and let soak for 30 minutes.
2   Drain the pears, reserving ¼ cup of the liquid. Put the liquid and pears into a food processor or blender. Add the ginger, cinnamon, orange juice, vanilla extract, and yogurt, and blend until smooth. Pour into a bowl and chill until required.
3   Thread the fruit alternately onto skewers and trickle the warmed honey over. Grill on an oiled rack until the fruit is lightly charred, about 5 minutes, turning once.
4   Finish the sauce by trickling the honey over the top and dusting with cinnamon. Serve with the hot brochettes.

357 PINEAPPLE WEDGES WITH HONEYED RUM

PREPARATION TIME *10 minutes* **COOKING TIME** *5–6 minutes* **SERVES 4**

1 ripe pineapple, peeled and quartered lengthwise	**2 tbsp dark rum** **2 tbsp clear honey** **1 tbsp lime juice**

1   Cut the core and "eyes" from the pineapple wedges, then cut the wedges across into 1-inch-thick triangular slices.
2   Stir the rum, honey, and lime juice together until smooth.
3   Brush the pineapple with the honeyed rum and grill on an oiled rack until lightly caramelized and hot, 5–6 minutes, turning once and brushing with the glaze. Serve straightaway, with any remaining glaze spooned over.

358 FUDGY BANANAS WITH RUM

PREPARATION TIME *5 minutes* **COOKING TIME** *4–5 minutes* **SERVES 4**

4 bananas, peeled	**3 oz vanilla fudge, coarsely chopped**	**¼ cup rum** **vanilla ice cream for serving**

1   Cut a slit along the length of each banana; don't cut all the way through. Place each banana on a large square of buttered heavy-duty foil and fill the slits with fudge. Fold up the edges of the foil and pour the rum over the bananas. Twist the edges of the foil together to seal.
2   Cook on the grill rack until hot, 4–5 minutes. Serve with vanilla ice cream.

359 SLICED COCONUT CAKE WITH CHERRY COMPOTE

PREPARATION TIME *5 minutes* **COOKING TIME** *20 minutes* **SERVES 4**

4 thick slices unfrosted coconut or pound cake	CHERRY COMPOTE	**½ tbsp sugar, or to taste**
sour cream for serving	**1 lb ripe but not too soft cherries, pitted**	**2 tbsp kirsch or brandy**
		1-2 tbsp red-currant jelly

1   Make the compote: Put the cherries into a saucepan with the sugar. Cover the pan and shake gently over low heat until the juices begin to run. Add the kirsch or brandy and cook until the cherries are soft, about 10 minutes longer. Stir in red-currant jelly to taste, then remove from the heat and let cool.
2   Grill the slices of cake until very lightly charred. Serve with the compote and sour cream.

360 CHOCOLATE BRIOCHE SANDWICHES

PREPARATION TIME *10 minutes* **COOKING TIME** *5 minutes* **SERVES 4**

8 slices brioche	**5-6 oz bittersweet**	**vanilla ice cream for**
good-quality apricot preserves for spreading	**chocolate with at least 70% cocoa solids, grated**	**serving**

1   Spread one side of each brioche slice with preserves. Divide the chocolate among half the apricot-covered slices, then cover with the other slices, apricot-side down. Press each sandwich together.
2   Grill on an oiled rack until the underside is beginning to color. Turn carefully and grill the other side until the chocolate has melted; press down gently with a metal spatula two or three times.
3   Serve immediately, topped with scoops of vanilla ice cream.

361 TROPICAL FRUIT PACKETS

PREPARATION TIME *15 minutes* **COOKING TIME** *4-5 minutes* **SERVES 4**

4 passion fruits	**2 bananas, thickly sliced**
4 oz lychees, peeled and pitted	**5 tbsp bottled sweetened lime juice**
flesh from 1 large mango, sliced, or 1 small to medium pineapple, peeled, cored, and sliced	**2 tbsp white rum (optional)**
	leaves from 2 small, fresh mint sprigs

1   Scoop the seeds and flesh from the passion fruits. Mix with the other fruits. Divide the fruits among four squares of heavy-duty foil large enough to enclose them.
2   Sprinkle with the lime juice and optional white rum. Reserve a few of the smallest mint leaves and chop the remainder. Add the chopped mint to the fruit. Fold the foil loosely over the fruit and twist the edges together firmly to seal.
3   Put the packets at the side of a grill rack and cook until heated through, 4-5 minutes. Decorate the fruit with the reserved mint leaves before serving.

362 SUMMER BERRIES EN PAPILLOTE WITH CARDAMOM CREAM

PREPARATION TIME *15 minutes, plus 30 minutes infusion* **COOKING TIME** *4–5 minutes* **SERVES 4**

1 lb prepared mixed
   red summer berries,
   such as ripe but firm
   strawberries (halved if
   large), pitted cherries,
   raspberries, blackberries,
   and blueberries

¼ cup framboise (raspberry
   eau-de-vie), white rum,
   or peach schnapps
¼ cup sugar
5 tbsp orange juice
1 tbsp lemon juice

CARDAMOM CREAM
1½ cups heavy cream
2–3 cardamom pods, split
about ½ tbsp sugar, or
   to taste

1 Make the cardamom cream: Heat the cream with the cardamom and sugar until it boils. Remove from the heat, cover, and let infuse for 30 minutes. Strain. Cool completely and then chill.

2 Divide the berries among four squares of heavy-duty foil large enough to enclose them.

3 Warm the framboise, sugar, and fruit juices in a small saucepan until the sugar has dissolved. Pour this syrup over the berries.

4 Fold the foil loosely over the berries and twist the edges together firmly to seal. Put the packets on the side of the grill rack and cook until heated through, 4–5 minutes.

5 Taste the cardamom cream for sweetness, then serve with the berries.

363 PINEAPPLE, MANGO, APRICOT, AND PEAR SKEWERS WITH MAPLE CREAM

PREPARATION TIME *15 minutes* **COOKING TIME** *5 minutes* **SERVES 4**

1 small pineapple, peeled

1 mango, peeled, pitted, and cut into 1-inch chunks

1 large, ripe but firm pear, cored and cut into 1-inch chunks

4 ripe but firm apricots, pitted and quartered

2 tbsp maple syrup

1 tbsp brandy or lemon juice

MAPLE CREAM

3-4 tbsp maple syrup

1 tbsp brandy

1 cup light cream or plain yogurt

1 Make the maple cream: Stir the maple syrup and brandy into the cream or yogurt. Cover and chill until required.

2 Quarter the pineapple lengthwise and cut away the core, then cut the flesh into 1-inch chunks.

3 Thread all the fruits alternately onto skewers.

4 Combine the maple syrup with the brandy or lemon juice and brush over the fruit. Grill on an oiled rack until piping hot and flecked with golden brown, about 5 minutes, turning regularly.

5 Serve the fruit with some of the maple cream trickled over. Serve the remaining cream separately.

364 SUMMER FRUIT BRUSCHETTAS

PREPARATION TIME *10 minutes* **COOKING TIME** *3-5 minutes* **SERVES 4**

1 large, ripe but still firm peach, pitted and cut into wedges	confectioners' sugar for sprinkling	½ cup clotted cream* unsweetened flaked coconut for serving
8 large strawberries	1 cup raspberries	
	4-6 slices brioche	

1 Halve the peach wedges crosswise. Thread onto bamboo skewers that have been soaked in water for 30 minutes. Thread the strawberries onto separate skewers. Sprinkle the peaches and strawberries with confectioners' sugar. Grill on an oiled rack for 3–5 minutes.

2 Meanwhile, put the raspberries onto a piece of heavy-duty foil. Form into a packet, if desired, and warm at the side of the grill rack. Toast the brioche at the side of the grill rack.

3 Divide the clotted cream among the brioche slices. Slip the strawberries off the skewers onto the clotted cream.

4 Slip the peaches off the skewers onto a plate and cut each wedge into two slices (use a fork to hold the fruit steady if too hot to handle). Divide among the toasts. Scatter the raspberries on top, sprinkle with the coconut, and serve.

* If clotted cream is not available, mascarpone cheese can be substituted. Or, for a lighter alternative, use sour cream.

365 FRUIT AND NUT BROCHETTES

PREPARATION TIME *15 minutes* **COOKING TIME** *8 minutes* **SERVES 4**

14 tbsp (3½ sticks) unsalted butter, chopped	1 cup finely chopped pistachios	2 large kiwi fruits, cut into bite-sized cubes
½ cup light brown sugar	flesh from 1 pineapple, cored and cut into bite-sized cubes	flesh from 1 papaya, cut into bite-sized cubes
2 tsp ground cinnamon		4 oz cape gooseberries, husks removed
1 cup shredded fresh coconut or unsweetened flaked coconut	flesh from 1 mango, cut into bite-sized cubes	

1 Gently heat the butter with the sugar and cinnamon, stirring until the sugar has dissolved. Boil until slightly syrupy, about 1 minute .

2 Spread the coconut and pistachios on separate deep plates.

3 Turn the pineapple and the mango separately in the spiced butter, remove with a slotted spoon, and let drain. Roll the pineapple in the coconut so the cubes are well coated. Roll the mango in the pistachios.

4 Stir the remaining fruit into the rest of the spiced butter.

5 Thread the fruit alternately onto eight skewers. Grill on an oiled rack until the coconut and nuts are toasted, about 5 minutes, turning frequently.

INDEX